MANUAL FOR

# Theory and Practice of Counseling and Psychotherapy

**4th Edition**

MANUAL FOR
# THEORY AND PRACTICE OF COUNSELING AND PSYCHOTHERAPY
## 4th Edition

## GERALD COREY

California State University, Fullerton

Diplomate in Counseling Psychology
American Board of Professional Psychology

Brooks/Cole Publishing Company
Pacific Grove, California

*To my students at California State University at Fullerton,*
*who have inspired me to keep my enthusiasm*
*and who have helped in refining the ideas in this manual*

Brooks/Cole Publishing Company
A Division of Wadsworth, Inc.

Printed in the United States of America

10  9  8  7  6

ISBN 0-534-13316-9


Sponsoring Editor: *Claire Verduin*
Editorial Assistant: *Gay Bond*
Production Coordinator: *Dorothy Bell*
Manuscript Editor: *William Waller*
Cover Design: *E. Kelly Shoemaker*
Word Processing: *Maxine Westby*
Printing and Binding: *Malloy Lithographing, Inc.*

# ACKNOWLEDGMENTS

I wish to thank my students at California State University at Fullerton, who have used the material in this manual and have provided helpful criticism and suggestions. They have my respect and affection for the challenge they continue to offer. My interactions with them are important sources of keeping me alive personally and professionally, and most of my ideas grow out of my involvement with students. I wish particularly to acknowledge several students who were closely involved in reading and reviewing the manuscript and who provided many helpful suggestions that were incorporated into this present revision: Helen Buzzella, Katie Dutro, Christine Heacox, Becky Mueller, and Michael Safko. Two professors who have used this manual provided constructive criticism and suggestions for change: Jorja Manos Prover of California State University, Fullerton; and David Van Doren of University of Wisconsin, Whitewater.

Special thanks go to my wife (and respected colleague), Marianne Schneider Corey, who read the manual and who patiently (and sometimes impatiently) discussed its ideas with me. Many of the ideas in the book are hers, and in many ways this manual is a joint effort.

The manual is more readable due to the editorial talents of Bill Waller. He has enhanced the style of this manual.

Writing a textbook is usually a one-way endeavor; the author talks to the reader and seldom receives feedback. To change that, I invite you to express your reactions to both this manual and the accompanying textbook, *Theory and Practice of Counseling and Psychotherapy*, Fourth Edition, by writing to me at Brooks/Cole Publishing Company, Pacific Grove, California 93950. I would also value your reactions to *Case Approach to Counseling and Psychotherapy*, Third Edition, which can be used in conjunction with the manual and textbook. For your convenience, there is a prepaid evaluation form at the end of this manual. I look forward to receiving your ideas on how to make both the text and the manual more useful.

*Gerald Corey*

# CONTENTS

MANUAL FOR

# THEORY AND PRACTICE
# OF COUNSELING AND
# PSYCHOTHERAPY

### 4th Edition

# 1

# INTRODUCTION AND OVERVIEW

## INTRODUCTION

This manual is designed to accompany my *Theory and Practice of Counseling and Psychotherapy*, Fourth Edition, and *Case Approach to Counseling and Psychotherapy*, Third Edition (both Brooks/Cole, 1991). The manual is aimed at helping you and your instructor personalize the process by which you learn about counseling theories and therapeutic practice. It emphasizes the *practical application* of various therapeutic approaches to your personal growth. And it stresses the critical evaluation of each therapy as you are called on to use the skills of each approach in exercises, activities, and consideration of case examples and problems. The manual thus demands that you become an *active learner*, both inside and outside the classroom, in your growth as a person and as a future counselor.

The manual is appropriate for courses in counseling theory and practice, intervention strategies, and human services and also for internship experiences. It is well suited to practicum courses during which you apply your knowledge of the helping process to specific, practical field experiences.

Key features of the manual are as follows:

- self-inventories to assess your attitudes and beliefs about counseling theory and practice, the counselor as a person, and ethical issues

- a summary overview of each major theory of counseling

- a review of the highlights of each theory

- questions for discussion and evaluation

- a prechapter self-inventory for each approach

- the professional codes of ethics of AACD and APA

- sample forms and charts for some chapters

- assessment forms for the appraisal of life patterns

- case examples and cases for practice

- experiential activities for inside and outside of class

- ethical and professional issues for exploration

- issues basic to your personal development

- a glossary of key terms for each theory

- a quiz on each theory

- a list of addresses of major professional organizations

# HOW TO USE THE MANUAL WITH THE TEXTBOOK

Let me suggest some ways of deriving the maximum benefit from the combined use of the textbook and the manual. These suggestions are based on student input and my experiences in teaching counseling courses.

1. Begin with the manual. Skim the entire manual to get some "feel" for the program.

2. Then take the survey questionnaire in this chapter of the manual. (Students have found it useful to take it again at the end of the course to assess any changes in their attitudes toward counseling and the helping process.)

3. Before you read and study a textbook chapter on one of the nine theories, take the manual's corresponding prechapter self-inventory, which is based on the key concepts of an approach as discussed in the textbook. The purpose of the inventories is to assess your degree of agreement or disagreement with the concepts of a theory, *not* to seek the "right answer." My students have said that the inventories give them a clear focus as they read the chapter material.

4. Also before reading each theory chapter, carefully study the manual's overview of the theory treated in the chapter. The overview provides a framework, in capsule form, for the entire textbook chapter. A glossary of key terms and several questions for discussion and evaluation are also included in the manual, to assist you in considering important issues before you read the textbook chapter. Students report that the overviews, by summarizing the key ideas of each theory, give an organizational framework from which to better grasp the textbook material.

5. After reading and studying a textbook chapter, turn again to the manual.

   a. Review the questions (for critique and personal applications).

   b. Retake (or at least review) the self-inventory.

   c. Look over again and think about the overview (for focusing on key ideas of the theory).

   d. Review the key terms that are defined in the glossary.

   e. Select a *few* key questions or exercises that are most meaningful to you, and clarify your position on the issues underlying the questions.

   f. Circle the above questions or exercises, think of any of your own questions you would like to pursue, and bring both sets to class for further discussion.

   g. Apply to the theory the list of questions found in the next section of this chapter, entitled "Reviewing the Highlights of a Theory."

   h. Formulate your own critique of the approach, and think about aspects that you would most like to incorporate in your own personal style of counseling.

   i. Fill in the incomplete sentences in the section near the end of each theory chapter entitled "Reviewing the Highlights."

   j. Take the quizzes at the end of each theory chapter and score them, referring to the key in Appendix 1.

6. Realize that in most of the chapters in this manual I have intentionally provided an abundance of exercises and questions, more than can be expected to be integrated within one course. I recommend looking over all the material in a chapter and then selecting the questions and exercises that seem the most relevant, stimulating, and interesting to you. I hope that at the end of the course you will review the material in this manual. At that time you may want to consider questions or activities that you omitted in your initial reading.

7. In reading and thinking about Chapter 2 ("The Counselor as a Person and as a Professional") do your best to relate to the issues in a personal manner. This chapter will

set the tone for the book by raising issues that you can explore as you study each of the theory chapters. Students have found that they get a lot more from this course (and from the textbook and manual) by relating to what they read in a *personal* way. Thus, in studying each theory you have some excellent opportunities to apply what you are learning about the theory to your own life. By bringing yourself into this reading you make the course much more interesting than if you merely studied abstract theories in an impersonal and strictly academic manner.

8.  I recommend at least an initial skimming of the last two chapters in the book. Chapter 13 (the case study of Stan) will provide you with a general overview of applying techniques from the various theories to this single case. As you study each theory, reflect on how you would approach working with Stan from that theoretical perspective. This manual will give you ideas of how to counsel him from each approach. Chapter 14, "An Integrative Perspective," will be most meaningful as a review once you have completed your study of the theories. I have placed these two chapters at the end of the book because I think they should be studied in depth as a summarizing and integrating activity after you have examined the theories. However, an initial reading of these chapters will surely help you integrate the material and see comparisons among the therapies as you study them separately.

9.  As you read and study the chapters in both the textbook and this manual, attempt to compare the approaches. Look for common denominators among all the theories with respect to key concepts and practices. Look for major points of disagreement. And begin to think of selecting certain aspects of each approach that seem suited to your personality and style of counseling as well as to the type of work you expect to do.

10. Many students have found it very valuable to keep a journal, in which they do some extensive writing about their experience in the course or elaborate on particular activities, questions, and issues in the manual. A spiral notebook is an ideal companion to this manual for keeping a record of your thoughts, reactions, and experiences. Students often find it worthwhile to read their journal later in their career, for in this way they achieve a sense of how their thinking evolved as they gained more experience. Those who take the time to keep such a journal typically say that doing so was well worth the effort.

11. As I mentioned, I have also written a book devoted to working with clients. With each therapy approach I demonstrate how I would counsel several clients and provide cases for you to work with. This book, *Case Approach to Counseling and Psychotherapy*, Third Edition, is designed for use as a combined package with the textbook and this manual.

12. Consider organizing and participating in a *study group* as a way of reviewing for tests and as a help in applying the material to yourself personally. If you meet with your small group at various times in the semester, you will have opportunities to learn from one another. A number of students have told me that by teaching or coaching fellow students they really learned the material. This process helped them crystallize key concepts and see differences and similarities among the approaches. A study group is particularly useful in exploring ethical, legal, and professional issues. Of course, this process of meeting for study sessions will be invaluable as a way to review for major tests and the final examination.

## REVIEWING THE HIGHLIGHTS OF A THEORY

*Directions*: This set of questions has been designed to apply to each of the counseling theories after you have studied it. As a way to help you get the approach into clearer focus, give a few concise summary statements in your own words in answer to each question. Use this outline to write your *critical evaluation* of each of the therapeutic approaches. This outline (and the quizzes for each chapter) would be very helpful for either studying on your own or as a basis for discussion in a study group, should you decide to organize one. Bring your critiques to class as a basis for active participation in discussion.

1. Key concepts

    a. What is the theory's *view of human nature*, and what are the *basic assumptions* underlying the approach?

    b. What primary characteristics distinguish the approach? What are its major areas of focus and emphasis? What are the fundamental ideas?

2. The therapeutic process

    a. What are the therapeutic goals?

    b. What are the functions and role of the therapist?

    c. What is the client's role in the therapeutic process? What is expected of the client? What does the client do?

    d. What is the nature of the relationship between the client and the therapist?

3. Applications: techniques and procedures

    a. What are the major techniques and methods?

    b. Where is the approach *most* applicable? To what types of client? To what types of problem? In what settings? How would this approach work in counseling clients from various cultures?

    c. What is *your evaluation* of the approach? What are the limitations? unique contributions? aspects you most like and least like?

    d. What are some specific aspects of this approach (*concepts and techniques*) that you would most want to incorporate in your own counseling style? Why?

    e. In what ways can you apply this approach to yourself *personally* as a basis for self-understanding and for ideas that you might use in your daily life?

    f. What are some of the most significant and personally meaningful questions that you would like to pursue further?

# SURVEY OF ATTITUDES AND VALUES
# RELATED TO COUNSELING AND PSYCHOTHERAPY:
# A SELF-INVENTORY AND PRETEST

*Directions*: This is *not* a traditional multiple-choice test in which you must select the correct answer. Instead, it is a survey of *your* basic beliefs, attitudes, and values related to counseling and psychotherapy. Circle the letter beside the response that most closely reflects *your viewpoint* at this time. *You may circle more than one response* for each item. Notice that a blank line ("e") is included in each item. If none of the provided options seems appropriate or if you have what you consider a better answer, write your response (or responses) on the line. Bring the completed inventory to class during one of the beginning sessions of the course, and compare your viewpoints with those of other students. It would be of interest to take the inventory again at the end of the course to see whether, or to what degree, any of your beliefs, attitudes, and values have changed.

1. I think that the purpose of counseling and psychotherapy is to

    a. make people socially adjusted.
    b. tell others how best to run their life.
    c. make clients happy and contented.
    d. always provide an answer or solution to the client's problem.
    e. _____

2. My view of human nature is that

    a. people are born basically good.
    b. people are born basically evil.
    c. people are born basically neutral.
    d. people can create their own nature.
    e. _____

3. Regarding the issue of human freedom, I believe that

    a. we create our own destiny by making choices.
    b. we possess *limited* degrees of freedom.
    c. we are almost totally the products of conditioning.
    d. we are what our genetic makeup and environment make us.
    e. _____

4. Regarding the issues of who should select the goals of counseling, I believe that

    a. it is primarily the client's responsibility.
    b. it is primarily the therapist's responsibility.
    c. it is a joint venture of the client and the therapist.
    d. society should dictate what the goals are.
    e. _____

5. From my viewpoint psychotherapy should be aimed primarily at

    a. providing conditions for maximizing self-awareness.
    b. making the unconscious conscious.
    c. acquiring a more tolerant and rational philosophy of life.
    d. learning realistic and responsible behavior.
    e. _____

6. Counseling should focus mainly on

    a. what people are thinking.
    b. what people are feeling.
    c. what people are doing.
    d. each of these, depending on the stage of therapy.
    e. _____

7. As I see counseling, it is a process of

    a. reeducation.
    b. helping clients make life decisions.
    c. learning to integrate one's feeling and thinking.
    d. all of the above.
    e. _____

8. Counseling and therapy should focus on

    a. the client's past experiences.
    b. the client's experience in the here and now.
    c. the client's strivings toward the future.
    d. whatever the client decides.
    e. _____

9. Counseling and therapy should focus primarily on

    a. changing behavior.
    b. providing insight.
    c. changing attitudes and feelings.
    d. challenging values.
    e. _____

10. When I think of a mentally and emotionally healthy person, the characteristic that seems most important is

   a. living within the framework of socially acceptable morality.
   b. the ability fo fully live and experience the present moment.
   c. the absence of any problems, conflicts, or struggles.
   d. being involved in doing good for others.
   e. _____

11. Abnormal behavior is best explained as

   a. the result of faulty learning.
   b. the failure to resolve a specific psychosexual conflict during the early years.
   c. thinking and behaving in irrational ways.
   d. genetic factors, biochemical factors, or both.
   e. _____

12. In thinking about practicing counseling in a multicultural society, I think that it is essential

   a. to have specialized course work on various cultures.
   b. to get fieldwork experience in multicultural settings.
   c. to come to terms with my own culture.
   d. to develop skills in working with culturally different clients.
   e. _____

13. I think that specific knowledge about cultural differences is

   a. essential for effective counseling.
   b. dangerous because of the tendency to stereotype.
   c. impossible to acquire because of the number of cultures.
   d. useful in providing a conceptual framework.
   e. _____

14. A person's early-childhood experiences are

   a. not really important material for therapy.
   b. the determinants of the person's present adjustments.
   c. experiences that must be explored in therapy.
   d. of interest but not much significance for who one is today.
   e. _____

15. Of the following I deem the most important function of a therapist to be

   a. being present for and with the client.
   b. interpreting the meaning of the client's symptoms.
   c. creating trust that allows the client to freely explore feelings and thoughts.
   d. giving the client specific suggestions for things to do outside the therapy sessions.
   e. _____

16. I believe that counselors should be

   a. active and directive.
   b. relatively nondirective, allowing the client to direct.
   c. whatever the client wants them to be.
   d. directive or nondirective, depending on the client's capacity for self-direction.
   e. _____

17. Concerning clients' potential or capacity for resolving their own emotional problems, I think that

   a. the therapist needs to be directive and provide answers for clients.
   b. clients can resolve their own problems if they feel accepted by their therapist.

c.  clients can resolve their conflicts without therapy.
d.  clients want someone to provide them with solutions to their problems, and they need direction.
e.  _____

18. I believe that the power of a therapist

a.  should be used to manipulate the client in the direction the therapist deems best for the client.
b.  should be minimized because of its danger.
c.  can be a vital force that the therapist can use in modeling for a client.
d.  is always a sign of a therapist's need to reinforce his or her own ego.
e.  _____

19. I believe that in order to help a client a therapist

a.  needs to have had a problem similar to the client's problem.
b.  must be free of any conflicts in the area he or she is exploring with the client.
c.  must share similar life experiences and values with the client.
d.  must like the client personally.
e.  _____

20. I believe that for those wishing to become therapists undergoing therapy

a.  is an absolute necessity.
b.  is not an important factor in a therapist's capacity to work with others.
c.  is necessary only when a therapist has severe personal problems.
d.  should be encouraged strongly but not required.
e.  _____

21. Regarding the client/therapist relationship, I think that

a.  the therapist should be a friend to the client.
b.  the therapist must remain relatively anonymous.
c.  a personal and warm relationship is not essential.
d.  it is the core of the counseling process.
e.  _____

22. Regarding value judgments in therapy, I believe that therapists should

a.  remain neutral and keep their values out of the therapeutic process.
b.  make value judgments regarding their clients' behavior.
c.  actively teach their values to clients.
d.  encourage their clients to make value judgments about the quality of their own behavior.
e.  _____

23. Regarding the role of theory in counseling, I think that a counselor should

a.  select one theory and work strictly within that framework for the sake of consistency.
b.  ignore theory, since it is not related to practical applications.
c.  strive to combine a couple of theoretical approaches.
d.  integrate all the theories by applying the appropriate concepts and techniques to each client.
e.  _____

24. Of the following, the most important feature of effective therapy is

a.  knowledge of the theory of counseling and behavior.
b.  skill in using techniques appropriately.

    c.  genuineness and openness on the therapist's part.

    d.  the therapist's ability to specify a treatment plan and evaluate the results.

    e.  _____

25.  Regarding the value of psychotherapy, I think that

    a.  it generally produces good results.

    b.  it can very easily be more harmful than helpful.

    c.  the outcomes are due mainly to the quality of the therapist.

    d.  it makes little difference in changing a person's behavior.

    e.  _____

*Directions*: *T = True. F = False.* For items 26 through 60 circle the answer (T, F, or both) that best fits your belief. Then, on the line provided, give a reason for your answer.

*Example*:   T  (F)  Giving advice is an important function of therapists.

             *This is the easy way out, but it is not therapy.*

T  F  26.  Therapists should work only with clients whom they really like and care for.

            _____

T  F  27.  As long as I counsel others, I should be open to the idea of receiving therapy myself.

            _____

T  F  28.  I have goals for my clients in advance of seeing them.

            _____

T  F  29.  My values should be kept out of the therapy process.

            _____

T  F  30.  Confidentiality is an absolute, and I would never disclose anything a client revealed during therapy, regardless of the circumstances.

            _____

T  F  31.  To work with a client effectively, the therapist must first be aware of the person's cultural background.

            _____

T  F  32.  I should model certain behaviors that I expect my clients to learn.

            _____

T  F  33.  My own levels of self-actualization and mental health are probably the most important variables that determine the success or failure of counseling.

            _____

T  F  34.  I should be completely open, honest, and transparent with my clients.

            _____

T  F  35.  It is appropriate for me to discuss my personal conflicts at length with my clients, for they can be helped if they know that I have problems, too.

            _____

T  F  36.  It is essential to understand the origin and causes of our problems before we can change.

            _____

T  F  37.  To be an effective therapist, I need to have an attitude of unconditional positive regard for and acceptance of my clients.

T  F  38.  The kind of person who I am is more important than my theoretical orientation and my use of techniques.

T  F  39.  Knowledge of my own cultural background is as important as knowing about the cultural background of my client.

T  F  40.  Intellectual insight is a necessary and sufficient condition for change.

T  F  41.  As children we learn certain life scripts that are programmed into us, and these scripts have a great deal to do with our present attitudes toward ourselves.

T  F  42.  Therapy needs to be aimed at social and political change if any real personal change is to occur.

T  F  43.  My job as a therapist is basically that of a teacher, for I am reeducating clients and teaching them coping skills.

T  F  44.  My central task as a therapist is to guide my clients in accepting reality and in functioning in the social world in a responsible way.

T  F  45.  Because confrontation might cause great pain or discomfort in a client, I think it is generally unwise to use this technique.

T  F  46.  My own needs are really not important in the therapeutic relationship with a client.

T  F  47.  Because silences during a therapy session are generally considered a sign of boredom, care should be taken to avoid them.

T  F  48.  Suggestion and persuasion are parts of the therapeutic process.

T  F  49.  The therapeutic relationship should be characterized by the same degree of sharing by both the client and the therapist.

T  F  50.  I must be careful to avoid mistakes, for my clients will lose respect for me if they observe me faltering.

T  F  51.  Therapy need not be a personal relationship, for it can be effective if the therapist possesses technical skill.

T   F   52.   A good therapist is born, not made.

_____

T   F   53.   Therapy can have either a positive or a negative effect on a client.

_____

T   F   54.   There is no personal change or growth unless a person is open to anxiety and pain.

_____

T   F   55.   As a counselor I want to be flexible and modify the techniques I use, especially in counseling culturally diverse clients.

_____

T   F   56.   As a counselor I want to strive to be objective and not become personally involved with my clients.

_____

T   F   57.   As a therapist I should not judge my client's behavior, for therapy and value judgments are incompatible.

_____

T   F   58.   If I experience intense feelings toward my client (anger or sexual desire, for example), I have lost my potential effectiveness to counsel that person, and I should terminate the relationship.

_____

T   F   59.   It is inappropriate to touch clients, under any circumstances.

_____

T   F   60.   I would not accept an involuntary client.

_____

# 2

# THE COUNSELOR AS A PERSON AND AS A PROFESSIONAL

## A SURVEY OF YOUR ATTITUDES AND BELIEFS ABOUT THE COUNSELOR AS A PERSON AND AS A PROFESSIONAL

*Directions*:   This self-inventory is designed to clarify your thinking on issues raised in the textbook on the counselor as a person and a professional. You may want to select more than one answer; notice also that line "e" is for any qualifying responses you want to make or any other answer you would like to provide.

1. Which of the following do you think is *most* important as a determinant of the outcome of therapy?

    a.   the skills and techniques the counselor possesses
    b.   the particular theoretical orientation of the counselor
    c.   the kind of person the counselor is
    d.   the quality of the counselor's life experiences
    e.   _____

2. What is the most important component of therapist authenticity?

    a.   willingness to be totally open with the client on all matters
    b.   caring for the client
    c.   willingness to confront the client
    d.   modeling of those qualities the therapist expects of the client
    e.   _____

3. Of the following, which is the most important attribute, or personal characteristic, of effective therapists?

    a.   the degree to which they are alive
    b.   the degree to which they are open to change
    c.   the degree to which they are willing to be themselves
    d.   the degree to which they have resolved any pressing personal conflicts
    e.   _____

4. As it applies to you, what is your position with respect to receiving personal therapy before you begin working with clients?

    a.   I don't feel the need, because I have few pressing problems.
    b.   I am willing to get involved in my own therapy as a client.
    c.   I see it as an ethical obligation to experience my own therapy before I expect to counsel others.
    d.   I would do it only if it were required that I do so.
    e.   _____

5. If you were to become a client, what issue(s) might you most focus on in your therapy sessions?

   a. the reasons why I want to become a counselor
   b. unfinished situations from my past, especially relationships with my parents
   c. my fear of overidentifying with my clients' problems
   d. my anxieties over my ability to work effectively with various types of clients
   e. _____

6. Over which of the following issues do you have the greatest degree of *anxiety* when you think about beginning as a counselor?

   a. that I will not have the knowledge or skills to be effective
   b. that I will make a mistake (or mistakes) that will damage the client
   c. that clients will demand too much from me and that I will not be able to meet these demands
   d. that I will find that I was never really cut out to be a therapist in the first place
   e. _____

7. When you think of "being yourself" as a counselor, what comes to your mind?

   a. that I function in a professional role yet still retain human qualities and make personal contact with clients
   b. that I be without roles of any kind
   c. that I relate to my clients as I would to any close friend
   d. that I say whatever I am thinking or feeling in sessions, without censoring myself
   e. _____

8. How would you determine what constitutes *appropriate* and *facilitative* self-disclosure as a counselor?

   a. by doing whatever feels comfortable to me at the time
   b. by observing the reactions of my client to my disclosures
   b. by observing the degree to which the client engages in deeper self-exploration
   d. by assessing the degree of risks I take in the disclosures
   e. _____

9. When do you think that it is important to disclose yourself to your clients?

   a. when they ask for it or when I sense that this is what they need
   b. whenever I have persistent negative or positive feelings
   c. when I want to influence them to choose a certain course
   d. when nothing much is happening in the sessions
   e. _____

10. What is your greatest fear as it relates to disclosing to your clients?

    a. that what I say will be inappropriate and that it will take the focus off of them and put it on me
    b. that my clients will lose respect for me because of what I tell them
    c. that I will lose my stature as a professional
    d. that I will get so involved in my own emotions that I will tune out the client
    e. _____

11. How does the issue of *perfectionism* apply to you as a counselor?

    a. I am sure that I will demand perfection of myself, which means that I cannot tolerate making any mistakes in my sessions.
    b. Whatever I do will never quite be enough.
    c. If I failed with a client, I think I would be devastated.
    d. Although I will strive to be the best I can I will not burden myself with the demand that I never make mistakes.
    e. _____

12. What is your policy on being honest with your clients?

    a. I believe in being completely frank and totally open with them regarding any impressions I may have toward them.

    b. I believe that I should carefully weigh what I say for fear of damaging our relationship.

    c. If I did not think I were competent to deal with a particular client, I would want to tell the person so.

    d. If I expect them to be honest with me, I had better be honest with them.

    e. _____

13. How do you think you would tend to deal with *silences* during a counseling session?

    a. I would be threatened and tend to think that I had done something wrong.

    b. I would ask the client questions to get him or her going again.

    c. I would discuss with the client my own feelings about the silence.

    d. I would sit it out and wait for the client to take the initiative.

    e. _____

14. How can you be on guard against both client self-deception and your own self-deception concerning the progress of a client?

    a. I would ask clients to demonstrate to me that they were making the changes they claimed to be making.

    b. I would bring up for discussion the tendency to deceive ourselves.

    c. I would be highly skeptical about most of what my clients said.

    d. I would recognize my own need to actually see clients' progress so that I would feel effective.

    e. _____

15. What is your view on the role of *giving advice* in counseling?

    a. Because I see the counseling process as guiding clients, I would freely give advice if I thought this was what the client wanted.

    b. I would rarely, if ever, give advice, for even if the advice was good, it would tend to make the client dependent on me.

    c. If I did not give advice, I would not feel as though I were helping the client.

    d. I think I would tend to give advice to clients when I had a strong preference for a direction I hoped they would choose.

    e. _____

16. What are your views concerning the use of *humor* in therapy?

    a. Whenever possible I would interject humor in a session, because I see laughter as potentially very therapeutic.

    b. I think I would tend to fall back on humor whenever I felt some degree of uncomfortableness in a session.

    c. I would avoid humor, as I think it can easily distract a client from dealing with the serious matters of therapy.

    d. I would use humor when my client got into "heavy feelings" to lighten things up a bit, so that neither of us would get depressed.

    e. _____

17. How do you expect that you will go about developing your own counseling style?

    a. by following pretty closely one theoretical approach

    b. by modeling myself after a supervisor

    c. by combining several therapeutic approaches

    d. by keeping a journal of what I do and experience as I work with clients

    e. _____

18. What do you think would be the major cause of *burnout* for you personally in your work as a counselor?

    a. not seeing the results that I had expected from clients
    b. not working well in the system
    c. receiving criticism from colleagues for my enthusiasm and optimism
    d. growing tired of hearing the same old problems
    e. _____

19. How do you think that you can best *prevent burnout*?

    a. by not blaming people or things outside of me for my feelings of devitalization and helplessness
    b. by taking the time to play and engage in hobbies
    c. by making sure that my personal needs are being met in my life away from work
    d. by quitting a job as soon as I find that I am losing interest or when I am feeling ineffective
    e. _____

20. As a counselor I expect that my values will affect the counseling process

    a. in those cases in which I have values strongly divergent from my client's.
    b. only in cases in which I attempt to sway the client to my way of thinking.
    c. at all times, because I cannot separate my values from my work as a counselor.
    d. when I have strong negative reactions to certain behaviors or values of my client.
    e. _____

21. My position on the ethics involved in the role of values in therapy is that

    a. therapists should never impose their values on a client.
    b. therapists should teach the client proper values.
    c. therapists should openly share their values when appropriate.
    d. values should be kept out of the relationship.
    e. _____

22. Of the following motivations, the one that best expresses my reason for wanting to be in this helping profession is

    a. my desire to nurture others.
    b. my desire to straighten others out.
    c. my desire to get confirmation of my value as a person.
    d. my need to be needed and to feel that I am helping others.
    e. _____

23. If I had strong feelings, positive or negative, toward a client, I think that I would probably

    a. discuss my feelings with my client.
    b. keep them to myself and hope they would eventually disappear.
    c. discuss my feelings with a supervisor or colleague.
    d. accept my feelings as natural unless they began to interfere with the counseling relationship.
    e. _____

24. I won't feel ready to counsel others until

    a. my own life is free of problems.
    b. I've experienced counseling as a client.
    c. I feel very confident and know that I'll be effective.
    d. I've become a self-aware person and developed the ability to continually reexamine my own life and relationships.
    e. _____

25. If a client evidenced strong feelings of attraction or dislike for me, I think that I would

    a. help the client work through these feelings and understand them.
    b. enjoy these feelings if they were positive.
    c. refer my client to another counselor.
    d. direct the sessions into less emotional areas.
    e. _____

## SUGGESTIONS ON HOW TO USE THIS INVENTORY

1. Now that you have finished this inventory, go back over it, and circle a few of the items that had the greatest meaning to you. Bring these issues to class, and compare your reactions with those of fellow students. You might also discuss why these issues held special meaning for you.

2. Discuss with others in class what it was like for you to go through this inventory. What did it stir up in you? What did you learn about yourself?

3. Go back to the initial "Survey of Attitudes and Values Related to Counseling and Psychotherapy: A Self-Inventory and Pretest" in Chapter 1 of this manual. Look over your responses to determine the degree of consistency between these two surveys. I strongly recommend that you also circle several of the items that you would *most* like to bring up for class discussion. It is a good idea to review your initial responses at the end of the semester in small groups. This process can help you examine any shifts in your thinking.

# ISSUES FOR PERSONAL APPLICATION

## DEALING WITH VALUE CONFLICTS

At times you and a client may experience value clashes that make it very difficult for you to work together. To help you identify such circumstances, complete the following inventory, and determine when you might refer a client to someone else because of a conflict of value systems. Use this code:

1 = I definitely would work well with this type of person.

2 = I probably would find working with this type of person extremely difficult.

3 = I am certain that I would not work well with this type of person.

_____ 1. an adolescent girl who wants to explore her feelings about whether to have an abortion

_____ 2. an adolescent boy who is convinced that living *for drugs* and *on drugs* is the way to live

_____ 3. a homosexual couple who want to explore relationship problems

_____ 4. a homosexual couple who want to discuss their desires to adopt a child

_____ 5. a man who is deeply troubled over his extramarital affairs but is not ready to give them up

_____ 6. a woman who is deeply troubled over her extramarital affairs but is not willing to give them up

_____ 7. a very dogmatic individual who is convinced that all of his problems would be solved if he did God's will and made the Lord the center of his life

_____ 8. an individual who has a great deal of hostility toward any form of religion and who wants to explore her negative feelings in this area

_____ 9. a person who has extremely strong fundamentalist religious beliefs and is not willing to explore these beliefs in counseling

_____ 10. a person whose basic value system includes the attempt to use and exploit others for his own gain

_____ 11. a person who lives by the basic belief that this is a cutthroat world and that she has to live aggressively in order to avoid getting squashed

_____ 12. someone who deeply believes that people should be able to work out their problems by themselves and that therapy is of little value in helping anyone make real-life changes

_____ 13. a person with a great deal of racial prejudice and hatred

_____ 14. an individual who is convinced that his way is "right" and who wants to impose his values on everyone with whom he has contact

_____ 15. a married person who wants to leave her family so that she can "be free from the burdens of responsibility"

**SOME QUESTIONS YOU MIGHT EXPLORE**

1. What specific kinds of clients might you have difficulty working with because of a clash of values?

2. How would you handle the situation if you discovered that you were not being effective with a client because of a difference in values?

3. What are some of your central values and beliefs, and how do you think they will either inhibit _or_ facilitate your work as a counselor?

4. Interview some practicing counselors about their experiences with values in the counseling process. You could ask questions such as these: "What kinds of clients have you had difficulty working with because of your value system? How do you think your values influence the way you counsel? How are your clients affected by your values? What are some of the main value issues that clients bring into the counseling process?"

I suggest that you bring the results of this inventory to class and form small groups to discuss ways to deal with situations in which you have a value system different from your client's. There are some excellent possibilities for role-playing these situations in a small group. As much as possible, role-play the situation first, and then discuss the issues and your experience in the exercise.

# SUGGESTED ACTIVITY: PERSONAL ISSUES IN COUNSELING AND PSYCHOTHERAPY

_Directions_: Fill in the blanks with the answers you think are appropriate for you. Of course, there are no "correct" answers. Try to give your immediate response to each question. Bring your answers to class for discussion.

1. What are three of your major qualities, or strengths, that you think will be assets for you as a counselor? _____

_____

_____

2. List three of your main weaknesses, or areas that you need to examine, that might interfere with your work as a counselor. _____

_____

_____

_____

3. What are some areas of personal information that you would be willing to disclose to your clients? _____

_____

_____

4. What are some areas of personal information that you would *not* be willing to disclose to your clients? _____

_____

_____

_____

5. What are a few of your specific concerns, or fears, regarding your work as a beginning counselor? _____

_____

_____

_____

6. How would you respond if you were required to undergo psychotherapy as a basic part of your degree program? _____

_____

_____

_____

7. Can you think of specific instances in which you might give your clients advice?

_____

_____

_____

8. What are some possible advantages or problems associated with combining a therapeutic relationship with a social relationship? _____

_____

_____

_____

9. What might you do if your client had values sharply contrasting with your own, to the point where you found that it interfered with the therapeutic relationship? _____

_____

_____

_____

10. What personal values do you think you might impose on your clients? (What are specific values you would be inclined to "push"?) _____

_____

_____

_____

11. Assume that a client requests you as a therapist but that you feel a dislike for the person and do not want to counsel him or her. What might you say to the person? _____

_____

_____

_____

12. What might you say to clients who assert that they are progressing in therapy when you see little progress and judge that they are deceiving themselves? _____

_____

_____

_____

13. What might you say to a client who continually looks to you for approval and for suggestions about how he or she should lead his or her life? _____

_____

_____

_____

14. Assume that a client consistently telephones you at home at inconvenient hours to discuss what was said in a therapy session. How might you respond? _____

_____

_____

_____

15. What life experiences do you see as having the greatest influence on your ability as a therapist? _____

_____

_____

_____

16. How do you typically deal with crisis situations?   with your own personal problems?

_____

_____

_____

17. How effective do you think you would be in counseling clients who are culturally different from you? _____

_____

_____

18. What, if anything, might get in the way of your counseling clients of a different gender? _____

_____

_____

_____

19. What can you do to increase your awareness and knowledge in the area of cultural diversity? _____

_____

_____

_____

20. What is one specific way in which your cultural experiences could help you understand clients from different cultures? _____

_____

_____

_____

21. What one skill would you most like to acquire to make you more effective in counseling those from various cultures? _____

_____

_____

_____

22. How do you think that working within a system would affect your ability to do what you believe as a counselor? _____

_____

_____

_____

23. Knowing what you do of yourself, what factors in your life and your personality might contribute most to your own burnout? _____

_____

_____

_____

24. What are a few important steps you would be willing to take to prevent burnout?

_____

_____

_____

25. How do you think that you can best ensure that you will be able to keep yourself alive both as a person and as a professional? _____

_____

_____

# CASES DEALING WITH VALUE ISSUES

The following are several cases for you to role-play in class and for discussion. It is best for someone to assume the client's role, and then several different students can role-play various alternative ways of dealing with each situation. I have found that discussion of cases generally proves to be lively if it follows a brief role enactment in class. Attempt to focus on your own values, and identify any areas where you might tend to impose them on a client. Discuss how you see your values either helping or hindering your intervention in each of these cases.

## 1. A Client Who Has Not Questioned Her Religious Beliefs

Brenda, age 22, comes to see you because of problems in living at home with her family. She tells you that she feels dependent both financially and emotionally on her parents and that although she would like to move out and live with a girlfriend, she has many fears of taking this step. She also says that her religion is extremely important to her and that she feels a great deal of guilt over the conflict she has with her parents. After some discussion you find that she has never really questioned her religious values and that it appears that she has completely accepted the beliefs of her parents. Brenda says that if she followed her religion more closely, she would not be having all these difficulties with her folks. She is coming to you because she would "like to feel more like an independent adult who could feel free enough to make her own decisions."

- Where would you begin with Brenda? With her stated goals? With her religious beliefs? With her fear of moving away from home? With her conflicts and guilt associated with her parents? With her dependence/independence struggles?

- Would your religious values influence the direction you were likely to take with Brenda?

- Do you see any connection between her dependence on her parents and her guilt over not following her religion closely enough?

## 2. A Woman Struggling over an Abortion Decision

This case involves Melinda, a 25-year-old Latina who wants to have an abortion. She has been married for three years, already has two children, and says: "We had to get married because I was pregnant. We didn't have money then. The second kid was not planned either. But now we really can't afford another child." Her husband is a policeman going to law school at night. She works as a housekeeper and plans to return to school once her husband finishes his studies and it is "her turn." He should graduate in another year, at which time she is scheduled to enroll in classes at the community college. Having another baby at this time would seriously hamper those arrangements in addition to imposing the previously mentioned financial burden. But the client reports:

> I go to call the clinic, and I just can't seem to talk. I hang up the minute they answer. I just can't seem to make the appointment for the abortion, let alone have one. I was never much of a Catholic, and I always thought you should be able to get an abortion if you wanted one. What's wrong with me? And what am I going to do? I don't exactly have a lot of time.

- With the information given here, what do you see as the major value issues that need to be explored?

- How much focus would you place on factors such as what is stopping her from making the call? her ambivalence between wanting to have the abortion and not wanting it?

- If she asked you for your advice, what do you think you would tell her? If you gave her this advice, what might your advice tell you about yourself?

- How would your views on abortion influence the interventions you made with Melinda? Would anything stop you from entering into a counseling relationship with her?

### 3. Value Issues Pertaining to Cultural and Family Background

Michael and Amy appear at your office for crisis counseling. Michael, 22, comes from a somewhat controlling Italian family. Amy, 20, comes from a large and powerful Japanese family that settled in California five generations before. They want to get married in the fall, but they fear the reactions of their families. After dating casually for six months they were forced to end their relationship because of objections on both sides. But after not seeing each other for two months they began to meet in secret and are now determined to marry. Amy has threatened to become pregnant if their decision to get married is not accepted by their families. No one in either of their families is aware of their plans, but they know they must act quickly. They decided to seek counseling.

- How do you approach this case?
- What kind of information about Amy's and Michael's families would you be interested in, and what would you ask each of them?
- Would you involve both families in the counseling process? Why or why not?
- What value issues are operating in this case, and how would you explore them in counseling?

### 4. Difficulties of a Person Adjusting to Two Cultures

Greta is a young woman who has been in the United States for six months. After living all of her life in Norway she immigrated as the bride of an American college professor. Ever since arriving she has suffered homesickness and difficulty in adjusting to modern American life. Her husband, who showered her with attention during their courtship, has become distant and preoccupied with schoolwork. When she tries to make friends, she is shunned by the other academic wives. All she really wants now is a divorce and a return ticket to Norway. Greta would like you as her therapist, but there is a complicating factor. You are a close friend and professional colleague of her husband. When you suggest to her that perhaps she should see another counselor, she begins to cry and tells you that she is not comfortable with many Americans and that it is a relief to be able to talk to you. She begs you not to reject her.

- What reactions do you have toward Greta?
- What would you do or say when she begged you not to reject her?
- Would the fact that you were a close friend and a colleague present ethical problems for you that would make it necessary for you to refer her? What exactly is your responsibility to her?
- Assume that you did not know her husband and that she asked for your help. What values do you have (and what life experiences have you had) that are likely to increase your chances of working with her? What might get in the way of your providing her with this help?

### 5. A Woman Who Wants Her Marriage and Her Affair

Loretta and Bart come to you for marriage counseling. In the first session you see them as a couple. Loretta says that she can't keep going on the way they have been for the past several years. She tells you that she would very much like to work out a new relationship with him. He says that he does not want a divorce and is willing to give counseling his "best shot." Loretta comes to the following session alone because Bart had to work overtime. She tells you that she has been having an affair for two years and hasn't yet mustered up the courage to leave Bart for this other man, who is single and is pressuring her to make a decision. She relates that she feels very discouraged about the possibility of anything changing for the better in her marriage. She would, however, like to come in for some sessions with Bart because she doesn't want to hurt him.

- What would you be inclined to say to Loretta based on what she has told you privately?

- Would you be willing to work with Loretta if her aim was to continue her affair and keep her marriage? Why or why not?

- How would your views on extramarital affairs influence the interventions you made with Loretta and Bart?

- Would you encourage Loretta to divulge what she had told you privately in a later session with Bart? Why or why not?

- Would the element of "the other man" pressuring Loretta to make a decision have a bearing on your intervention in this case?

# 3

# ETHICAL ISSUES IN
# COUNSELING PRACTICE

## ETHICAL ISSUES AND PROBLEMS FOR EXAMINATION

The following groups of questions correspond to the various sections that deal with ethical issues in Chapter 3 of the textbook. Make at least a brief outline of your position on each of the issues.

### QUESTIONS FOR DISCUSSION AND EVALUATION

1. *Introduction*

   As a future counselor consider the following statement: "In short, psychological counselors are discovering that to bring about significant *individual* change, they cannot remain blind and deaf to the major *social* ills that often create and foster individual sickness. They must become active agents of constructive social change."

   a. Do you think the statement is realistic?

   b. If you accept the premise, what *specifically* do you envision yourself as being able to do to change society?

   c. If you cannot deal with social ills, do you imagine that your inability to do so could lead to feelings of powerlessness?

2. *Therapist competence, education, and training*

   a. What would you do if the agency that employed you expected you to perform psychological services that you judged yourself incompetent to perform because of lack of education or training?

   b. Assume that you are a counselor intern in a community agency. You were promised close on-the-job supervision, plus weekly sessions with your supervisor, but you've seen her briefly only a few times. A whole semester has passed, and so far you have had no private consultation with her. What would you do?

   c. There is a debate over professional licensing and certification. Essentially, what are the pros and cons of licensure or certification procedures? What is your position on this issue?

   d. Most professional organizations for mental-health practitioners strongly endorse continuing education as a condition for relicensing and recertification. Do you think that once a professional attains an advanced degree and a license to practice, continuing education should be mandatory? Or should it merely be strongly encouraged? What are some professional activities you would want for yourself as a way to keep current in your specialization? If you had to present a plan for expanding your knowledge in your field and upgrading your skills over a three-year period, what proposal might you make to your professional organization?

3. *Ethical issues in a multicultural perspective*

    a. It has been argued that established ethical codes are frequently insensitive to the client's cultural values. What is your view?

    b. Do you think that a separate set of ethical guidelines is needed for multicultural counseling? Why or why not?

    c. What ethical questions, if any, should be raised if you counsel someone who differs from you with respect to race? culture? sexual orientation? gender? socioeconomic status?

    d. What life experiences have you had that would either aid or hinder you in working with clients from diverse ethnic and cultural backgrounds?

4. *Foundations of ethical practice*

    a. The ethical codes of most professional organizations require that clients be presented with enough data to make informed choices about entering and continuing the client-therapist relationship. What are some matters you would explore with your clients at the first and second counseling sessions? What do you see as the client's work? What is your work as a counselor?

    b. Assume that the supervisor in your practicum asks you to tape-record your counseling sessions. You ask a prospective client for permission to tape the session, and he refuses. What would you say to the prospective client? What would you say to your supervisor?

    c. Assume that you work for an agency that has a policy to report the names of clients who use drugs but that you do not agree with the policy. Would you follow the policy as long as you were employed there, or would you keep information about your clients' use of drugs to yourself? Explain the implications of your position.

    d. What is your position on "mandatory counseling"? Do you believe counseling can be effective only if your client is willing to cooperate?

    e. How might you resolve a clash between what a client judged to be in her best interest and your judgment? What if her judgment was clearly self-destructive?

    f. What would you do if you decided to terminate counseling with a client because you felt quite sure that neither of you was making any progress? What would you do if your client objected to terminating even though he agreed that it was not "doing any good"? What would you do if your client wanted to continue because he wanted friendship with you, felt lonely, and liked being with you?

    g. What would you do with a client whom you judged to be in need of referral if there was no referral source available?

    h. Assume that you are employed in a mental hospital. The patients are being given a variety of drugs, not for their benefit but so that they are easier for the staff to manage. What is your position on the misuse of drugs? What might you say or do?

5. *Issues in the client/therapist relationship*

    a. What are your views about forming social relationships with clients? What are the arguments for and against combining social and therapeutic relationships?

    b. What guidelines would you use to determine when touching clients in nonerotic ways would be appropriate?

    c. Sexual contact in the therapeutic relationship has been termed "professional incest." What are your thoughts about the potential harm done to clients in such a relationship? What measures can you think of to prevent sex from entering the client/therapist relationship?

d. What are your thoughts about developing a romantic relationship with a *former* client? Would the amount of time that had elapsed since the end of therapy be an issue? Would the circumstances surrounding termination be an issue? What other ethical issues, if any, are involved?

e. How well prepared do you feel in dealing with potential sexual attractions to your clients? How ready are you to deal with clients who tell you that they are sexually attracted to you?

6. *Ethical and legal aspects of confidentiality*

a. What kind of information would you give your clients about the nature and purpose of confidentiality? What would you say if a client asked you what reasons would cause you to break confidentiality? How would you explain the limits of confidentiality to your client during an early session?

b. Some states allow children and adolescents to participate in psychological counseling without parental knowledge and consent. Do you agree or disagree with this practice? What particular areas do you think might justify minors' receiving treatment without parental consent? Why? What would you tell minors about confidentiality as it pertains to talking to their parents about them?

c. Assume that you are counseling an elementary schoolchild in a community clinic and that the child's parents show up one day and want to know from you what is going on. What kind of information would you *not* share with them? How would you cope with your responsibility to the parents without divulging certain confidences revealed to you by the child?

d. What issues of confidentiality can you think of in counseling clients who either think they have AIDS or have been diagnosed as having AIDS?

7. *Legal liability and malpractice*

a. At a time when malpractice suits are becoming increasingly common in many professions, what practical steps can you take to lessen the chances of being embroiled in such a legal battle? How can you keep aware of the legal and ethical values of professional practice and at the same time not be overly inhibited by restrictions? What are the main legal safeguards for clinical practice?

b. What are the main grounds for lawsuits against mental-health practitioners?

c. What responsibility do you see yourself as having for *predicting* violent behavior and suicidal tendencies on the part of your clients? What guidelines are most important in working with clients who might pose a danger to themselves or others?

# SELF-INVENTORY OF ATTITUDES RELATING TO ETHICAL ISSUES

This inventory is designed to assess your attitudes and beliefs on specific ethical issues. Select the response that comes closest to your position, or write your own response in "e." Bring the completed inventory to class as material for discussion.

1. A therapist's primary responsibility is to

   a. the client.
   b. the therapist's agency.
   c. society.
   d. the client's family.
   e. _____

2. Counseling or therapy should be aimed primarily at

   a. bringing about radical social and political change.
   b. eliminating the social ills that lead to powerlessness.
   c. individual change.
   d. change or adjustment within the family structure.
   e. _____

3. A therapist should terminate a therapeutic relationship when

   a. the client decides to terminate.
   b. the therapist judges that it is time to terminate.
   c. it is reasonably clear that the client is not benefiting from therapy.
   d. the client reaches an impasse.
   e. _____

4. Concerning the tape-recording of counseling sessions, I believe that

   a. it should be done only when I have the client's permission.
   b. it is ethical to secretly tape some sessions so that the client will not be self-conscious.
   c. it should never be done unless the supervisor requests it.
   d. it is advisable only when the therapist deems it so.
   e. _____

5. Regarding confidentiality, my position is that

   a. it is never ethical to disclose anything a client tells me under any circumstances.
   b. it is ethical to break a confidence when the therapist deems that the client might do harm to himself or herself or to others.
   c. confidences can be shared with the parents of the client if the parents request information.
   d. it applies only to licensed therapists.
   e. _____

6. The best way I can think of to avoid becoming involved in a malpractice lawsuit is

   a. to be extremely legalistic in my practice as a counselor.
   b. to decide to avoid taking any risks as a counselor.
   c. by turning to a supervisor any time I encounter difficulties.
   d. by keeping myself informed of local and state laws but not letting this knowledge immobilize my activity as a counselor.
   e. _____

7. A sexual relationship between a client and a therapist is

   a. ethical if the client initiates such a relationship.
   b. ethical if the therapist decides it would be in the best interests of the client.
   c. ethical only when both the therapist and the client discuss the issue and agree to such a relationship.
   d. never ethical under any circumstances.
   e. _____

8. Regarding the issue of counseling friends, I think that

   a. it is acceptable to accept a valued friend for a client.
   b. it should be done rarely and then only if it is clear that the friendship will not interfere with the therapeutic relationship.
   c. friendship and therapy should not be mixed.
   d. a friend could be accepted as a client only when the friend asks to be.
   e. _____

9. Concerning the issue of physically touching clients, my position is that

    a. touching is an important part of the therapeutic process.
    b. touching a client is not wise, because it can be misinterpreted by the client.
    c. touching a client is ethical when the client requests physical closeness with the therapist.
    d. it should be done only when the therapist feels like doing so.
    e. _____

10. The way I can best determine my level of competence in working with a given type of client is

    a. by having training, supervision, and experience in the areas in which I am practicing.
    b. by asking my clients whether they feel they are being helped.
    c. by possessing an advanced degree and a license.
    d. by relying on reactions and judgments from colleagues who are familiar with my work.
    e. _____

11. If I thought that my supervision as a counselor intern was inadequate, I would

    a. take the initiative and talk to my supervisor about it.
    b. seek supervision elsewhere, even if I had to pay for it.
    c. continue to work without complaining.
    d. attempt to compensate for the lack of supervision by doing extensive reading, attending conferences and workshops, and talking with fellow interns about my work.
    e. _____

12. Continuing education for those who counsel others

    a. should be mandated by professional organizations.
    b. should be left to the discretion of the practitioner.
    c. should be a requirement for relicensure of mental-health professionals.
    d. is appropriate primarily for professionals who are open to new learning, because requiring it will simply lead to complying with the letter of the law.
    e. _____

13. I would tend to refer a client to another professional

    a. if it were clear that the client was not benefiting in the relationship with me.
    b. if I felt a strong sexual attraction to the person.
    c. if the client continually stirred up painful feelings in me (reminded me of my mother, father, ex-spouse, and so on).
    d. if I had a hard time caring for or being interested in the client.
    e. _____

14. Regarding the ethics of social and personal relationships with clients, it is my position that

    a. it is never wise to see or to get involved with clients on a social basis.
    b. it is an acceptable practice to strike up a social relationship once the therapy relationship has ended if both want to do so.
    c. with some clients a personal and social relationship might well enhance the therapeutic relationship by building trust.
    d. it is ethical to combine a social and therapeutic relationship if both parties agree.
    e. _____

15. One of the best ways that I can think of to help me determine on what occasions and under what circumstances I would break confidentiality with a client is

    a. to confer with a supervisor or a consultant.
    b. to check out my perceptions with several colleagues.
    c. to follow my own intuitions and trust my own judgment.
    d. to discuss the matter with my client and solicit his or her opinion.
    e. _____

16. If I were an intern and became convinced that my supervisor was encouraging trainees to participate in unethical behavior in an agency setting, I would

    a. encourage those trainees involved to report the situation to the director.
    b. report the supervisor to the director of the agency myself.
    c. ignore the situation, because there is really not much I could do about it.
    d. look the other way out of fear of making the situation even worse.
    e. _____

17. I believe that the real reason for professional licensing and certification is

    a. to protect the public by setting minimum standards of competent practice.
    b. to protect licensed people from competition from unlicensed people and to preserve a "union shop."
    c. to increase the stature of the profession.
    d. to give the consumer a sense of confidence in the counseling profession.
    e. _____

18. My view of supervision is that it is

    a. a threat to my status as an independent professional.
    b. essential whenever I feel that I am at an impasse with a client.
    c. something that I could use on a continuing basis.
    d. a way that I can keep growing both personally and professionally.
    e. _____

19. If I thought that a client was at high risk for committing suicide, my course of action would be to tell my client that

    a. I would offer support for whatever decision she made.
    b. it would help to look at all the positive things to live for.
    c. I had certain legal and ethical responsibilities to take action to prevent her suicide.
    d. I intended to seek consultation with another professional because of my concern in this case.
    e. _____

20. In terms of appreciating and understanding the value systems of clients who are culturally different from me,

    a. I see it as my responsibility to learn about their values and not impose mine on them.
    b. I would encourage them to accept the values of the dominant culture for survival purposes.
    c. I would attempt to modify my counseling procedures to fit their cultural values.
    d. it is imperative that I learn about the specific cultural values my clients hold.
    e. _____

21. In working with clients from different ethnic groups, I think it is most important to

    a. be aware of the sociopolitical forces that have affected these clients.
    b. understand how language can act as a barrier to effective cross-cultural counseling.
    c. refer these clients to some professional who shares their ethnic and cultural background.
    d. help these clients modify their views so that they will be accepted and not have to suffer rejection.
    e. _____

22. To be effective in counseling clients from a different culture, a counselor must

    a. possess specific knowledge about the particular group he or she is counseling.
    b. be able to accurately "read" nonverbal messages.
    c. have had direct contact with this group.
    d. treat these clients no differently from clients from his or her own cultural background.
    e. _____

23. If my philosophy were in conflict with that of the institution I worked for, I would

   a. seriously consider whether I could ethically remain in that position.
   b. attempt to change the policies of the institution.
   c. agree to whatever was expected of me in that system.
   d. quietly do what I wanted to do, even if I had to be devious about it.
   e. _____

24. Of the following, I consider the most unethical form of counselor behavior to be

   a. using the client to satisfy my personal needs.
   b. promoting a dependent relationship.
   c. continuing therapy with a client when it seems clear that the client is not benefiting from it.
   d. practicing beyond my level of competence.
   e. _____

25. My definition of an ethical therapist is one who

   a. knows the right thing to do in each problem situation in counseling.
   b. follows all of the ethical codes of the profession.
   c. continually devotes time to self-examination on issues.
   d. does not take advantage of the client.
   e. _____


## SOME SUGGESTIONS FOR USING THIS SELF-INVENTORY

- On completing this inventory look over the items, and circle those you would like to bring to class and discuss with others. Limit yourself to a few issues that have stimulated your thinking the most.

- Look over the initial inventory that you completed in Chapter 1 of this manual. Compare the general tone of your responses in the two surveys.

- Work in pairs on certain questions. Compare your positions on each issue.

- Divide the class into small groups, each group taking one of the issues for discussion: confidentiality, mandatory counseling, therapist responsibility, the client/therapist relationship, therapist competence, therapist values and needs, and so on.

- Next, each group can report a consensus to the rest of the class. Some good material for debates can be generated when divergent viewpoints are established within or between groups.


# CASES INVOLVING ETHICAL DILEMMAS

Try your hand at dealing with these cases. Look for what you consider to be the core of the ethical dilemma in each case. Identify the issues, and clarify the position you would take in each situation. Working with these cases in class is an excellent way for you to expand your awareness of the ethical dimension of practice, and it will help you learn a process of ethical decision making. I suggest that you try role-playing these vignettes first. After you have had opportunities to be both the client and the counselor, discuss the issues involved in each situation.

## 1. Case of Dealing with Sexual Attractions

You have been treating client A for six weeks and find that your sexual attraction to him or her has been growing as the counseling relationship develops. It is becoming more and more difficult to focus on the therapy process because of your attraction. You feel, in turn, that A is flirtatious, although you have begun to doubt your own judgment and objectivity. You find yourself thinking about your client often, and you would like to extend the time you have together beyond the counseling sessions. You have had two sexual dreams involving the client. Although you are concerned about A's best interests, it is difficult for you to really listen, and you are aware of being preoccupied with being liked and accepted by A. At this point you are feeling some guilt and wondering if these feelings are "normal" in this situation.

- Do you think that this attraction presents both a personal and a professional problem? If so, how?

- Might you be inclined to discuss your attraction with your client? Give your rationale for either doing so or not doing so.

- Would you discuss this situation with another professional, such as a colleague? your supervisor? your therapist?

- Do you think that you would continue working with A or would refer him or her to another counselor? If you chose the first course, how would you deal with both your feelings toward A and A's feelings toward you? If you took the latter course, what reasons would you give to A for wanting to make this referral?

## 2. A Case of Dealing with a Client's Initiative

Still considering the prior case, assume that before you had made a decision concerning the way you would proceed with A, he or she returned the next week and began the sessions by telling you:

> There is something I really need to talk about. Lately I've been thinking a lot about you, and I'd really like to spend more time with you—outside of this office. You are very exciting to me, not just sexually but as a person, and I'd so much like to get to know more about you. By the way, it's important for me to know how you feel about me.

- What are your feelings and thoughts as you listen to A?

- What might you tell A about your feelings for him or her?

- How would you deal with A's request to spend some time out of the office?

- What do you see as the ethical issues involved in the way you might proceed?

## 3. A Colleague Who Is Having an Affair with a Former Client

You have just found out that one of the psychologists who works in your student mental-health clinic is having an affair with one of his former clients. The affair began ten months after the student completed therapy. The psychologist was teaching a counseling-skills course on campus, the student was attending, and after the course ended, they began dating in earnest. There has been quite a lot of gossip and debate in the clinic about the relationship, but the psychologist refuses to discuss it. Your colleagues wonder if it violates professional ethics. There is also the question of whether it violates the ethics of the student/teacher relationship.

- What are your thoughts about a psychotherapist dating his or her former clients? What about a psychologist who is an educator and on rare occasions dates a former student? Do you see any difference between a therapist/client relationship and an instructor/student relationship?

- Given the fact that there is gossip, what might you say to your colleague? If your colleague refused to talk about the matter, what might you do?

- What are your thoughts about the ethics of forming social or intimate relationships with *former* clients? Besides the amount of time that has elapsed since the end of therapy, what other factors need to be considered?

- Assume that this psychologist approached you and *asked* for your reactions. For a start, what might you say? (This scenario would be a good one to role-play.)

### 4. Racism among Your Colleagues

What do you do when there is sexism or racism among your colleagues? You work in the Psychiatry Department of a major metropolitan hospital and have become quite disturbed at the element of bias that you see around you. You have heard several therapists refer to clients in derogatory terms. In particular, you fear that the attitudes of one White male therapist who is counseling several Black women may be affecting his professional judgment. From some comments that you have heard from this therapist, it sounds to you as if he has definite prejudices against minorities and women.

- Would you be likely to confront this therapist? Why or why not?
- What would you want to ask him or tell him?
- What ethical issues are involved in this situation?

### 5. Breaches of Confidentiality

You work in private practice and rent office space with several other counselors and social workers. Although you are not legally bound to one another, you have formed a loose professional confederation, helping one another cover clients when someone is out of town, taking night calls and just discussing professional issues and problems as they arise. You discuss everything from billing and insurance problems to the thornier questions of psychotherapy and counseling. You have always enjoyed this professional association, but lately you have noticed that one therapist is talking a little bit too much about her clients and is referring to them by first *and* last names. You have tried to overlook this breach of confidentiality, because it has always occurred within the office walls. But last Sunday you were at an afternoon brunch and overheard the same therapist discussing her clients *by name* with the wife of one of your colleagues. You feel that she was clearly violating confidentiality, because the woman she was talking with was not a professional colleague.

- What would you say or do in this situation?
- Do you think that the therapist would be breaking confidentiality if she did not use any names?
- What might you say to your colleague if after you confronted her with your reactions, she told you that she saw nothing wrong with what she was doing and that you were being overly sensitive?

## SUGGESTED ACTIVITIES AND EXERCISES

Following are activities that you can do on your own, in small groups in the classroom, in pairs, or by contacting professional counselors to sample their reactions to some of these ethical issues. Because there are more activities than you can probably realistically complete, select those topics that have the most meaning for you.

1. Assume that you are in a field placement as a counselor in a community agency. The administrators tell you that they do *not* want you to inform your clients that you are a student intern. They explain that your clients might feel that they were getting second-class service if they found out that you were in training. The administrators contend that your clients are paying for the services they receive (on a sliding scale based on their ability to pay) and that it would not be psychologically good to give them any information that might cause them to conclude that they were not getting the best help available. What would you say and do if you found yourself as an intern in this situation? Would it be ethical to follow this directive and not

inform your clients that you were a trainee and that you were receiving supervision? Do you agree or disagree with the rationale of the administrators? Might you accept the internship assignment under the terms outlined if you could not find any other field placements?

2. How might you proceed if you knew of the unethical practice of a colleague? What kinds of unethical behavior of your colleagues, if any, do you think you would report?

3. Discuss some ways in which you can prepare clients for issues pertaining to confidentiality. How can you teach them about its purposes and the legal restrictions on it? Think particularly about the counseling of minors.

4. What experiences have you had with people from a different cultural background? Did you learn anything about your potential prejudices? What prejudices, if any, did you feel directed at you? You might bring your experiences to class. Also, I suggest that you interview other students or faculty members who identify themselves as ethnically or culturally different from you. What might they teach you about differences that you as a counselor would need to take into consideration in order to work more effectively with them?

5. Assume that you are applying for a job or writing a resume to be used in private practice. Write your own professional-disclosure statement in a page or two. Consider writing the essence of your views about matters such as these: the nature and purpose of counseling; what clients might expect from the process; a division of responsibilities between your client and you; a summary of your theoretical position, including the main techniques you are likely to use; a statement of the kinds of clients and problems that you are best qualified to work with; matters that might affect your relationship with your clients (such as legal restrictions, agency policy, and limits of confidentiality); and any other topics that you think could help clients decide if they wanted to consult with you. Another suggestion is to bring your disclosure statement to class and have fellow students review what you've written. They can then interview you, and you can get some practice in talking with "prospective clients." This exercise can help you clarify your own positions and give you valuable practice for job interviews.

6. Write an *informed-consent document* that you might give to clients. This could be in the form of a contract that outlines your responsibilities to clients. It can be considered an extension of the professional-disclosure statement that you wrote in the previous exercise. The informed-consent document that follows gives you a sample of some aspects you might include. The point of this exercise is to give you an opportunity to develop your own version of an information sheet that you might provide for your clients.

Your Name
Your Business Address
Your Business Phone Number

## INFORMATION AND CONSENT

I am pleased that you have selected me as your counselor. This document is designed to inform you about my background and to ensure that you understand our professional relationship.

I am licensed by (your state) as a Professional Counselor. In addition, I am certified by the National Board for Certified Counselors, a private national counselor certifying agency. My counseling practice is limited to (types of clients—that is, adolescents, couples, or the like).

I hold a(n) (your degree) from (name of institution).

I have been a professional counselor since (year). I accept in my private practice only clients who I believe have the capacity to resolve their own problems with my assistance. I believe that as people become more accepting of themselves, they are more capable of finding happiness and contentment in their lives. However, self-awareness and self-acceptance are goals that sometimes take a long time to achieve. Some clients need only a few counseling sessions to achieve these goals, whereas others may require months or even years of counseling. As a client you are in complete control and may end our counseling relationship at any point. I will be supportive of that decision. If counseling is successful, you should feel that you are able to face life's challenges in the future without my support or intervention.

Although our sessions may be very intimate psychologically, it is important for you to realize that we have a *professional* relationship rather than a personal one. Our contact will be limited to the paid sessions you have with me. Please do not invite me to social gatherings, offer gifts, or ask me to relate to you in any way other than in the professional context of our counseling sessions. You will be best served if our relationship stays strictly professional and if our sessions concentrate exclusively on your concerns. You will learn a great deal about me as we work together during your counseling experience. However, it is important for you to remember that you are experiencing me only in my professional role.

I will keep confidential anything you say to me, with the following exceptions: (1) you direct me to tell someone else, (2) I determine you are a danger to yourself or others, or (3) I am ordered by a court to disclose information.

If at any time for any reason you are dissatisfied with my services, please let me know. If I am not able to resolve your concerns, you may report your complaints to the Board for Professional Counselors in (your state) at (phone number) or the National Board for Certified Counselors in Alexandria, Virginia, at 703-461-6222.

In the return for a fee of $ _____ per session, I agree to provide counseling services for you. Sessions are ( ) minutes in duration. The fee for each session will be due and must be paid at the conclusion of each session. Cash or personal checks are acceptable for payment. I will provide you with a monthly receipt for all fees paid. In the event that you are unable to keep an appointment, you must notify me 24 hours in advance. If I do not receive such advance notice, you will be responsible for paying for the session you missed.

I assure you that my services will be rendered in a professional manner consistent with accepted ethical standards. Please note that it is impossible to guarantee any specific results regarding your counseling goals. However, together we will work to achieve the best possible results for you.

If you wish to seek reimbursement for my services from your health-insurance company, I will be happy to complete any forms related to your reimbursement provided by you or the insurance company. Because you will be paying me each session for my services, any later reimbursement from the insurance company should be sent directly to you. Please do not assign any payments to me.

Some health-insurance companies will reimburse clients for my counseling services, and some will not. Those that do reimburse usually require that a standard amount be paid by you before reimbursement is allowed, and then usually only a percentage of my fee is reimbursable. You should contact a company representative to determine whether your insurance company will reimburse you and about what schedule of reimbursement is used.

Health-insurance companies often require that I diagnose your mental condition and indicate that you have an "illness" before they will agree to reimburse you. In the event a diagnosis is required, I will inform you of the diagnosis I plan to render before I submit it to the health-insurance company. Any diagnosis made will become a part of your permanent insurance records.

If you have any questions, feel free to ask. Please sign and date both copies of this form.


_____          _____
Counselor's name & signature             Client's signature


_____          _____
Date                                     Date

*Note:* This form was designed by Theodore P. Remley, Jr. of Mississippi State University, who is both a counselor educator and an attorney at law, and is reproduced with his permission.

# STUDY, CRITIQUE, AND DISCUSSION OF ETHICAL STANDARDS

Read over the professional code of ethics of the American Association for Counseling and Development, which follows. In my classes students form in small discussion groups for the purpose of "picking apart" the codes. Remember, these are not written in cement, and they are only guides to ethical practice. One of their purposes is to stimulate thought and discussion.

In your study of these standards ask yourself: What guidelines do you think are the *most* important? Do you find yourself in disagreement with any specific guidelines? Do you think these ethical codes adequately cover the special concerns of all ethnic and cultural groups? Do you agree or disagree with the view of some writers that the codes are restricted in their applicability to multicultural issues in counseling? Do you see any specific guidelines that might be insensitive to the client's cultural values? Discuss these and other points with fellow students in discussion groups.

---

## ETHICAL STANDARDS

### American Association for Counseling and Development

## Preamble

*The Association is an educational, scientific, and professional organization whose members are dedicated to the enhancement of the worth, dignity, potential, and uniqueness of each individual and thus to the service of society.*

*The Association recognizes that the role definitions and work settings of its members include a wide variety of academic disciplines, levels of academic preparation, and agency services. This diversity reflects the breadth of the Association's interest and influence. It also poses challenging complexities in efforts to set standards for the performance of members, desired requisite preparation or practice, and supporting social, legal, and ethical controls.*

*The specification of ethical standards enables the Association to clarify to present and future members and to those served by members the nature of ethical responsibilities held in common by its members.*

*The existence of such standards serves to stimulate greater concern by members for their own professional functioning and for the conduct of fellow professionals such as counselors, guidance and student personnel workers, and others in the helping professions. As the ethical code of the Association, this document establishes principles that define the ethical behavior of Association members.*

*Additional ethical guidelines developed by the Association's Divisions for their specialty areas may further define a member's ethical behavior.*

## Section A: General

1. The member influences the development of the profession by continuous efforts to improve professional practices, teaching, services, and research. Professional growth is continuous throughout the member's career and is exemplified by the development of a philosophy that explains why and how a member functions in the helping relationship. Members must gather data on their effectiveness and be guided by the findings. Members recognize the need for continuing education to ensure competent service.

2. The member has a responsibility both to the individual who is served and to the institution within which the service is performed to maintain high standards of professional conduct. The member strives to maintain the highest levels of professional services offered to the individuals to be served. The member also strives to assist the agency, organization, or institution in providing the highest

caliber of professional services. The acceptance of employment in an institution implies that the member is in agreement with the general policies and principles of the institution. Therefore the professional activities of the member are also in accord with the objectives of the institution. If, despite concerted efforts, the member cannot reach agreement with the employer as to acceptable standards of conduct that allow for changes in institutional policy conducive to the positive growth and development of clients, then terminating the affiliation should be seriously considered.

3. Ethical behavior among professional associates, both members and nonmembers, must be expected at all times. When information is possessed that raises doubt as to the ethical behavior of professional colleagues, whether Association members or not, the member must take action to attempt to rectify such a condition. Such action shall use the institution's channels first and then use procedures established by the Association.

4. The member neither claims nor implies professional qualifications exceeding those possessed and is responsible for correcting any misrepresentations of these qualifications by others.

5. In establishing fees for professional counseling services, members must consider the financial status of clients and locality. In the event that the established fee structure is inappropriate for a client, assistance must be provided in finding comparable services of acceptable cost.

6. When members provide information to the public or to subordinates, peers, or supervisors, they have a responsibility to ensure that the content is general, unidentified client information that is accurate, unbiased, and consists of objective, factual data.

7. Members recognize their boundaries of competence and provide only those services and use only those techniques for which they are qualified by training or experience. Members should only accept those positions for which they are professionally qualified.

8. In the counseling relationship, the counselor is aware of the intimacy of the relationship and maintains respect for the client and avoids engaging in activities that seek to meet the counselor's personal needs at the expense of that client.

9. Members do not condone or engage in sexual harassment which is defined as deliberate or repeated comments, gestures, or physical contacts of a sexual nature.

10. The member avoids bringing personal issues into the counseling relationship, especially if the potential for harm is present. Through awareness of the negative impact of both racial and sexual stereotyping and discrimination, the counselor guards the individual rights and personal dignity of the client in the counseling relationship.

11. Products or services provided by the member by means of classroom instruction, public lectures, demonstrations, written articles, radio or television programs, or other types of media must meet the criteria cited in these Standards.

## Section B: Counseling Relationship

This section refers to practices and procedures of individual and/or group counseling relationships.

The member must recognize the need for client freedom of choice. Under those circumstances where this is not possible, the member must apprise clients of restrictions that may limit their freedom of choice.

1. The member's primary obligation is to respect the integrity and promote the welfare of the client(s), whether the client(s) is(are) assisted individually or in a group relationship. In a group setting, the member is also responsible for taking reasonable precautions to protect individuals from physical and/or psychological trauma resulting from interaction within the group.

2. Members make provisions for maintaining confidentiality in the storage and disposal of records and follow an established record retention and disposition policy. The counseling relationship and information resulting therefrom must be kept confidential, consistent with the obligations of the member as a professional person. In a group counseling

setting, the counselor must set a norm of confidentiality regarding all group participants' disclosures.

3. If an individual is already in a counseling relationship with another professional person, the member does not enter into a counseling relationship without first contacting and receiving the approval of that other professional. If the member discovers that the client is in another counseling relationship after the counseling relationship begins, the member must gain the consent of the other professional or terminate the relationship, unless the client elects to terminate the other relationship.

4. When the client's condition indicates that there is clear and imminent danger to the client or others, the member must take reasonable personal action or inform responsible authorities. Consultation with other professionals must be used where possible. The assumption of responsibility for the client's(s') behavior must be taken only after careful deliberation. The client must be involved in the resumption of responsibility as quickly as possible.

5. Records of the counseling relationship, including interview notes, test data, correspondence, tape recordings, electronic data storage, and other documents are to be considered professional information for use in counseling, and they should not be considered a part of the records of the institution or agency in which the counselor is employed unless specified by state statute or regulation. Revelation to others of counseling material must occur only upon the expressed consent of the client.

6. In view of the extensive data storage and processing capacities of the computer, the member must ensure that data maintained on a computer is: (a) limited to information that is appropriate and necessary for the services being provided; (b) destroyed after it is determined that the information is no longer of any value in providing services; and (c) restricted in terms of access to appropriate staff members involved in the provision of services by using the best computer security methods available.

7. Use of data derived from a counseling relationship for purposes of counselor training or research shall be confined to content that can be disguised to ensure full protection of the identity of the subject client.

8. The member must inform the client of the purposes, goals, techniques, rules of procedure, and limitations that may affect the relationship at or before the time that the counseling relationship is entered. When working with minors or persons who are unable to give consent, the member protects these clients' best interests.

9. In view of common misconceptions related to the perceived inherent validity of computer generated data and narrative reports, the member must ensure that the client is provided with information as part of the counseling relationship that adequately explains the limitations of computer technology.

10. The member must screen prospective group participants, especially when the emphasis is on self-understanding and growth through self-disclosure. The member must maintain an awareness of the group participants' compatibility throughout the life of the group.

11. The member may choose to consult with any other professionally competent person about a client. In choosing a consultant, the member must avoid placing the consultant in a conflict of interest situation that would preclude the consultant's being a proper party to the member's efforts to help the client.

12. If the member determines an inability to be of professional assistance to the client, the member must either avoid initiating the counseling relationship or immediately terminate that relationship. In either event, the member must suggest appropriate alternatives. (The member must be knowledgeable about referral resources so that a satisfactory referral can be initiated.) In the event the client declines the suggested referral, the member is not obligated to continue the relationship.

13. When the member has other relationships, particularly of an administrative, supervisory, and/or evaluative nature with an individual seeking counseling services, the member must not serve as the counselor but should refer the individual to another professional. Only

in instances where such an alternative is unavailable and where the individual's situation warrants counseling intervention should the member enter into and/or maintain a counseling relationship. Dual relationships with clients that might impair the member's objectivity and professional judgment (e.g., as with close friends or relatives) must be avoided and/or the counseling relationship terminated through referral to another competent professional.

14. The member will avoid any type of sexual intimacies with clients. Sexual relationships with clients are unethical.

15. All experimental methods of treatment must be clearly indicated to prospective recipients, and safety precautions are to be adhered to by the member.

16. When computer applications are used as a component of counseling services, the member must ensure that: (a) the client is intellectually, emotionally, and physically capable of using the computer application; (b) the computer application is appropriate for the needs of the client; (c) the client understands the purpose and operation of the computer application; and (d) that a follow-up of client use of a computer application is provided to both correct possible problems (misconceptions or inappropriate use) and assess subsequent needs.

17. When the member is engaged in short-term group treatment/training programs (e.g., marathons and other encounter-type or growth groups), the member ensures that there is professional assistance available during and following the group experience.

18. Should the member be engaged in a work setting that calls for any variation from the above statements, the member is obligated to consult with other professionals whenever possible to consider justifiable alternatives.

19. The member must ensure that members of various ethnic, racial, religious, disability, and socioeconomic groups have equal access to computer applications used to support counseling services and that the content of available computer applications does not discriminate against the groups described above.

20. When computer applications are developed by the member for use by the general public as self-help stand-alone computer software, the member must ensure that: (a) self-help computer applications are designed from the beginning to function in a stand-alone manner, as opposed to modifying software that was originally designed to require support from a counselor; (b) self-help computer applications will include within the program statements regarding intended user outcomes, suggestions for using the software, a description of the conditions under which self-help computer applications might not be appropriate, and a description of when and how counseling services might be beneficial; and (c) the manual for such applications will include the qualifications of the developer, the development process, validation data, and operating procedures.

## Section C: Measurement and Evaluation

The primary purpose of educational and psychological testing is to provide descriptive measures that are objective and interpretable in either comparable or absolute terms. The member must recognize the need to interpret the statements that follow as applying to the whole range of appraisal techniques including test and nontest data. Test results constitute only one of a variety of pertinent sources of information for personnel, guidance, and counseling decisions.

1. The member must provide specific orientation or information to the examinee(s) prior to and following the test administration so that the results of testing may be placed in proper perspective with other relevant factors. In so doing, the member must recognize the effects of socioeconomic, ethnic, and cultural factors on test scores. It is the member's professional responsibility to use additional unvalidated information carefully in modifying interpretation of the test results.

2. In selecting tests for use in a given situation or with a particular client, the member must consider carefully the specific validity, reliability, and appropriateness of the test(s). General validity, reliability, and related issues may be

questioned legally as well as ethically when tests are used for vocational and educational selection, placement, or counseling.

3. When making any statements to the public about tests and testing, the member must give accurate information and avoid false claims or misconceptions. Special efforts are often required to avoid unwarranted connotations of such terms as IQ and grade equivalent scores.

4. Different tests demand different levels of competence for administration, scoring, and interpretation. Members must recognize the limits of their competence and perform only those functions for which they are prepared. In particular, members using computer-based test interpretations must be trained in the construct being measured and the specific instrument being used prior to using this type of computer application.

5. In situations where a computer is used for test administration and scoring, the member is responsible for ensuring that administration and scoring programs function properly to provide clients with accurate test results.

6. Tests must be administered under the same conditions that were established in their standardization. When tests are not administered under standard conditions or when unusual behavior or irregularities occur during the testing session, those conditions must be noted and the results designated as invalid or of questionable validity. Unsupervised or inadequately supervised test-taking, such as the use of tests through the mails, is considered unethical. On the other hand, the use of instruments that are so designed or standardized to be self-administered and self-scored, such as interest inventories, is to be encouraged.

7. The meaningfulness of test results used in personnel, guidance, and counseling functions generally depends on the examinee's unfamiliarity with the specific items on the test. Any prior coaching or dissemination of the test materials can invalidate test results. Therefore, test security is one of the professional obligations of the member. Conditions that produce most favorable test results must be made known to the examinee.

8. The purpose of testing and the explicit use of the results must be made known to the examinee prior to testing. The counselor must ensure that instrument limitations are not exceeded and that periodic review and/or retesting are made to prevent client stereotyping.

9. The examinee's welfare and explicit prior understanding must be the criteria for determining the recipients of the test results. The member must see that specific interpretation accompanies any release of individual or group test data. The interpretation of test data must be related to the examinee's particular concerns.

10. Members responsible for making decisions based on test results have an understanding of educational and psychological measurement, validation criteria, and test research.

11. The member must be cautious when interpreting the results of research instruments possessing insufficient technical data. The specific purposes for the use of such instruments must be stated explicitly to examinees.

12. The member must proceed with caution when attempting to evaluate and interpret the performance of minority group members or other persons who are not represented in the norm group on which the instrument was standardized.

13. When computer-based interpretations are developed by the member to support the assessment process, the member must ensure that the validity of such interpretations is established prior to the commercial distribution of such a computer application.

14. The member recognizes that test results may become obsolete. The member will avoid and prevent the misuse of obsolete test results.

15. The member must guard against the appropriation, reproduction, or modification of published tests or parts thereof without acknowledgment and permission from the previous publisher.

## Section D: Research and Publication

1. Guidelines on research with human subjects shall be adhered to, such as:
   a. Ethical Principles in the Conduct of

Research with Human Participants, Washington, D.C.: American Psychological Association, Inc., 1982.

   b. Code of Federal Regulations, Title 45, Subtitle A, Part 46, as currently issued.

   c. *Ethical Principles of Psychologists*, American Psychological Association, Principle #9: Research with Human Participants.

   d. Family Educational Rights and Privacy Act (the "Buckley Amendment").

   e. Current federal regulations and various state rights privacy acts.

2. In planning any research activity dealing with human subjects, the member must be aware of and responsive to all pertinent ethical principles and ensure that the research problem, design, and execution are in full compliance with them.

3. Responsibility for ethical research practice lies with the principal researcher, while others involved in the research activities share ethical obligation and full responsibility for their own actions.

4. In research with human subjects, researchers are responsible for the subjects' welfare throughout the experiment, and they must take all reasonable precautions to avoid causing injurious psychological, physical, or social effects on their subjects.

5. All research subjects must be informed of the purpose of the study except when withholding information or providing misinformation to them is essential to the investigation. In such research the member must be responsible for corrective action as soon as possible following completion of the research.

6. Participation in research must be voluntary. Involuntary participation is appropriate only when it can be demonstrated that participation will have no harmful effects on subjects and is essential to the investigation.

7. When reporting research results, explicit mention must be made of all variables and conditions known to the investigator that might affect the outcome of the investigation or the interpretation of the data.

8. The member must be responsible for conducting and reporting investigations in a manner that minimizes the possi-

bility that results will be misleading.

9. The member has an obligation to make available sufficient original research data to qualified others who may wish to replicate the study.

10. When supplying data, aiding in the research of another person, reporting research results, or in making original data available, due care must be taken to disguise the identity of the subjects in the absence of specific authorization from such subjects to do otherwise.

11. When conducting and reporting research, the member must be familiar with and give recognition to previous work on the topic, as well as to observe all copyright laws and follow the principles of giving full credit to all to whom credit is due.

12. The member must give due credit through joint authorship, acknowledgment, footnote statements, or other appropriate means to those who have contributed significantly to the research and/or publication, in accordance with such contributions.

13. The member must communicate to other members the results of any research judged to be of professional or scientific value. Results reflecting unfavorably on institutions, programs, services, or vested interests must not be withheld for such reasons.

14. If members agree to cooperate with another individual in research and/or publication, they incur an obligation to cooperate as promised in terms of punctuality of performance and with full regard to the completeness and accuracy of the information required.

15. Ethical practice requires that authors not submit the same manuscript or one essentially similar in content for simultaneous publication consideration by two or more journals. In addition, manuscripts published in whole or in substantial part in another journal or published work should not be submitted for publication without acknowledgment and permission from the previous publication.

## Section E: Consulting

Consultation refers to a voluntary relationship between a professional helper and help-needing individual, group, or social unit in which the consultant is providing help to the client(s) in defining and solving a work-related problem or potential problem with a client or client system.

1. The member acting as a consultant must have a high degree of self-awareness of his/her own values, knowledge, skills, limitations, and needs in entering a helping relationship that involves human and/or organizational change and that the focus of the relationship be on the issues to be resolved and not on the person(s) presenting the problem.
2. There must be understanding and agreement between member and client for the problem definition, change of goals, and prediction of consequences of interventions selected.
3. The member must be reasonably certain that she/he or the organization represented has the necessary competencies and resources for giving the kind of help that is needed now or may be needed later and that appropriate referral resources are available to the consultant.
4. The consulting relationship must be one in which client adaptability and growth toward self-direction are encouraged and cultivated. The member must maintain this role consistently and not become a decision maker for the client or create a future dependency on the consultant.
5. When announcing consultant availability for services, the member conscientiously adheres to the Association's Ethical Standards.
6. The member must refuse a private fee or other remuneration for consultation with persons who are entitled to these services through the member's employing institution or agency. The policies of a particular agency may make explicit provisions for private practice with agency clients by members of its staff. In such instances, the clients must be apprised of other options open to them should they seek private counseling services.

## Section F: Private Practice

1. The member should assist the profession by facilitating the availability of counseling services in private as well as public settings.

2. In advertising services as a private practitioner, the member must advertise the services in a manner that accurately informs the public of professional services, expertise, and techniques of counseling available. A member who assumes an executive leadership role in the organization shall not permit his/her name to be used in professional notices during periods when he/she is not actively engaged in the private practice of counseling.
3. The member may list the following: highest relevant degree, type and level of certification and/or license, address, telephone number, office hours, type and/or description of services, and other relevant information. Such information must not contain false, inaccurate, misleading, partial, out-of-context, or deceptive material or statements.
4. Members do not present their affiliation with any organization in such a way that would imply inaccurate sponsorship or certification by that organization.
5. Members may join in partnership/corporation with other members and/or other professionals provided that each member of the partnership or corporation makes clear the separate specialties by name in compliance with the regulations of the locality.
6. A member has an obligation to withdraw from a counseling relationship if it is believed that employment will result in violation of the Ethical Standards. If the mental or physical condition of the member renders it difficult to carry out an effective professional relationship or if the member is discharged by the client because the counseling relationship is no longer productive for the client, then the member is obligated to terminate the counseling relationship.
7. A member must adhere to the regulations for private practice of the locality where the services are offered.
8. It is unethical to use one's institutional affiliation to recruit clients for one's private practice.

## Section G: Personnel Administration

It is recognized that most members are employed in public or quasi-public institutions. The functioning of a member within an institution must contribute to the goals of the institution and vice versa if either is to accomplish their respective goals or objectives. It is therefore essential that the member and the institution function in ways to: (a) make the institution's goals explicit and public; (b) make the member's contribution to institutional goals specific; and (c) foster mutual accountability for goal achievement.

To accomplish these objectives, it is recognized that the member and the employer must share responsibilities in the formulation and implementation of personnel policies.

1. Members must define and describe the parameters and levels of their professional competency.
2. Members must establish interpersonal relations and working agreements with supervisors and subordinates regarding counseling or clinical relationships, confidentiality, distinction between public and private material, maintenance and dissemination of recorded information, work load, and accountability. Working agreements in each instance must be specified and made known to those concerned.
3. Members must alert their employers to conditions that may be potentially disruptive or damaging.
4. Members must inform employers of conditions that may limit their effectiveness.
5. Members must submit regularly to professional review and evaluation.
6. Members must be responsible for in-service development of self and/or staff.
7. Members must inform their staff of goals and programs.
8. Members must provide personnel practices that guarantee and enhance the rights and welfare of each recipient of their service.
9. Members must select competent persons and assign responsibilities compatible with their skills and experiences.
10. The member, at the onset of a counseling relationship, will inform the client of the member's intended use of supervisors regarding the disclosure of information concerning this case. The member will clearly inform the client of the limits of confidentiality in the relationship.
11. Members, as either employers or employees, do not engage in or condone practices that are inhumane, illegal, or unjustifiable (such as considerations based on sex, handicap, age, race) in hiring, promotion, or training.

**Section H: Preparation Standards**

Members who are responsible for training others must be guided by the preparation standards of the Association and relevant Division(s). The member who functions in the capacity of trainer assumes unique ethical responsibilities that frequently go beyond that of the member who does not function in a training capacity. These ethical responsibilities are outlined as follows:

1. Members must orient students to program expectations, basic skills development, and employment prospects prior to admission to the program.
2. Members in charge of learning experiences must establish programs that integrate academic study and supervised practice.
3. Members must establish a program directed toward developing students' skills, knowledge, and self-understanding, stated whenever possible in competency or performance terms.
4. Members must identify the levels of competencies of their students in compliance with relevant Division standards. These competencies must accommodate the paraprofessional as well as the professional.
5. Members, through continual student evaluation and appraisal, must be aware of the personal limitations of the learner that might impede future performance. The instructor must not only assist the learner in securing remedial assistance but also screen from the program those individuals who are unable to provide competent services.
6. Members must provide a program that includes training in research commensurate with levels of role functioning. Paraprofessional and technician-level personnel must be trained as consumers of research. In addition, personnel must learn how to evaluate their own and their program's effectiveness. Graduate training, especially at the doctoral level, would include preparation for original research by the member.
7. Members must make students aware of

the ethical responsibilities and standards of the profession.

8. Preparatory programs must encourage students to value the ideals of service to individuals and to society. In this regard, direct financial remuneration or lack thereof must not influence the quality of service rendered. Monetary considerations must not be allowed to overshadow professional and humanitarian needs.

9. Members responsible for educational programs must be skilled as teachers and practitioners.

10. Members must present thoroughly varied theoretical positions so that students may make comparisons and have the opportunity to select a position.

11. Members must develop clear policies within their educational institutions regarding field placement and the roles of the student and the instructor in such placement.

12. Members must ensure that forms of learning focusing on self-understanding or growth are voluntary, or if required as part of the educational program, are made known to prospective students prior to entering the program. When the educational program offers a growth experience with an emphasis on self-disclosure or other relatively intimate or personal involvement, the member must have no administrative, supervisory, or evaluating authority regarding the participant.

13. The member will at all times provide students with clear and equally acceptable alternatives for self-understanding or growth experiences. The member will assure students that they have a right to accept these alternatives without prejudice or penalty.

14. Members must conduct an educational program in keeping with the current relevant guidelines of the Association.

---

## STUDY QUESTIONS FOR THE AACD ETHICAL STANDARDS

To guide you in your study and discussion of professional ethics, I've prepared some questions that are keyed to various topics in each section of the AACD *Ethical Standards* (numbers refer to the corresponding subsections under the given heading of the *Ethical Standards*). You can pick out other topics in the standards that you would like to discuss.

### Section A: General

5. *Establishing fees.* Do you think that ethical practice dictates a sliding scale of fees? How would you determine an appropriate fee structure for a client?

7. *Boundaries of competence.* Assume that you recognize the boundaries of your competence but that your employer asks you to perform services for which you think you have not had the training or experience necessary to render quality service. What would you say to your employer?

8. *Counselor's personal needs.* How would you assess those activities that "meet [your] personal needs at the expense of the client?" Do you think that it is possible to continue your work as a counselor if you do not meet your own needs?

9. *Sexual harassment.* What might you do if an employer, a supervisor, or a professor were sexually harassing you?

10. *Stereotyping of clients.* How would you guard against racial and sexual stereotyping in counseling relationships with your clients?

### Section B: Counseling Relationship

3. *Relationships with other therapists.* Assume that you discover that one of your clients (whom you have seen twice) is also seeing another therapist. Your client does not want to

terminate with his other therapist, yet he would like to continue seeing you. What would you do?

4. *Seeking consultation.* How would you determine when your "client's condition indicates that there is clear and imminent danger to the client or others"? How would you assess the degree of danger? When would you seek consultation with another professional?

8. *Informed consent.* What procedures would you use to inform prospective clients about the nature of counseling at the beginning of therapy? In the case of counseling with minors, how would you protect their best interest?

10. *Screening.* If you set up a group without screening prospective members, would that be unethical? Is it always possible to screen group members?

12. *Terminating and referring.* What would you do if you thought you could not be of help to a client, yet the client wanted to continue seeing you? What action would you take if this client refused to accept a referral?

13. *Dual relationships.* Do you think that all forms of dual relationships are unethical? What would you be likely to do when dual relationships were inevitable and could not be avoided?

14. *Sexual intimacies.* What do you think you would say to a client who sought your services and told you that her prior therapist had initiated and continued sexual contact with her for several months before she terminated therapy with him? What action, if any, would you take?

## Section C: Measurement and Evaluation

1. *Interpreting test scores.* How can counselors "recognize the effects of socioeconomic, ethnic, and cultural factors on test scores"? Practically speaking, how can you take these factors into account in working with culturally diverse clients?

12. *Evaluating test performance.* How would you "proceed with caution when attempting to evaluate and interpret the test performance of minority group members"?

14. *Obsolete test results.* Suppose your supervisor asks you to send a client's intelligence-test scores, which are five years old, to the client's high school principal. What factors do you have to consider before releasing these records?

## Section D: Research and Publication

5. *Informing research subjects.* In doing research with human subjects, what steps would you take to avoid injurious psychological and social effects on them?

6. *Participation in research.* Do you think that research must make use of voluntary subjects only?

## Section E: Consulting

4. *Client dependency.* In a consulting relationship what would be the ethical course to take if a client seemed to be dependent on the consultant?

6. *Consultation and private practice.* If Mr. X seeks out personal therapy with a psychologist who is consulting in Mr. X's agency, is it ethical for the psychologist to accept him as a client?

## Section F: Private Practice

3. *Advertising.* If you knew of a colleague in private practice who was providing inaccurate information about his background and qualifications in his advertisement, what would you say or do?

8. *Recruiting clients.* What might you do if one of your professors used her affiliation with the university as a way to actively solicit clients for her private practice? Do you think it is always unethical for a professor to recruit clients from students?

## Section G:  Personnel Administration

4. *Informing employers.* Assume that you inform your employer of conditions that may limit your effectiveness and that your employer disagrees with your assessment of the situation. What will you do?

10. *Limits of confidentiality.* What kind of information would you give to your clients about the limitations of confidentiality?

## Section H:  Preparation Standards

5. *Evaluating and screening students.* What are the ethical and legal ramifications of instructors' "screening from the program those individuals who are unable to provide competent services"? On what basis are these decisions made?

10. *Theoretical positions.* Assume that a given graduate counseling program is heavily slanted toward a single theoretical orientation. What do you think of the ethics of this practice?

12. *Self-understanding and growth experiences.* Some counselor-education programs require a personal-growth group or some other form of a self-exploration workshop. The leader of this growth group might also be a professor who teaches required courses in the program (and has the responsibility of grading students in those courses). What are your thoughts about the ethics of this practice?

13. *Alternatives to growth experiences.* If a counseling program clearly states from the outset that a self-exploration course (group experience) is a required part of the program, do you think that those in charge of the program are behaving unethically if they do not "provide students with clear and equally acceptable alternatives for self-understanding or growth experiences"?

*Note*:  In considering the entire AACD *Ethical Standards*, do you think that any areas are not addressed adequately? What aspects of the present code would you like to change (and how) if you were on the Ethics Committee charged with the revision of these codes? With your fellow students, identify specific changes that you would recommend.

For your study of the AACD code I highly recommend reading *Ethical Standards Casebook*, Fourth Edition (by B. Herlihy and L. Golden, 1990), which contains a variety of useful cases that are geared to the Code. The examples illustrate and clarify the meaning and intent of the standards. There are also case studies demonstrating that ethical dilemmas are rarely simple. Included in this casebook are a number of stimulating essays written by various counselor educators on topics such as confidentiality, advertising, multicultural counseling, dual relationships, child abuse, counseling records, and counselor impairment. The appendix contains the divisional codes of ethics for the ACPA, AMHCA, ARCA, ASCA, ASGW, and NCDA and the ethical standards of the National Board for Certified Counselors. Also described are the specific steps to be followed in reporting and processing allegations of unethical behavior by members. (This casebook can be purchased from the AACD, 5999 Stevenson Avenue, Alexandria, VA 22304; telephone:  703-823-9800.)

# 4

# PSYCHOANALYTIC
# THERAPY

## PRECHAPTER SELF-INVENTORIES

*Directions*: The purpose of this self-inventory scale is to identify and clarify your attitudes and beliefs related to the key concepts of and issues raised by each therapeutic approach. Complete the self-inventory before you read the corresponding textbook chapter. Then, after reading the chapter and discussing it in class, take the self-inventory again to determine whether you have modified your position on any of the issues. Respond to each statement, giving the initial response that most clearly identifies how you really think or feel. Remember that the idea is for you to express your view, not to decide which is the "correct" answer. Each statement is a true assumption of the particular approach. Thus, you are rating your degree of agreement or disagreement with the assumptions that are a part of each theory.

Using the following code, write the number of responses that most closely reflects your viewpoint on the line at the left of each statement:

5 = I *strongly agree* with this statement.

4 = I *agree*, in most respects, with this statement.

3 = I am *undecided* in my opinion about this statement.

2 = I *disagree*, in most respects, with this statement.

1 = I *strongly disagree* with this statement.

Compare your responses with those of your classmates, and use the statements as points for discussion in class sessions.

## PRECHAPTER SELF-INVENTORY

_____  1. Clients are ready to terminate therapy when they have clarified and accepted their current emotional problems, have understood the historical roots of their difficulties, and can integrate these awarenesses of their present problems with past relationships.

_____  2. Our infantile conflicts may never be fully resolved even though many aspects of transference are worked through with a therapist.

_____  3. We experience transference with many people, and our past is always a vital part of the person we are presently becoming.

_____  4. The transference situation is considered valuable in therapy because its manifestations provide clients with the opportunity to reexperience a variety of feelings that would otherwise be inaccessible.

_____  5. The key to understanding human behavior is understanding the unconscious.

_____ 6. Most psychological conflicts are not open to conscious control because their source has been repressed and remains unconscious.

_____ 7. The unconscious, even though it is out of awareness, has a great influence on behavior.

_____ 8. Development during the first six years of life is a crucial determinant of the later, adult personality.

_____ 9. Most personality and behavior problems have roots in a failure to resolve some phase of psychosexual development in early childhood.

_____ 10. One learns the basic sense of trust in one's world during the events during the first year of life.

_____ 11. In order to progress toward healthy development, one must learn how to deal with feelings of rage, hostility, and anger during the second and third years of life.

_____ 12. It is normal for children around the age of 5 to have concerns about their sexuality, their sex roles, and their sexual feelings.

_____ 13. Insight, understanding, and working through earlier, repressed material are essential aspects of therapy.

_____ 14. Therapists should engage in relatively little self-revelation and should remain anonymous.

_____ 15. For therapy to be effective, clients must be willing to commit themselves to an intensive and long-term therapeutic process.

_____ 16. Therapy is not complete unless the client works through the transference process.

_____ 17. Analysis and interpretation are essential elements in the therapeutic process.

_____ 18. It is important that a client relive the past in therapy.

_____ 19. Effective therapy cannot occur unless the underlying causes of a client's problem are understood and treated.

_____ 20. The basic aim of therapy is to make the unconscious conscious.

# OVERVIEW OF PSYCHOANALYTIC THERAPY

## KEY FIGURES AND MAJOR FOCUS

Original key figure: Sigmund Freud. Ego psychologist: Erik Erikson. Leading contemporary figures: Margaret Mahler, Otto Kernberg, and Heinz Kohut. Historically, psychoanalysis was the first system of psychotherapy. It is a personality theory, a philosophy of human nature, and a method of therapy.

## PHILOSOPHY AND BASIC ASSUMPTIONS

Although the Freudian view of human nature is basically deterministic and focuses on irrational forces, biological and instinctual drives, and unconscious motivation, later developments in psychoanalysis stressed social and cultural factors. Contemporary psychoanalytic thinking emphasizes the development of the ego and the differentiation and individuation of the self.

## KEY CONCEPTS

Key notions include the division of the personality into the id, ego, and superego; the unconscious; anxiety; the functioning of the ego-defense mechanisms; and a focus on the past for clues to present problems. Healthy personality development is based on successful resolution of both psychosexual and psychosocial issues at the appropriate stages. Psychopathology is the result of failing to meet some critical developmental task or becoming fixated at some early level of development. Freudian psychoanalysis is basically an id psychology, whereas the newer formulations of psychoanalytic therapy are based on an ego psychology. The contemporary trends stress psychosocial development throughout the life span.

## THERAPEUTIC GOALS

A primary goal is to make the unconscious conscious. Both psychoanalysis and psychoanalytically oriented therapy seek the growth of the ego through analysis of resistance and transference, allowing the ego to solve the unconscious conflicts. The restructuring of personality is more an aim than is solving immediate problems.

## THERAPEUTIC RELATIONSHIP

In classical psychoanalysis the anonymity of the therapist is stressed, so that clients can project feelings onto the therapist. With psychoanalytically oriented therapy the therapist tries to relate objectively with warm detachment but does not remain anonymous. Both transference and countertransference are central aspects in the relationship. The focus is on resistances that occur in the therapeutic process, on interpretation of these resistances, and on working through transference feelings. Through this process clients explore the parallels between their past and present experience and thus gain new understanding that can be the basis for personality change.

## TECHNIQUES AND PROCEDURES

All techniques are designed to help the client gain insight and bring repressed material to the surface so that it can be dealt with in a conscious way. Major techniques include maintaining the analytic framework, free association, dream analysis, and interpretation, analysis of resistance, and analysis of transference. These techniques are geared to increasing awareness, gaining intellectual insight, and beginning a working-through process that will lead to a reorganization of the personality.

## APPLICATIONS

Good candidates for analytic therapy include professionals who wish to become therapists as well as people who have been helped by intensive therapy and want to go further. This therapy demands sacrifices of time, money, and personal commitment and is typically a long-term process. Psychoanalytic concepts can be applied to understanding the psychodynamics of behavior on many levels and in many areas such as the arts, religion, education, and human development.

## CONTRIBUTIONS

Many other models have developed as reactions against psychoanalysis. The theory has had a powerful, revolutionary influence on all aspects of life in our time. It provides a comprehensive and detailed system of personality. It emphasizes the legitimate place of the unconscious as a determinant of behavior, highlights the profound effect of early childhood development, and provides procedures for tapping the unconscious. Several factors can be applied by practitioners with nonanalytic orientations, such as understanding of ways in which resistance is manifested, how early trauma can be worked through so that a client is not fixated, the manifestations of transference and countertransference in the therapy relationship, and the functioning of the ego-defense mechanisms.

## LIMITATIONS

Psychoanalysis involves lengthy training for the therapist and a great amount of time and expense for clients. There is limited delivery of services. The approach stresses the role of insight but does not give due recognition to the importance of action methods. The concepts cannot be verified by research methods. The model is based on the study of neurotics, not of healthy people. The orthodox Freudian approach, with its stress on instinctual forces, ignores social, cultural, and interpersonal factors. The techniques of this long-term approach are of limited applicability to crisis counseling, working with minorities, and social work.

# GLOSSARY OF KEY TERMS

**Abreaction.** The emotional release resulting from recalling and reliving painful and repressed experiences.

**Anal stage.** The second stage of psychosexual development, at which time pleasure is derived from retaining and expelling feces.

**Borderline personality.** A disorder characterized by instability, irritability, self-destructive acts, impulsivity, and extreme mood shifts. Such people lack a sense of their own identity and do not have a deep understanding of others.

**Countertransference.** The therapist's unconscious emotional responses to a client that are likely to interfere with objectivity; unresolved conflicts of the therapist that are projected onto the client.

**Ego.** The part of the personality that is the mediator between external reality and inner demands.

**Ego-defense mechanisms.** Intrapsychic processes that operate unconsciously to protect the person from threatening and, therefore, anxiety-producing thoughts, feelings, and impulses.

**Ego psychology.** The psychosocial approach of Erik Erikson; emphasizes the development of the ego or self at various stages of life.

**Electra complex.** The unconscious sexual desire of the female child for her father, along with feelings of hostility toward her mother.

**Fixation.** The condition of being arrested, or "stuck," at one level of psychosexual development.

**Free association.** A primary technique, consisting of spontaneous and uncensored verbalization by the client, which gives clues to the nature of the client's unconscious conflicts.

**Genital stage.** The final stage of psychosexual development, usually attained at adolescence, in which heterosexual interests and activities are predominant.

**Id.** The part of personality, present at birth, that is blind, demanding, and insistent. Its function is to discharge tension and return to homeostasis.

**Identity crisis.** A developmental challenge, occurring during adolescence, whereby the person seeks to establish a stable view of self and to define a place in life.

**Latency stage.** A period of psychosexual development, following the phallic stage, that is relatively calm before the storm of adolescence.

**Libido.** The instinctual drives of the id and the source of psychic energy.

**Narcissism.** Extreme self-love, as opposed to love of others. A narcissistic personality is characterized by a grandiose and exaggerated sense of self-importance and an exploitive attitude toward others, which hides a poor self-concept.

**Object-relations theory.** A newer version of psychoanalytic thinking, which focuses on predictable developmental sequences in which early experiences of self shift in relation to an expanding awareness of others. It holds that individuals go through phases of autism, normal symbiosis, and separation and individuation, culminating in a state of integration.

**Oedipus complex.** The unconscious sexual desire of the male child for his mother, along with feelings of hostility and fear toward his father.

**Oral stage.** The initial stage of psychosexual development, during which the mouth is the primary source of gratification. A time when the infant is learning to trust or mistrust the world.

**Phallic stage.** The third stage of psychosexual development, during which the child gains maximum gratification through direct experience with the genitals.

**Psychodynamics.** The interplay of opposing forces and intrapsychic conflicts, providing a basis for understanding human motivation.

**Psychosexual stages.** The Freudian chronological phases of development, beginning in infancy. Each is characterized by a primary way of gaining sensual and sexual gratification.

**Psychosocial stages.** Erikson's turning points, from infancy through old age. Each presents psychological and social tasks that must be mastered if maturation is to proceed in a healthy fashion.

**Reaction formation.** A defense against a threatening impulse, involving actively expressing the opposite impulse.

**Repression.** The ego-defense mechanism whereby threatening or painful thoughts or feelings are excluded from awareness.

**Resistance.** The client's reluctance to bring to awareness threatening unconscious material that has been repressed.

**Superego.** That aspect of personality that represents one's moral training. It strives for perfection, not pleasure.

**Transference.** The client's unconscious shifting to the therapist of feelings and fantasies, both positive and negative, that are displacements from reactions to significant others from the client's past.

**Transference neurosis.** The point in classical psychoanalysis when the patient's fantasies about the therapist are at their peak, at which time the therapeutic relationship becomes the focus of therapy.

**Unconscious.** That aspect of psychological functioning or of personality that houses experiences, wishes, impulses, and memories in an out-of-awareness state as a protection against anxiety.

**Working through.** A process of resolving basic conflicts that are manifested in the client's relationship with the therapist, achieved by the repetition of interpretations and by exploring forms of resistance.

# QUESTIONS FOR DISCUSSION AND EVALUATION

1. What degree of importance do you give to each of the following factors as a determinant of present personality problems? Explain.

   a. early-childhood experiences

   b. social and cultural factors

   c. unconscious factors

   d. relationship with one's parents

2. The analyst tends to maintain warm detachment, objectivity, and anonymity so as to foster transference. What are your reactions to the therapeutic value of the therapist's assuming such a role? How do you think a self-disclosing stance on the therapist's part would alter the course of psychotherapy?

3. Mention some psychoanalytic concepts that you think have validity and can be incorporated into a counseling approach even if you do not employ psychoanalytic techniques. Discuss how you see these concepts as useful.

4. This approach places considerable emphasis on therapists' awareness of their own needs and reactions toward clients (or awareness of countertransference). At this time what kind of client behavior do you think you'd find most difficult? Are you aware of any of your vulnerabilities, unresolved personal concerns, or unmet needs that might interfere with your objectivity and effectiveness as a therapist? How might you work with your countertransference reactions?

5. The evolution of psychoanalytic theory and practice is most clearly seen in self psychology and object-relations theory. How do these approaches contribute to a practitioner's understanding of borderline and narcissistic personality disorders?

# SUGGESTED ACTIVITIES AND EXERCISES

1. The following pages describe two case histories: Stan's case and Jack's case. As a role-playing technique have one volunteer play the role of Stan and another play the role of the psychoanalytic therapist. Then have both "Stan" and the "therapist" share with the class what the experience of assuming those roles was like. Other students can give them feedback concerning what they saw. Do the same for Jack's case.

2. Write a letter to Freud. Tell him what you think of his contribution to psychology and how his theory applies to your life (or how it does not apply). Bring your letter to class, and share it with the other members.

3. Reread the section in the text that discusses the importance of the first six years of life. Then do the following:

   a. Write down a few key questions about your own psychosexual and psychosocial development from birth through age 6 that you would like to have answered.

   b. Seek out your relatives, and ask them some of the questions.

   c. Gather up any reminders of your early years.

   d. If possible, visit the place or places where you lived.

   e. Attempt to answer your own questions briefly in written form.

   f. Construct a chart showing key influences on your development during those early years.

   g. If the class wishes, bring the charts to class, and discuss in small groups the effects of each member's developmental history on his or her present life.

4. Try this free-association exercise at home by yourself. Get a tape recorder and say aloud *whatever comes into your mind* for about 15 or 20 minutes. Then listen to the tape for pauses or hesitations, recurring themes, and key remarks. Then make a list of about ten key words based on this tape. Now, make another tape, this time by free-associating with each of the key words. Listen to the second tape. What do you hear? Do you notice any patterns? You might want to bring into class a brief written statement describing what the free-associating experience was like for you.

5. Refer to the textbook section on ego-defense mechanisms. What are some defenses that you have used to deal with anxiety?

# CASE EXAMPLES

## STAN'S CASE: A NOTE

I encourage you to read the case of Stan (Chapter 13) early in the course. Then, within each of the nine theory chapters in this manual I will briefly describe one or two focal points of that perspective. Let me stress that these brief discussions represent my own interpretation and application of each theoretical approach. I will show you how I might think in terms of each theory and then merely point to a direction I might take. Then you can follow up by addressing the questions I present and reviewing and applying to Stan what you have learned about each theory. If you do this for each theory, you will begin to get a sense of how Stan can be viewed from a variety of perspectives and how the same themes in his life can be explored from different angles.

## MY WAY OF WORKING WITH STAN
## FROM THE PSYCHOANALYTIC PERSPECTIVE

I value what I learn from the psychoanalytic model about the unconscious and early childhood experiences and about their influence on Stan's present personality. Drawing on this approach, I would encourage Stan to recall and talk about his early memories of his parents. I would use his reactions to me as one basis of making interpretations about his early childhood, thinking that he is relating to me in some ways as he did to other significant people in his life. I would also work with Stan's difficulties in relating to women by making some connections with his mother. Although I do not see that Stan is determined by his past, I do assume that for him to eventually be free he needs to understand his past as it is evident in his present.

As you review Stan's case and think about him from a psychoanalytic perspective, consider these questions:

1. What aspects of his past would you be most interested in hearing about? Why? Once you obtained this information, what uses would you make of it?

2. You could expect to work with Stan's transference feelings toward you. Do you have any ideas of what you would do or say if he began to see you and treat you as his father? as his mother? After reading his case carefully, what feelings do you have toward him? What countertransference issues might be brought up in you as you worked with Stan? (For example, might you identify with him in some ways? Might you get lost in his problem?)

3. As you worked in this model, what are a few of the dimensions of Stan's personality that you would be most inclined to focus on?

## JACK'S CASE

"Most of my life I have felt pushed and pulled. My father pushed me into school, sports, and so forth, and over the years my resentment grew for him, as he was always directing and controlling my life and beating me when I challenged his authority. My mother always gave me a warm, unconditional love and tried to pull me under her protective wing, something I have always resisted.

"My parents divorced when I was 16, and without parental control I began a life of permissiveness in my relationships with women and in my use of psychedelic drugs and marijuana.

"On graduating from college, I rejected my father's wishes to pursue a career and returned to school to seek another degree. In some ways it's just a place to be that I like. Most of my life revolves around living for today, a hedonistic style that has no concreteness of goals and aspirations, with a lack of definition of 'what a man should be.'

"I float in and out of people's lives. They see an image of me as a despoiler of women, a drug freak, and a cold bastard. My fear is that I am nothing more than that image, that I am empty inside. I want to be able to open up and let people see the warmer, more sensitive sides of me, but I have terrible difficulty doing that. I have a strong need to become close and intimate with others, yet I never let myself become vulnerable because I fear being dependent on them and trapped by their love."

*How would you work with Jack?* Jack's case was written by one of my students in an internship program. At the time he wrote it, he was himself undergoing both individual and group counseling. Assume that Jack comes to you for personal counseling and that all you know about him is what he wrote. Answer the following questions on how you might proceed with Jack within a *psychoanalytic* frame of reference:

1. Do you think that Jack's current unwillingness to become vulnerable to others out of his fear of "being dependent on them and trapped by their love" has much to do with his mother's unconditional love?

2. Was his mother's "warm, unconditional love" really without conditions? What do you suppose her conditions were for keeping Jack "under her protective wing"? How might this experience be related to Jack's relationships with women now?

3. Jack describes his father as an authoritarian, controlling, and cruel man who apparently had conventional ideas of what he wanted Jack to become. What are the underlying psychological aspects that you see involved with Jack's rejection of his father's wishes? How might you explain the fact that in many ways Jack became what his father did not want him to become?

4. How might you work with Jack's fear that he is nothing more than a "despoiler of women," "a drug freak," and a "cold bastard"?

5. How might you explain Jack's fear that he is "empty inside"? What are some possible causes of his feelings of emptiness? How would you work with this with him?

6. What else would you want to know about Jack? What specific factors in his case would you focus on, and what would be your treatment plan as you worked with him during the therapy sessions?

# REVIEWING THE HIGHLIGHTS

*Directions*: For the purpose of a concise review, complete these sentences in your own words. Also, look at the "Reviewing the Highlights of a Theory" in Chapter 1, and use them as a further way to review key psychoanalytic concepts.

1. The basic philosophical assumption underlying the psychoanalytic approach is _____

    _____

2. The key characteristic that distinguishes psychoanalysis is _____

    _____

3. The therapeutic goals of psychoanalytic therapy are _____

_____

4. The central role of the therapist is _____

_____

5. In the therapy process clients are expected to _____

_____

6. The relationship between the client and the therapist is characterized by_____

_____

7. Some of the major techniques are _____

_____

8. I think this approach is most applicable to those clients who _____

_____

9. The one aspect of psychoanalysis that I *like most* is _____

_____

10. The one aspect of psychoanalysis that I *like least* is _____

_____

Now (and in subsequent chapters) I recommend that you bring your responses to class. Discuss at least some of the answers, especially those dealing with aspects of the approach you like best and like least and with areas of application of the therapy.

## QUIZ ON PSYCHOANALYTIC THERAPY: A COMPREHENSION CHECK

Score ____%

*Note*: Please refer to Appendix 1 for the scoring key for these quizzes. Count 4 points for each error, and subtract the total from 100 to get your percentage score. I recommend that you review these comprehension checks for midterm and final examinations. I also suggest that you bring to class questions that you would like clarified. If you get a wrong answer that you believe is right, bring it up for discussion. My classes have had some lively discussions, which have helped students learn to defend their positions.

*True/false items*: Decide if the following statements are "more true" or "more false" as they apply to psychoanalytic therapy.

T F 1. The psychosocial perspective is not at all compatible with the psychosexual view of development.

T F 2. Children who do not experience the opportunity to differentiate self from others may later develop a narcissistic character disorder.

T F 3. Heinz Kohut is a leading contemporary psychoanalytic theorist.

T F 4. The phallic stage typically occurs during ages 1–3.

T F 5. Analytic therapy is oriented toward achieving insight.

T F 6. Working through in analysis is achieved almost totally by catharsis, including getting out deeply buried emotions.

T F 7. From the Freudian perspective, resistance is typically a conscious process, or a stubbornness on the client's part.

T F 8. The approach of Erik Erikson is known as object-relations theory.

T F 9. Object-relations theorists focus on matters such as symbiosis, separation, differentiation, and integration.

T F 10. In object-relations theory there is an emphasis on early development as a decisive factor influencing later development.

*Multiple-choice items*: Select the *one best answer* of those alternatives given. Consider each question within the framework of psychoanalytic therapy.

_____ 11. Who of the following is *not* considered an object-relations theorist?

    a. Heinz Kohut          c. Otto Kernberg
    b. Margaret Mahler      d. Erik Erikson

_____ 12. Of the following, who is considered an ego psychologist?

    a. Otto Kernberg        d. Carl Jung
    b. Erik Erikson         e. none of the above
    c. Erich Fromm

_____ 13. Which of the following is *not* a characteristic of the newer psychoanalytic thinking?

    a. Emphasis is on the origins, transformations, and organizational functions of the self.
    b. The contrasting experiences of others is highlighted.
    c. People are classified as compliant, aggressive, or detached types.
    d. Focus is on the differentiations between and integration of the self and others.
    e. Early development is seen as critical to understanding later development.

_____ 14. The personality disorder that is characterized by instability, irritability, impulsive anger, and external mood shifts is known as a(n)

    a. narcissistic disorder.      d. id disorder.
    b. borderline disorder.      e. neurotic disorder.
    c. ego disorder.

_____ 15. According to Erikson's psychosocial view, the struggle between industry and inferiority occurs during

    a. adolescence.         d. infancy.
    b. old age.             e. middle age.
    c. school age.

_____ 16. Erikson's preschool-age phase corresponds to which Freudian stage?

    a. oral               d. latency
    b. anal              e. genital
    c. phallic

_____ 17. Which term refers to the repetition of interpretations and the overcoming of resistance so that clients can resolve neurotic patterns?

    a. working through      d. catharsis
    b. transference neurosis   e. acting out
    c. countertransference

_____ 18. Analysis of transference is central to psychoanalysis because

    a. it keeps the therapist hidden and thus feeling secure.
    b. it allows clients to relive their past in therapy.
    c. it helps clients formulate specific plans to change behavior.
    d. it is considered the only way to get at unconscious material.
    e. it helps clients experience their emotions.

_____ 19. Resolution of sexual conflicts and sex-role identity is a critical task at the

    a. oral stage.                  d. latency stage.
    b. anal stage.                  e. genital stage.
    c. phallic stage.

_____ 20. The Electra complex and the Oedipus complex are associated with what psychosexual stage of development?

    a. oral stage.                  d. latency stage.
    b. anal stage.                  e. genital stage.
    c. phallic stage.

_____ 21. Borderline and narcissistic disorders tend to be rooted in traumatic events during which phase of development?

    a. normal infantile autism        d. movement toward self and object con-
    b. symbiosis                      stancy
    c. separation /individuation     e. none of the above

_____ 22. During psychoanalytic treatment clients are typically asked

    a. to monitor their behavioral changes by keeping a journal that describes what they do at home and at work.
    b. to make major changes in their lifestyle.
    c. not to make radical changes in their lifestyle.
    d. to give up their friendships.
    e. none of the above.

_____ 23. Countertransference refers to

    a. the irrational reactions that clients have toward their therapists.
    b. the irrational reactions that therapists have toward their clients.
    c. the projections of the client.
    d. the client's need to be special in the therapist's eyes.
    e. all except for (a).

_____ 24. "Maintaining the analytic framework" refers to

    a. the whole range of procedural factors in the treatment process.
    b. the analysts relative anonymity.
    c. agreement on the payment of fees.
    d. the regularity and consistency of meetings.
    e. all of the above.

_____ 25. In psychoanalytic therapy (as opposed to classical analysis), which of the following procedures is _least_ likely to be used?

    a. the client lying on the couch.
    b. working with transference feelings.
    c. relating present struggles with past events.
    d. working with dreams.
    e. interpretation of resistance.

_Note_: Another suggestion for feedback and for review is to retake the prechapter self-inventory. All 20 items are true statements as applied to the particular therapy, so thinking about them is a good way to review. You'll find these quizzes an excellent way to study and review.

# 5

# ADLERIAN THERAPY

## PRECHAPTER SELF-INVENTORY

*Directions*: Refer to page 46 for general directions. Use the following code:

5 = I *strongly agree* with this statement.

4 = I *agree*, in most respects, with this statement.

3 = I am *undecided* in my opinion about this statement.

2 = I *disagree*, in most respects, with this statement

1 = I *strongly disagree* with this statement.

_____ 1. The social determinants of personality development are more powerful than the sexual determinants.

_____ 2. Humans can be understood by looking at where they are going and what they are striving toward.

_____ 3. People are pushed by the need to overcome inferiority and pulled by the striving for superiority.

_____ 4. If a client is depressed, the proper focus of therapy is on the thinking patterns that lead to certain behaviors and feelings, not on feelings alone.

_____ 5. People are best understood by seeing through the "spectacles" by which they view themselves in relation to the world.

_____ 6. Although people are influenced by their early childhood experiences, they are not passively shaped by them; they are the actor and creator of their own life.

_____ 7. It is therapeutically useful to ask clients to recall their earliest memories.

_____ 8. Each person develops a unique lifestyle, which should be a focal point of examination in counseling.

_____ 9. Clients in counseling should not be viewed as being "sick" and needing to be "cured"; it is better to see them as being discouraged and in need of reeducation.

_____ 10. Knowing about one's position in the family is important as a reference point for therapy.

_____ 11. Typically, clients come to therapy with mistaken assumptions or faulty beliefs about life.

_____ 12. Because emotions are the result of our cognitive processes, it is appropriate that the counseling process be aimed at the exploration of the client's thoughts and beliefs.

_____ 13. Although a good client/therapist relationship is essential for counseling to progress, this relationship alone will not bring about change.

_____ 14. One of a counselor's main tasks is to gather information about family relationships and then to summarize and interpret this material.

_____ 15. People tend to remember only those past events that are consistent with their current view of themselves.

_____ 16. Dreams are rehearsals for possible future courses of action.

_____ 17. Conscious factors should be given more attention than unconscious factors in the therapy process.

_____ 18. Although insight is a powerful adjunct to behavioral change, it is not a prerequisite for change.

_____ 19. Insight can best be defined as translating self-understanding into constructive action.

_____ 20. At its best counseling is a cooperative venture, structured by a contract and geared toward helping clients identify and change their mistaken beliefs about life.

# OVERVIEW OF ADLERIAN THERAPY

## KEY FIGURES AND MAJOR FOCUS

Founder: Alfred Adler. Significant developers: Rudolf Dreikurs and Harold Mosak. *Individual Psychology* (a term Adler used to describe his approach's emphasis on the uniqueness and unity of the individual) began in Europe in the early 1900s under Adler's leadership. Dreikurs was the main figure responsible for transplanting Adlerian principles in the United States, especially in applying these principles to education, child guidance, and group work.

## PHILOSOPHY AND BASIC ASSUMPTIONS

More than any other theorist, Adler stresses social psychology and a positive view of human nature. He views human beings as influenced more by social than by biological forces. People are in control of their fate, not victims of it. Individuals create a distinctive lifestyle at an early age, rather than being merely shaped by childhood experiences. This lifestyle tends to remain relatively constant and defines our beliefs about life and ways of dealing with its tasks.

## KEY CONCEPTS

Consciousness, not the unconscious, is the center of personality. The Adlerian approach, based on a growth model, stresses the individual's positive capacities to live fully in society. It is characterized by seeing unity in the personality, understanding a person's world from a subjective vantage point, and stressing life goals that give direction to behavior. Humans are motivated by social interest, or a sense of belonging and having a significant place in society. Feelings of inferiority often serve as the wellspring of creativity, motivating people to strive for mastery, superiority, and perfection.

## THERAPEUTIC GOALS

Adlerians are mainly concerned with challenging clients' mistaken notions and faulty assumptions, which helps them develop on the useful side of life. Working cooperatively with clients, therapists try to provide encouragement so that clients can develop socially useful goals. Some specific goals include fostering social interest, helping clients overcome feelings of discouragement, changing faulty motivation, restructuring mistaken assumptions, and assisting clients to feel a sense of equality with others.

## THERAPEUTIC RELATIONSHIP

The client/therapist relationship is often structured by means of a therapeutic contract, which emphasizes joint responsibility for the therapeutic process. The relationship is based on mutual respect and equality, and both client and counselor are active. The focus is on examining the client's lifestyle, which is expressed in everything that the client does. Therapists frequently interpret this lifestyle by demonstrating a connection between the past, the present, and the client's future strivings.

## TECHNIQUES AND PROCEDURES

Adlerians have developed a variety of techniques and therapeutic styles. They are not bound to follow a specific set of procedures; rather, they can tap their creativity by applying those techniques that they think are most appropriate for each client. They share many methods with other approaches and select according to the unique needs of their clients. Some of the specific techniques they often employ are attending, encouragement, confrontation, paradoxical intention, summarizing, interpretation of the family constellation and early recollections, suggestion, and homework assignments. Most of these procedures were originally developed by Adler.

## APPLICATIONS

As a growth model Adlerian theory is concerned with helping people reach their full potential. Its principles have been applied to a broad range of human problems and to alleviating social conditions that interfere with growth. The theory has been widely adopted in education, child-guidance work, parent/child counseling, individual therapy, and social work. Being grounded in the principles of social psychology, it is ideally suited for working with groups, couples, and families.

## CONTRIBUTIONS

Adler founded one of the major humanistic approaches to psychology. The approach's greatest contribution is the Adlerian ideas that have been integrated into other therapies. The model is a forerunner of most current approaches to counseling. Its focus on consciousness foreshadowed the cognitive-behavioral approaches; its recognition of the social context and of parent/child interaction paved the way for some of the various family therapies. Adler's influence has extended into the community mental-health movement. The interpersonal emphasis is most appropriate for counseling culturally diverse populations.

## LIMITATIONS

Some of the approach's basic concepts are vague and not precisely defined, which makes it difficult to validate them empirically. Critics contend that the approach oversimplifies complex human functioning and is based too heavily on a common-sense perspective.

# GLOSSARY OF KEY TERMS

**Basic mistakes.** Faulty, self-defeating perceptions, attitudes, and beliefs, which may have been appropriate at one time but are no longer. These myths are influential in the shaping of personality. Examples include denying one's worth, an exaggerated need for security, and impossible goals.

**Convictions.** Conclusions based on life experiences and the interpretation of such experiences.

**Courage.** The willingness to take risks.

**Early recollections.** Specific, detailed childhood memories, which can be thought of as capsule summaries of one's present philosophy of life.

**Encouragement.** The process of increasing one's courage to face life tasks. Used throughout therapy as a way to counter discouragement and to help people set realistic goals.

**Family constellation.** The social and psychological structure of the family system. Includes birth order, the individual's perception of self, sibling characteristics and ratings, and parental relationships.

**Fictional finalism.** An imagined central goal that gives direction to behavior and unity to the personality. An image of what people would be like if they were perfect and perfectly secure.

**Holism.** Studying people as integrated beings with a focus on the ways in which they proceed through life. A reaction against separating personality into parts.

**Inferiority feelings.** The ever-present determining force in behavior; the source of human striving. Humans attempt to compensate for both imagined and real inferiorities, which helps them overcome handicaps.

**Life tasks.** Adler's notion that all humans must face and solve certain problems universal in human life, including the tasks of friendship (or community), work (or a division of labor), and intimacy (or love and marriage).

**Priorities.** Characteristics that involve a dominant behavior pattern with supporting convictions that an individual uses to cope. Examples include superiority, control, comfort, and pleasing.

**Social interest.** A sense of identification with humanity; a feeling of belonging; an interest in the common good.

**Striving for superiority.** A strong inclination toward becoming competent, toward mastering our environment, and toward self-improvement. The striving for perfection is a movement toward enhancement of self and is known as the "growth force."

**Style of life.** An individual's way of thinking, acting, and feeling. A conceptual framework by which the world is perceived and by which people are able to cope with life tasks. The person's personality.

**Teleology.** The study of goals and the goal-directedness of human behavior. Humans live by aims and purposes, not by being pushed by outside forces.

## QUESTIONS FOR DISCUSSION AND EVALUATION

1. Adlerians contend that first we think, then we act, and then we feel. Their emphasis is thus on cognition (thinking, beliefs, assumptions about life, attitudes). What are the strengths and limitations of this type of focus for a counselor?

2. Compare and contrast the basic concepts of the psychoanalytic and Adlerian approaches. What are some of the major differences: What are the implications of these differences for therapeutic practice?

3. Adlerians typically begin the counseling process with a lifestyle assessment, which focuses on the family constellation and early recollections. Within these areas what kinds of information would you be most interested in learning about as you faced a new client?

4. How can you apply Adlerian concepts to understanding and working with your own life?

5. When you think of yourself working with clients from diverse cultural and socioeconomic backgrounds, what aspects of Adlerian therapy do you think would be most useful? What techniques might you be inclined to use?

# PERSONAL APPLICATION:   THE LIFESTYLE ASSESSMENT

The lifestyle assessment is typically done at the initial phase of therapy as a way to obtain information about the client's family constellation, early recollections, dreams, and strengths as a person.  This information is then summarized and interpreted, especially in light of the client's faulty assumptions about life (or "basic mistakes").  From the results of this assessment procedure, counselors make tentative interpretations about the client's lifestyle.

Although there are a number of formal formats for the lifestyle questionnaire, counselors may develop their own variation by focusing on information deemed most valuable for exploration in therapy.  What follows is an example of a lifestyle questionnaire that has been modified and adapted from various sources.  To give you an experiential sense of the process of thinking and responding to this early life-history material, take the following questionnaire and apply it to yourself.  As much as possible, try to give your initial responses, without worrying about what you can and cannot remember or about any "correct" responses.  I strongly encourage you to fill in the blanks and to make brief summaries after each section.  Assume that you are interested in being a *client* in Adlerian therapy.  Based on the outcomes of this questionnaire, what areas of your life would you most like to explore?  How much help is this questionnaire in getting you focused on what you might want from a therapeutic relationship?

## Family Constellation:   Birth Order and Sibling Description

1. List the siblings from oldest to youngest.  Give a brief description of each (including your-self).  What most stands out for each sibling?

   _____

   _____

   _____

   _____

   _____

2. Do a rating of each of the siblings, from the highest to the lowest, on each of the following personality dimensions.  Include your own position in relationship to your siblings.

   | *Most to Least* | *Most to Least* |
   |---|---|
   | intelligence_____ | feminine_____ |
   | achievement-oriented_____ | masculine_____ |
   | hardworking_____ | easygoing_____ |
   | pleasing_____ | daring_____ |
   | assertive_____ | responsible_____ |
   | charming_____ | idealistic_____ |
   | conforming_____ | materialistic_____ |
   | methodical_____ | fun-loving_____ |
   | athletic_____ | demanding_____ |
   | rebellious_____ | critical of self_____ |
   | spoiled_____ | sociable_____ |
   | critical of others_____ | withdrawn_____ |
   | bossy_____ | sensitive_____ |

3. Which sibling(s) is(are) the most different from you, and how? _____
_____
_____

4. Which is most like you, and how? _____
_____

5. Which played together? _____

6. Which fought together? _____

7. Who took care of whom? _____

8. Any unusual achievements by the siblings? _____
_____

9. Any accidents or sickness? _____
_____

10. What kind of child were you? _____
_____
_____

11. What was school like for you? _____
_____

12. What childhood fears did you have?_____
_____

13. What were your childhood ambitions? _____
_____

14. What was your role in your peer group? _____
_____
_____

15. Any significant events in your physical and sexual development? _____
_____
_____

16. Any highlights in your social development? _____
_____

17. What were the most important values in your family? _____
_____
_____

18. What stands out the most for you about your family life? _____
_____
_____

**Family Constellation:  Parental Figures and Relationships**

1. Your father's current age. _____  Mother's age. _____

2. His occupation. _____  Her occupation. _____

3. What kind of person is he? _____  What kind of person is she? _____
   _____  _____
   _____  _____

4. His ambitions for the children. _____  Her ambitions for the children. _____
   _____  _____
   _____  _____

5. Your childhood view of your father. _____  Your childhood view of your mother. _____
   _____  _____
   _____  _____

6. His favorite child, and why? _____  Her favorite child, and why? _____
   _____  _____
   _____  _____

7. Relationship to children. _____  Relationship to children. _____
   _____  _____
   _____  _____

8. Sibling most like father.  In what ways?   Sibling most like mother.  In what ways?
   _____  _____
   _____  _____
   _____  _____

9. Describe your parents' relationship with each other. _____
   _____
   _____

10. In general, how did each of the siblings view and react to your parents? _____
   _____
   _____

11. In general, what was your parents' relationship to the children? _____
   _____
   _____

12. Besides your mother and father, were there any other parental figures in your life?  Who
    were they? How did they affect you? _____
   _____
   _____

**Early Recollections and Dreams**

1. What is your earliest single and specific memory? _____
_____
_____
_____

2. What are some other early recollections? Be as detailed as possible._____
_____
_____
_____
_____

3. What feelings are associated with any of the above early memories?_____
_____
_____

4. Can you recall any childhood dreams? _____
_____
_____

5. Do you have any recurring dreams? _____

**Lifestyle Summary**

1. Give a summary of your family constellation. (What stands out most about your role in your family? Are there any themes in your family history?) _____
_____
_____
_____
_____
_____

2. Summarize your early recollections. (Are there any themes running through your early memories? Do you see any meaning in your early recollections?) _____
_____
_____
_____

3. List your mistaken self-defeating perceptions. (What do you see as your "basic mistakes"?)
_____
_____
_____

4. Summarize what you consider to be your strengths as a person. (What are your assets?)
_____
_____
_____

Now that you are finished with this lifestyle questionnaire:

- What did you learn from taking it and reviewing it?

- Assuming you will be a client in counseling, what theme(s) do you most want to address?

- Do you see connections between your past and the person you are today? What about any continuity from your past and present to your strivings toward the future?

- Do you see any patterns in your life? Are there any themes running through from childhood to the present?

- Consider bringing the results of your lifestyle summary to class. Form small groups, and exchange with others what you learned from taking this self-assessment questionnaire.


# CASE EXAMPLES

## MY WAY OF WORKING WITH STAN FROM AN ADLERIAN PERSPECTIVE

To provide more background material on Stan's developmental history, I will make use of the lifestyle questionnaire that Adlerians typically give during the assessment and analysis phase of therapy. This questionnaire taps information about his family constellation, early recollections, dreams, and basic mistakes. When this family material is summarized and interpreted, it will provide a rich background for understanding him as he experiences counseling with the other therapeutic approaches.

### Family Constellation: Birth Order and Sibling Description

1. List all the siblings from oldest to youngest, giving a brief description of each.

| *Judy +7* | *Frank +5* | *Stan 25* | *Karl −3* |
|---|---|---|---|
| attractive | athletic | immature | spoiled |
| brilliant | fun-loving | depressed a lot | devilish |
| out of my class | sociable | slow learner | demanding |
| highly capable | bright | a loner | overprotected |
| accomplished | masculine | scared | got his way |
| mature | well-liked | self-critical | argued with me |
| hard worker | respected | not too accomplished | liked by mother |
| responsible | made fun of me | the rejected child | daring |
| sensitive | didn't like me | one who tried hard | sensitive |

2. Rate the siblings on these traits, from most to least (*J* refers to Judy, *F* to Frank, *S* to Stan, and *K* to Karl).

| | | | | | | | | | | |
|---|---|---|---|---|---|---|---|---|---|---|
| intelligent | J | F | K | S | | feminine | J | | | |
| achievement-oriented | F | J | K | S | | masculine | only F | | | |
| hardworking | F | J | S | K | | easygoing | none of us | | | |
| pleasing | J | F | K | S | | daring | K | F | J | S |
| assertive | K | F | J | S | | responsible | J | F | S | K |
| charming | K | J | F | S | | idealistic | J | F | S | K |
| conforming | none | | | | | materialistic | K | S | F | J |
| methodical | J | F | K | S | | fun-loving | F | K | J | S |
| athletic | only F | | | | | demanding | K | F | S | J |
| rebellious | S | K | F | J | | critical of self | S | J | F | K |
| spoiled | only K | | | | | withdrawn | S | J | K | F |
| critical of others | F | K | S | J | | sensitive | J | K | S | F |
| bossy | K | F | S | J | | | | | | |

3. Which sibling(s) is(are) the most different from you, and how? _Judy and Frank. They were both achievement oriented, intelligent, respected by my parents, and liked by other kids. Whatever they did, they excelled in._

4. Which sibling(s) is(are) most like you? _Really none. I always felt like the oddball in my family!_

5. Which played together? _Really nobody._

6. Which fought together? _Mainly my younger brother, Karl, and I._

7. Who took care of whom? _Judy was responsible for taking care of me when I was a young kid._

8. Any unusual achievements? _Judy won just about every award that was given out at school. Frank was at the top of his class and won athletic trophies._

9. Any accidents or sickness? _I was hit by a car when I was 11 while I was riding my bicycle. My younger brother seemed sick a lot._

10. What kind of child were you? _As a child I was lonely, felt hurt a lot, was withdrawn, felt like I could never measure up to Frank and Judy, felt unwanted, and didn't feel the other kids wanted to play with me._

11. What was school like for you? _For me, school was a real drag._

12. What childhood fears did you have? _I was afraid of being picked on, afraid of being alone, and scared that I would fail at whatever I did._

13. What were your childhood ambitions? _To build a race car and drive it!_

14. What was your role in your peer group? _The one who was chosen last._

15. Any significant events in your physical and sexual development? _I was smaller than most other guys, and didn't mature physically until late. I remember being scared of the sexual changes in my body—and confused!_

16. Any highlights in your social development? _I felt retarded. I always felt like I was out of step, especially with girls._

17. What were the most important values in your family? _To be honest, to work hard, and to get ahead._

18. What stands out the most for you about your family life? _How I never really felt a part of the family, and how distant my older brother seemed to me._

**Family Constellation: Parental Figures and Relationships**

_Father (+31)_

1. Current age. _56_
2. Occupation. _High-school teacher_
3. Kind of person. _Devoted to his work, detached, distant at home, passive._

_Mother (+27)_

1. Current age. _52_
2. Occupation. _Housewife (Part-time nurse)_
3. Kind of person. _Bossy, dominant, very hard to please, capable, aggressive. Demands her way._

4. His ambitions for the children. _Strive_
   _and do well academically; never bring_
   _shame to the family._

   Her ambitions for the children. _To keep out_
   _of trouble, to succeed, to show respect for_
   _authority._

5. Your childhood view of him. _Hard worker,_
   _dominated by my mother, passive, and_
   _quiet, distant from me._

   Your childhood view of her. _Rejecting of_
   _me, depressed a lot, responsible. Expected_
   _too much of me._

6. His favorite child. _Frank—he admired_
   _his academic and athletic accom-_
   _plishments._

   Her favorite child. _Karl—she could see no_
   _wrong that the little brat could do._

7. Relationship to children. _He really_
   _liked Frank and Judy and did a lot with_
   _Frank. He ignored me and didn't have_
   _much to do with Karl._

   Relationship to children. _She seemed to_
   _like and have time for all the kids, except for_
   _me._

8. Sibling most like father. _Frank, in_
   _that he was smart and really loved_
   _school._

   Sibling most like mother. _Really none,_
   _except Judy might be most like her in that_
   _both are responsible and highly capable._

9. Describe your parents' relationship to each other. _Horrible! She berated him and ran over_
   _him, and he would never stand up to her. He escaped into his work. They were never really_
   _affectionate or close with each other._

10. Siblings' relationship to parents. _Frank and Judy got along well with both mother and_
    _father; Karl did well by mother, but not with father; I wasn't given much attention, and I_
    _didn't want much from them._

11. Parents' relationship to the children. _Good for Frank and Judy, OK with mother to Karl,_
    _and rotten with me._

12. Besides your parents, who was another parental figure in your life? _My uncle, who seemed_
    _to take an interest in me and liked me._

**Early Recollections and Dreams**

1. What is your earliest single and specific memory? _I was about 6. I went to school, and I_
   _was scared of the other kids and the teacher. When I came home, I cried and told my_
   _mother I didn't want to go back to school. She yelled at me and called me a baby._

2. What are some other early recollections?
   a. _Age 6-1/2: My family were visiting my grandparents. I was playing outside, and some_
      _neighborhood kid hit me for no reason. We got in a big fight, and my mother came out_
      _and scolded me for being such a rough kid. She wouldn't believe me when I told her he_
      _had started the fight._

b.  *Age 8:  I stuck some nails in the neighbor's tires, and he caught me in the act.  He took me by the neck to my folks.  They both yelled at me and punished me.  My father didn't talk to me for weeks.*

c.  *Age 11:  I was riding my bike to school, and all of a sudden a car hit me from the side.  I remember lying there thinking I might die.  I went to the hospital with a broken leg and concussion.  Being in that hospital was lonely and scary.*

3.  What feelings are associated with these early memories?  *I often felt that I could do no right.  I was scared most of the time, felt lonely, and never really felt understood or cared for.*

4.  Can you recall any childhood dreams?  *I recall nightmares of being chased a lot.  I would wake up crying.  All I can remember is seeing something ugly chasing me, and sometimes catching me.*

5.  Any recurring dreams?  *A dream I have had often is being alone in a desert, dying of thirst.  I see people with water, but nobody seems to notice me, and nobody comes over to me to give me any water.  I also have had a dream a number of times that I was falling—like falling out of the sky—and I would wake up petrified.*


**Lifestyle Summary**

1.  Summary of Stan's family constellation:  Stan was the third in a family of four children.  The values of the family were achieving and doing well, yet Stan felt that he could never measure up to the standards of achievement of his older brother and sister.  A central theme for Stan was that he felt excluded and unwanted.  The attention was directed to the other siblings, and the only attention he could get was through negative means.  He saw a cold war between his parents, and he learned to fear intimacy.  Although he tried to make his parents feel proud of him, he was really never able to succeed in this.  He kept to himself most of the time.

2.  Summary of Stan's early recollections:  (1) No matter how hard I try to do the right thing, I am ineffective in (2) a world that just isn't fair.  Therefore, (3) to keep safe I must not trust others or get close to them, and I've got to fight my own way in this cruel world.

3.  Summary of Stan's basic mistakes:  Stan's pattern and profile show a number of mistaken and self-defeating perceptions, some of which are:

    a.  Be a man, which means be strong and never show emotions.

    b.  Don't get close to people, especially women, because they will suffocate and control you if they can.

    c.  If you can't do anything right, why try at all?

    d.  I was an accident—unwanted—and therefore, the best way for me is to be invisible.

    e.  I should be perfect, and if I become perfect, my folks will love me.

    f.  Because my father was a weak man, I will follow in his footsteps in being weak.

    g.  If people don't like me or approve of me, that is horrible;  I'll try to do what people expect.

    h.  If I don't let myself feel, I won't get hurt.

4.  Summary of Stan's assets:   Some of Stan's strengths that can be built on are:

    a.  He has courage and is willing to look at his life.

    b.  He is willing to question assumptions he has made that he did not question earlier.

    c.  He realizes that he puts himself down a great deal, and he is determined to learn to accept and like himself.

    d.  He has some clear goals—namely, to graduate and to work with kids as a counselor.

    e.  He is motivated to work to feel equal to others, and he no longer wants to feel apologetic for his existence.

    You proceed in working with Stan from an Adlerian perspective:

1.  As you review Stan's lifestyle assessment, what stands out for you the most?  What direction would you be inclined to pursue with Stan?

2.  As you can see, Stan has made several "basic mistakes." How would you work with him on correcting some of these mistaken perceptions?  How would you work with him on a cognitive level, as a way of changing his behavior and his feelings?

3.  Stan comes to counseling as a discouraged person who feels victimized. Do you have any ideas on applying encouragement in your counseling with him?  What might you do if he persisted in his vision of himself as a victim who is powerless to make changes now?

## ALICE AND JAVIER:  A COUPLE SEEKING COUNSELING

Assume that a social worker whom who know conducts groups for couples.  In one of these groups a couple indicates to her that they would like to have at least a few counseling sessions with someone different to get another perspective on the problems they are having in their relationship.   The counselor knows that your orientation is Adlerian (hers happens to be psychoanalytic).  She wants to refer this couple to you, and before you see them, she gives you the following background information.

### Some Background Data

Alice and Javier have been married for 17 years and have three children.  This is an interracial marriage.  Javier is Hispanic, and Alice is a Pacific Islander.  Neither his family nor hers was very supportive of their marrying a person "not of your own kind."  Consequently, Javier and Alice do not see their parents very often.  She feels a real gap without this connection with her family;  he maintains that if that's the way his family wants it, so be it.

They have been having a great deal of difficulty as family for several years.  The social worker sees Javier as being extremely defensive in his dealings with Alice.  He shouts a lot, gets angry, and then slams the door and refuses to talk to her for days at a time.  Although he never strikes her, he has threatened to do so, and she is intimidated by his tirades and displays of anger.  He has put his fist through the bathroom door, as well as breaking objects in the house.  Alice seems to think that Javier is far too strict with the children, demanding full obedience without question.  Javier admits he is a hard taskmaster, but he says that's the way it was for him in his family.  He insists on being the boss in the family.  He is constantly yelling at them for making messes as well as for a multitude of offenses in his eyes.  He rarely spends time with his two teenage daughters (who see him as a stranger), but he often takes his 10-year-old son on fishing and camping trips.  They appear to have a fairly good relationship.

Alice would like to get a job, yet she stops herself from considering it because Javier becomes extremely upset when she even mentions the issue.  His response is "Why can't you be satisfied with what you have?  Don't I make enough money for this damn family?  It reflects poorly on me if you have to go outside and get work!"  Alice has tended to assume the role of keeping peace in the family, almost at any price.  This means *not* doing many of the things she would like to do, lest it lead to an escalation of the conflicts between them. The social worker perceives Alice as quiet, submissive to Javier, very bright and attractive, afraid of the prospects of a divorce, and very disenchanted with her life with him. Alice has finally decided that even if it rocks the boat and causes a storm, she cannot continue living as she has. She has asked Javier to go to counseling with her. He has agreed, reluctantly, mostly to understand her better and "do whatever can be done to help her." His reaction is that he should be able to solve any problems in his family without the help of some professional. Again, he thinks that seeking counseling is somewhat of a slap in his face.

As a couple they rarely have any time together except for Wednesday evenings, when they attend a couples group they recently joined. Alice says she would like to go away to spend at least a weekend alone with Javier, which she cannot ever remember doing. He complains that doing so is too expensive, that it is a problem to get someone to be with the children, and that they could have as much fun by hanging around the house. She feels continually rebuffed when she asks him for time together. He feels typically defensive that he is being asked for more and more, and he thinks he is doing enough in what he refers to as "this damn family."

## How Would You Work with Javier and Alice?

Using an Adlerian perspective, show how you might proceed in counseling this couple, assuming that you would see them for four to six sessions. Following are some questions to guide you:

1. If you were to use the lifestyle questionnaire, would you want to administer it to each person, with the spouse in the room at the time? What advantages and disadvantages do you see in this procedure?

2. From the background data given, what guesses do you have about Alice's family background? Javier's family constellation? How might you work with each of their family backgrounds in relation to their current difficulties as a couple?

3. Would the fact that he is Hispanic and she is a Pacific Islander be something that you would explore with the couple, especially since their parents were not supportive of their marrying each other? Would you want to discuss the impact of their families of origin on their current family dynamics?

4. How do you see Alice? How do you see Javier? How do you see them as a couple? Do their respective cultural backgrounds provide you with any information about their behavior and their roles in their marriage? Because they are from different ethnic backgrounds, would you be inclined to work with them differently than you would if they shared the same cultural background?

5. Do you think you have enough knowledge about the cultural backgrounds of Javier and Alice to work effectively with them? If you do not have this knowledge, how might you go about acquiring it? What special problems, if any, might you encounter by not sharing the same cultural background?

6. As an Adlerian counselor you will want to make sure that your goals and the goals of Alice and of Javier are in alignment. How might you go about this? What if Javier and Alice have different goals? What kind of contract might you envision developing with them?

7. If you had to speculate at this moment, what are Alice's "basic mistakes"? Javier's? Do you have any ideas of ways in which you might work on such mistaken beliefs with each of them? With them as a couple?

8. What specific Adlerian techniques might you be most inclined to employ in working with this couple? Toward what goals?

# REVIEWING THE HIGHLIGHTS

*Directions*: Fill in the sentence-completion form, and bring in your responses as a basis of class discussion. Also, refer to the questions under "Reviewing the Highlights of a Theory" in Chapter 1 as a more detailed way of reviewing key concepts of this approach.

1. This approach views human nature as _____

   _____

2. The key characteristic that distinguishes this approach is _____

   _____

3. The therapeutic goals of this approach are _____

   _____

4. The central role of the therapist is _____

   _____

5. In the therapy process clients are expected to _____

   _____

6. The relationship between the client and the therapist is characterized by_____

   _____

7. Some of the major techniques are _____

   _____

8. I think this approach is most applicable to those clients who _____

   _____

9. The one aspect of Adlerian therapy that I like most is _____

   _____

10. The one aspect of Adlerian therapy that I like least is _____

   _____

# QUIZ ON ADLERIAN THERAPY:
## A COMPREHENSION CHECK          Score ____%

*Note*: Please refer to Appendix 1 for the scoring key.

*True/false items*: Decide if the following statements are "more true" or "more false" as they apply to Adlerian therapy.

T  F  1. The Adlerian approach is primarily a cognitive perspective.

T  F  2. Fictional finalism refers to the central goal that guides a person's behavior.

T  F  3. Striving for superiority is seen as a neurotic manifestation.

T  F  4. Adler maintained that our style of life is not set until middle age.

T  F  5. Adlerian counselors place emphasis on confronting faulty beliefs.

T  F  6. Adlerians typically do not use the technique of interpretation, for they believe that clients can make their own interpretations without therapist interventions.

T F 7. Adlerians place relatively little importance on the quality of the client/therapist relationship.

T F 8. Analysis and assessment are a basic part of the counseling process.

T F 9. Insight is best defined as understanding translated into action.

T F 10. Contracts are rarely used in Adlerian therapy.

*Multiple-choice items*: Select the *one best answer* of those alternatives given. Consider each question within the framework of Adlerian therapy.

_____ 11. According to Adler, childhood experiences

    a. are not relevant to the practice of counseling.
    b. determine the adult personality.
    c. passively shape us.
    d. in themselves are not as crucial as our attitude toward these experiences.
    e. should provide the focus of therapy.

_____ 12. The Adlerian point of view toward the role of insight in therapy is best stated as:

    a. Insight is a prerequisite to any personality change.
    b. To be of value, insight must be translated into a constructive action program.
    c. People will not make changes until they know the precise causes of their personality problems.
    d. Emotional insight must precede intellectual insight.
    e. Cognitive understanding is absolutely essential before significant behavior changes can occur.

_____ 13. Which of the following statements is *not* true as it is applied to Adlerian therapy?

    a. Consciousness, not the unconscious, is the center of personality.
    b. The approach is grounded on the medical model.
    c. It is a phenomenological and humanistic orientation.
    d. Feelings of inferiority can be the wellspring of creativity.
    e. Early influences can predispose the child to a faulty lifestyle.

_____ 14. Which of the following comes closest to the therapeutic goal of Adlerians?

    a. behavior modification.
    b. symptom removal
    c. experiencing feelings as intensely as possible
    d. motivation and modification
    e. both (a) and (b)

_____ 15. The lifestyle assessment includes information based on

    a. the family constellation.
    b. early recollections.
    c. dreams
    d. mistaken, self-defeating perceptions.
    e. all of the above.

_____ 16. Which is the correct sequence of human experiencing from an Adlerian perspective?

    a. First we feel, then we think, then we act.
    b. First we act, then we feel, then we think.
    c. First we think, then we act, then we feel.
    d. First we feel, then we act, then we think.
    e. none of the above.

_____ 17. Adlerians could best be described as using which techniques?

   a. They use strictly cognitive techniques.
   b. They use emotive and behavioral techniques to get people to think.
   c. They are bound by a clear set of therapeutic techniques.
   d. They are largely eclectic in that they fit a variety of techniques to the needs of each client.
   e. They have an aversion to using techniques because they see the therapeutic relationship alone as the healing factor.

_____ 18. How would the Adlerian therapist view the personal problems of clients?

   a. as the result of cultural conditioning
   b. as the end result of a process of discouragement
   c. as deeply embedded neurotic tendencies
   d. as the product of our innate tendencies toward self-destruction
   e. none of the above

_____ 19. What is the principle that accounts for the consistency and directionality of an individual's psychological movement?

   a. lifestyle
   b. fictional goals
   c. basic mistakes
   d. social interest
   e. phenomenology

_____ 20. Which term does _not_ fit Adlerian therapy?

   a. holistic
   b. social
   c. teleological
   d. deterministic
   e. phenomenological

_____ 21. Which of the following does Adler _not_ stress?

   a. the unity of personality
   b. reliving early childhood experiences
   c. direction in which people are headed
   d. unique style of life that is an expression of life goals
   e. feelings of inferiority

_____ 22. The phenomenological orientation pays attention to

   a. the events that occur at various stages of life.
   b. the manner in which biological and environmental forces limit us.
   c. the way in which people interact with each other.
   d. the internal dynamics that drive a person.
   e. the way in which individuals perceive their world.

_____ 23. The concept of fictional finalism refers to

   a. an imagined central goal that guides a person's behavior.
   b. the hopeless stance that leads to personal defeat.
   c. the manner in which people express their need to belong.
   d. the process of assessing one's style of life.
   e. the interpretation that individuals give to life events.

_____ 24. Adlerians consider which factor(s) to be influential in an individual's life?

   a. psychological position in the family
   b. birth order
   c. interactions among siblings
   d. parent/child relationships
   e. all of the above

_____ 25. Adlerians value early recollections as an important clue to the understanding of

      a. one's sexual and aggressive instincts.
      b. the bonding process between mother and child.
      c. the individual's lifestyle
      d. the unconscious dynamics that motivate behavior.
      e. the origin of psychological trauma in early childhood.

_Note_: As regular practice, after completing these quizzes, it would be a good idea to retake the prechapter self-inventory. Each of these items is true as applied to a given theory. It is useful to see if any of your ratings have changed _after_ your study of the chapter.

# 6

# EXISTENTIAL THERAPY

## PRECHAPTER SELF-INVENTORY

*Directions*:   Refer to page 46 for general directions.  Use the following code:

5 = I *strongly agree* with this statement.

4 = I *agree*, in most respects, with this statement.

3 = I am *undecided* in my opinion about this statement.

2 = I *disagree*, in most respects, with this statement.

1 = I *strongly disagree* with this statement.

_____ 1.   The basic goal of therapy is to expand self-awareness and thus to increase potentials for choice.

_____ 2.   The therapist's main task is to attempt to understand the subjective being of the client.

_____ 3.   Psychotherapy should be viewed as an approach to human relationships rather than as a set of techniques.

_____ 4.   The final decisions and choices rest with the client.

_____ 5.   People define themselves by the choices they make.

_____ 6.   The therapeutic relationship should be based on a human-to-human encounter.

_____ 7.   Therapist authenticity is one of the most crucial qualities in an effective therapeutic relationship.

_____ 8.   Humans possess the capacity for self-awareness, and that quality makes them unique among animals.

_____ 9.   Responsibility, which is the crux of human existence, is based on the capacity for consciousness.

_____ 10.   Freedom, self-determination, willingness, and decision making are qualities that form the very center of human existence.

_____ 11.   The nature of freedom lies in the capacity to shape one's own personal development by choosing among alternatives.

_____ 12.   Even though there are limits to freedom (environment and genetic endowment), humans have the capacity to choose.

_____ 13.   The central issues in counseling and therapy are freedom and responsibility.

_____ 14.   Ultimately, we are alone.

_____ 15.   The failure to establish relatedness to others results in a condition marked by alienation, estrangement, and isolation.

_____ 16.   The human being by nature seeks meaning and purpose.

_____ 17. Guilt and anxiety do not necessarily need to be cured, for they are part of the human condition.

_____ 18. Anxiety can be the result of the person's awareness of his or her aloneness, finiteness, and responsibility for choosing.

_____ 19. The reality of death gives significance to living.

_____ 20. Humans have a tendency toward self-actualization—that is, toward becoming all they are able to become.

# OVERVIEW OF EXISTENTIAL THERAPY

## KEY FIGURES AND MAJOR FOCUS

Key figures in existential philosophy, which serves as a backdrop for existential therapy, are Dostoyevski, Kierkegaard, Nietzsche, Heidegger, Sartre, and Buber. Early European existential therapists are Ludwig Binswanger, Medard Boss, and Viktor Frankl. Major contemporary spokespeople are Rollo May and Irvin Yalom. The approach focuses on central concerns that are rooted in the person's existence, such as loneliness, isolation, alienation, and meaninglessness.

## PHILOSOPHY AND BASIC ASSUMPTIONS

The significance of the approach is that it reacts against the tendency to view therapy as a system of well-defined techniques; it affirms looking at those unique characteristics that make us human and building therapy on them. It emphasizes choice, freedom, responsibility, and self-determination. In essence, we are the author of our life. Thrust into a meaningless and absurd world, we are challenged to accept our aloneness and create meanings in life. The awareness of our eventual nonbeing acts as a catalyst for finding meaning.

## KEY CONCEPTS

There are six key propositions of existential therapy: (1) We have the capacity for self-awareness. (2) Because we are basically free beings, we must accept the responsibility that accompanies our freedom. (3) We have a concern to preserve our uniqueness and identity; we come to know ourselves in relation to knowing and interacting with others. (4) The significance of our existence and the meaning of our life are never fixed once and for all; instead, we recreate ourselves through our projects. (5) Anxiety is part of the human condition. (6) Death is also a basic human condition, and awareness of it gives significance to living.

## THERAPEUTIC GOALS

The basic aim is to enable individuals to accept the freedom and responsibility that go along with action. This approach to therapy is an invitation to clients to recognize the ways in which they are not living authentically and to challenge them to make choices that will lead to their becoming what they are capable of being. Some basic therapeutic goals are (1) to help people see that they are free and become aware of their possibilities, (2) to challenge clients to recognize that they are doing something that they formerly thought was happening to them, and (3) to recognize factors that block freedom.

## THERAPEUTIC RELATIONSHIP

The approach places primary emphasis on understanding the client's current experience, not on using techniques. Thus, therapists are _not_ bound by any prescribed procedures, so they can use techniques from other schools. Interventions are used in the service of broadening the ways in which clients live in their world. Techniques are tools to help clients become aware of their choices and their potential for action.

## APPLICATIONS

The approach is especially appropriate for those seeking personal growth. It can be useful for clients who are experiencing a developmental crisis (career or marital failure, retirement, transition from one stage of life to another). Clients experience anxiety rising out of existential conflicts, such as making key choices, accepting freedom and the responsibility that goes with it, and facing the anxiety of their eventual death. These existential realities provide a rich therapeutic context.

## CONTRIBUTIONS

The essential humanity of the individual is highlighted. The person-to-person therapeutic relationships lessens the chances of dehumanizing therapy. The approach has something to offer counselors regardless of their theoretical orientation. It stresses self-determination, accepting the personal responsibility that accompanies freedom, and viewing oneself as the author of one's life. Further, it provides a perspective for understanding the value of anxiety and guilt, the role of death, and the creative aspects of being alone and choosing for oneself.

## LIMITATIONS

The approach lacks a systematic statement of principles and practices of therapy. Many existential writers use vague and global terms or abstract concepts that are difficult to grasp. The model has not been subjected to scientific research as a way of validating its procedures. It has limited applicability to lower-functioning clients, clients in extreme crisis who need direction, poor clients, and those who are nonverbal.

# GLOSSARY OF KEY TERMS

**Existential guilt.** The result of, or the consciousness of, evading the commitment to choosing for ourselves.

**Existential neurosis.** Feelings of despair and anxiety that result from inauthentic living, a failure to make choices, and an avoidance of responsibility.

**Existential vacuum.** A condition of emptiness and hollowness that results from meaninglessness in life.

**Existentialism.** A philosophical movement associated with writers such as Dostoyevski, Kierkegaard, Nietzsche, Heidegger, Sartre, and Buber. The movement stresses individual responsibility for creating one's ways of thinking, feeling, and behaving.

**Freedom.** An inescapable aspect of the human condition. Implies that we are the author of our life, and therefore, are responsible for our destiny and are accountable for our actions.

**Logotherapy.** Developed by Frankl, this brand of existential therapy literally means "healing through reason." Focus on challenging clients to search for meaning in life.

**Phenomenology.** A method of exploration that uses subjective human experiencing as its focus. The phenomenological approach is a part of the fabric of existentially oriented therapies, of Adlerian therapy, of person-centered therapy, of Gestalt therapy, and of reality therapy.

**Restricted existence.** The state of functioning with a limited degree of awareness of oneself and being vague about the nature of one's problems.

# QUESTIONS FOR DISCUSSION AND EVALUATION

1. If you embrace the existential philosophy of human nature, what implications do you see for the actual practice of therapy?

2. How can you imagine guilt and anxiety as being explored in therapy?

3. Can it be true that one is essentially free while at the same time being shaped by environmental and genetic factors? Why or why not?

4. What problems might the therapist have in grasping the subjective world of the client if the therapist has not experienced a world similar to the client's?

5. If you were working with a culturally diverse client population in a community agency what existential concepts might you draw from, if any? What do you see as the major strengths and weaknesses of this approach as it is applied to multicultural counseling?

# ISSUES AND QUESTIONS FOR PERSONAL APPLICATION

## PERSONAL FREEDOM AND RESPONSIBILITY

My assumption is that as therapists and counselors we cannot help clients come to grips with the issues of personal freedom and responsibility unless we have wrestled with those very issues in our own life. Ask yourself the following questions to see where you stand on the issues:

1. What does freedom mean to you? Do you believe in the concept of personal freedom? Do you accept that you are what you are now largely as a result of your choices, or do you feel that you are the product of your circumstances? Or is freedom a combination of some of these factors?

2. What are some critical decisions that you have made? How might your life be different now had you decided differently?

3. In what ways do you choose to give away your freedom? How do you attempt to escape from freedom? What is it like for you to accept that you must make certain decisions alone?

4. Would you be more inclined to give up some of your autonomy for the security of being taken care of by another? What price do you pay when you look to another for your answers?

5. Can you recall any periods in your life when you experienced anxiety over the necessity of making choices? Do you believe that a burden of responsibility comes with choosing for oneself?

6. When others in your life made decisions for you that you could have made yourself, what did they tell you? How did you respond at such times?

7. How, in your view, is a sense of self-trust related to an acceptance of the weight of freedom? Can you increase your capacity for self-trust by risking to choose for yourself?

8. If you do not accept the concept of choice, how will this influence your work as a counselor?

## OTHER QUESTIONS FOR PERSONAL REFLECTION

Ask yourself the following questions to attempt to clarify both how you now see yourself and the ways in which you'd like to change. Bring these questions into class for discussion.

1. Do you believe that you are ultimately alone? What are the creative aspects of being alone? What for you is the difference between being alone and feeling isolated and lonely?

2.  What are the sources of meaning and purpose in your life? What do you have or do that gives you a sense of significance? If you do not experience a meaningful direction in your life, what is that like?

3.  When do you experience anxiety? What is the experience like for you? How do you cope with anxiety? What ways have you used in an attempt to escape from anxiety?

4.  What are your views, attitudes, and feelings relating to your own eventual death? How well do you accept that reality? In what ways do you deny your eventual nonbeing? How do you suppose your acceptance or denial is important in terms of the quality of your day-to-day living?

5.  Do you agree with the existentialists' assertion that the price for denying death is undefined anxiety and self-alienation? If you knew that you were going to die soon, what would you be able to say about your life? What is some significant unfinished business that you'd most like to complete before dying?

## SUGGESTED ACTIVITIES AND EXERCISES

### WAYS OF BEING "DEAD" BUT STILL EXISTING

In counseling situations I find it useful to ask people to examine parts of themselves that they feel are "dead." In what ways are you dead? How do you prevent yourself from experiencing life? What would happen if you chose to live fully instead of settling for your half-life/half-death existence?

*Directions*:    The following is a list of comments that express some ways in which clients may choose "death" over "life." As you read them, reflect on questions such as "How fully alive do I feel? When do I feel most alive? least alive? What parts within me are 'dead' or 'dying'? What would it take for me to experience a new surge of vitality in these areas?" Then discuss in class, either in small groups or in dyads, the degree to which you feel fully alive. Also, share how the reality of death can give life a sense of meaning.

1.  "I'll kill in me what is real, and I'll try to be what you want so that you'll approve of me."

2.  "I'll cut off all my feelings—that way I won't hurt. I've become a good computer, and I'll never experience pain."

3.  "I'll be the 'helpless one' so that you'll take care of me. I am without power. I am dead to my strength. I need you to make me alive."

4.  "I'm overweight and unattractive, and I work at keeping myself dead to my body. I have killed my sexuality because I'm scared of making choices."

5.  "I am dead, hollow, empty, with nothing inside. I can't find any real purpose for living. I just exist and wait for each day to pass."

6.  "I live in isolation from people. I don't want to get close, so I just seal myself off from everyone."

Now list some possible ways in which parts of *you* are not fully "alive":

1.  _____

2.  _____

3.  _____

4.  _____

## WILL WE REALLY CHANGE?

According to the existentialists, the best means of understanding individuals is watching their striving for the future. Because humans are always emerging and becoming, the future is the dominant mode of time for them. Persons can be understood as they project themselves forward.

One technique that I have often used in group situations is to ask each person to fantasize his or her life as he or she would like it to be. I have asked such questions as "What future do you want for yourself? What do you want to be able to say about yourself in relation to the significant people in your life? What would you like to have inscribed on your tombstone? What are you doing now, or what can you do now to make your vision a reality?" A look into the future can be a stimulus for people to see choices they have made and the ways in which they can create and shape their own future. In some real ways they can be the architect of their future life.

*Directions*: Write down a brief response to the following questions. Then discuss your answers in class, either in small groups or in dyads.

1. What do you think your future will be like if you stay very much as you are now? Complete the following statement:  If I make no major changes, then I expect _____

   _____

   _____

2. List some things, situations, or people that you see as preventing your change or as making your change difficult._____

   _____

   _____

   _____

3. If you could make *one* significant change in your personality or behavior *now*, what would it be?_____

   _____

4. What do you see that you can do *now* to make that one change?_____

   _____

5. Write your own epitaph._____

   _____

   _____

# CASE EXAMPLES

## MY WAY OF WORKING WITH STAN FROM THE EXISTENTIAL PERSPECTIVE

One of my basic assumptions is that people are more than mere victims of their past and that they can assume responsibility for changing those aspects that they most want to change. Therefore, I might work with Stan by focusing on his fear of suicide. I take this fear to mean that he is tired of living a half-dead existence, that he wants to live in new ways, and that he will no longer settle for some of the deadening ways in which he has lived. I would probably ask him to look at what it would be like if he were to die now. One of the things I value from the existential model is the view that death is a stimulus to living; death jars us into taking a look at how we are living to determine if we are merely existing or are really alive. In keeping with this notion, I might ask Stan to relate all the ways in which he feels that he has been a victim and how he has kept himself a prisoner of his past. This would be a starting point for working with the choices that are open to him.

I make the assumption that his anxiety is a motivating force and that his anxiety attacks are really significant existential messages indicating that it is time for him to take inventory and realize his options. On this basis I would also explore with him how he has been numbing himself with alcohol as an attempt to avoid dealing with the anxiety he feels over the freedom that comes with choosing for himself.

As you review Stan's case and think about him from an existential perspective, consider these questions:

1. To what degree have you dealt with your own feelings of death? How would this affect your ability to work with Stan on his fear of suicide?

2. Do you have an ideas about how you might work with his overwhelming anxiety? Do you see any connections between his restricted existence and his anxiety?

3. What steps would you most like to see Stan take? How can he begin to move toward increased freedom?

## RALPH: FEELING TRAPPED IN HIS JOB

Ralph is a 47-year-old father of four children (all of whom are adolescents or older). He says that he is coming to you for counseling in order to find a way to free himself from feeling trapped by meaningless work. He was referred to you by a friend, and he tells you the following at the intake session:

I feel a need to take some action at this point in my life—I suppose you could say I'm going through a late identity crisis. By now, you'd expect that a guy of my age should know where he's going in life, but all I know is that I feel blah. Just sorta like a zombie!

I attribute most of my problems to my job. I've worked with this department store chain for more years than I can remember. I'm the manager of a store with quite a few people under me. But how I've come to hate that job! There's nothing to look forward to anymore. It's no challenge. Part of me wants to junk the entire thing, even though I'm not that far away from retirement with a nice pension and many fringe benefits. So the conservative part of me says stay and put up with what you've got! Then another side of me says leave and find something else more challenging. Don't *die* living for a stinking pension plan!

So I'm really torn whether I should stay or leave. I keep thinking of my kids. I feel I should support them and see them through college—and if I go to another job I'll have to take a big pay cut. I feel guilty about even thinking of letting my kids down when they expect me to see them through. And then my wife tells me I should just accept that what I'm feeling is normal for my age—a midlife crisis, she calls it. She says I should get rid of foolish notions about making a job change at my age. Then there's always the fear that I'll get out there and make that big change and then get fired. What would I do without a job? Who would I be if I couldn't work? I just feel as though there are heavy rocks on my shoulders weighing me down every time I think about being stuck in my job. I sure hope you'll help me get rid of this burden and help me make a decision about what to do with this work situation.

1. Based on his story, what are your impressions of Ralph? Would you like to work with him? Why or why not? Would you share with him any of your initial reactions and thoughts from the intake session? If so, what do you think you would tell him?

2. How might you work with the two sides of Ralph: the part of him that wants to stay in his job versus the part that wants to leave?

3. Check what your goals might be in working with Ralph:

_____ to provide him with information about the job market
_____ to give him advice about whether he should remain in his job or look for a new career in life
_____ to encourage him to work with his feelings of "blahness" and guilt over not providing for his children
_____ to help him deal with his fear of changing jobs and then failing
_____ to help him look at what he would be without his work
_____ to challenge him to deal with his feelings toward his wife

4. Depending on which of the above goals you see as being most pressing, how do you think you would work differently with him?

5. Do you have any ideas about how to work with his burden of carrying heavy rocks on his shoulders?

6. What ideas do you have about helping him explore his feeling of being trapped?

## REVIEWING THE HIGHLIGHTS

*Directions*: Fill in the sentence-completion form, and bring in your responses, as a basis for class discussion. Also, refer to the questions under "Reviewing the Highlights of a Theory" in Chapter 1 as a more detailed way of reviewing key concepts of this approach.

1. This approach views human nature as _____

_____

2. The key characteristic that distinguishes this approach is _____

_____

3. The therapeutic goals of this approach are _____

_____

4. The central role of the therapist is _____

_____

5. In the therapy process clients are expected to _____

_____

6. The relationship between the client and the therapist is characterized by_____

_____

7. Some of the major techniques are _____

_____

8. I think this approach is most applicable to those clients who _____

_____

9. One aspect of the existential approach that I like most is _____

_____

10. One aspect of the existential approach that I like least is _____

_____

# QUIZ ON EXISTENTIAL THERAPY:
## A COMPREHENSION CHECK    Score ____%

*Note*:   Refer to Appendix 1 for the scoring key.

*True/false items*:   Decide if the following statements are "more true" or "more false" as they apply to existential therapy.

T   F    1.   Existential therapy is best considered as a system of highly developed techniques designed to foster authenticity.

T   F    2.   Existential therapists show wide latitude in the techniques they employ.

T   F    3.   According to Sartre, existential guilt is the consciousness of evading commitment to choose for ourselves.

T   F    4.   Existentialists maintain that our experience of aloneness is a result of our making inappropriate choices.

T   F    5.   Techniques are secondary in the therapeutic process, and a subjective understanding of the client is primary.

T   F    6.   To its credit, existential therapy derives its findings from empirical testing.

T   F    7.   Part of the human condition is that humans are both free and responsible.

T   F    8.   Anxiety is best considered as a neurotic manifestation;  thus, the primary aim of therapy is to eliminate anxiety.

T   F    9.   Existential therapy is primarily classified as a cognitive approach.

T   F   10.   The existential approach is a reaction against *both* psychoanalysis and behaviorism.


*Multiple-choice items*:   Select the *one best answer* of those alternatives given.   Consider each question within the framework of existential therapy.

_____   11.   The basic goal(s) of existential therapy is(are)

   a.   to expand self-awareness.
   b.   to increase potentials for choice.
   c.   to help clients accept the responsibility of choosing.
   d.   to help clients experience authentic existence.
   e.   all of the above.

_____   12.   Which is not a key concept of existential therapy?

   a.   It is based on a personal relationship between client and therapist.
   b.   It stresses personal freedom in deciding one's fate.
   c.   It places primary value on self-awareness.
   d.   It is based on a well-defined set of techniques and procedures.
   e.   None of the above is a key concept.

_____   13.   The function of the existentially-oriented counselor is

   a.   to develop a specific treatment plan that can be objectively appraised.
   b.   to challenge the client's irrational beliefs.
   c.   to understand the client's subjective world.
   d.   to explore the client's past history in detail.
   e.   to assist the client in working through transference.

_____ 14. According to the existential view, anxiety is

    a. a result of repressed sexuality.
    b. a part of the human condition.
    c. a neurotic symptom that needs to be cured.
    d. a result of faulty learning.

_____ 15. Existential therapy is best considered as

    a. an approach to understanding humans.
    b. a school of therapy.
    c. a system of techniques designed to create authentic humans.
    d. a strategy for uncovering game playing.

_____ 16. Which might be considered the most crucial quality of a therapist in building an effective therapeutic relationship with a client?

    a. the therapist's knowledge of theory
    b. the therapist's skill in using techniques
    c. the therapist's ability to diagnose accurately
    d. the therapist's authenticity

_____ 17. The central issue in therapy is

    a. freedom and responsibility.
    b. resistance.
    c. transference.
    d. examining irrational beliefs.
    e. none of the above.

_____ 18. Guilt and anxiety are viewed as

    a. behaviors that are unrealistic.
    b. the result of traumatic situations in childhood.
    c. conditions that should be removed or cured.
    d. all of the above
    e. none of the above.

_____ 19. The existential emphasis is based on

    a. specific behaviors that can be assessed.
    b. a scientific orientation.
    c. a teaching/learning model that stresses the didactic aspects of therapy.
    d. the philosophical concern with what it means to be fully human.
    e. an analysis of our ego states.

_____ 20. Existential therapy is basically

    a. a behavioral approach.
    b. a cognitive approach.
    c. an experiential approach.
    d. an action-oriented approach.

_____ 21. Existential therapy places emphasis on

    a. a systematic approach to changing behavior.
    b. the quality of the client/therapist relationship.
    c. teaching clients cognitive and behavioral coping skills.
    d. uncovering early childhood traumatic events.
    e. working through the transference relationship.

_____ 22. Which person is not considered a European existential psychiatrist?

    a. Ludwig Binswanger      c. Medard Boss

    b. Margaret Mahler      d. Viktor Frankl

_____ 23. Two of the most significant spokespersons for the existential approach in the United States are:

    a. Heinz Kohut and Otto Kernberg.

    b. Medard Boss and Ludwig Binswanger.

    c. Rollo May and Irvin Yalom.

    d. Martin Buber and Jean-Paul Sartre.

    e. Erik Erikson and Margaret Mahler.

_____ 24. The concept of bad faith refers to

    a. not keeping up to date with paying one's therapist.

    b. leading an inauthentic existence.

    c. the failure to cooperate with the therapeutic venture.

    d. the experience of aloneness.

    e. the unwillingness to search for meaning in life.

_____ 25. Which of the following is a limitation of the existential approach in working with culturally diverse client populations?

    a. the focus on understanding and accepting the client

    b. the focus on finding meaning in one's life

    c. the focus on death as a catalyst to living fully

    d. the focus on one's own responsibility rather than on social conditions

# 7

# PERSON-CENTERED THERAPY

## PRECHAPTER SELF-INVENTORY

*Directions*:   Refer to page 46 for general directions.   Use the following code:

5 = I *strongly agree* with this statement.

4 = I *agree*, in most respects, with this statement.

3 = I am *undecided* in my opinion about this statement.

2 = I *disagree*, in most respects, with this statement.

1 = I *strongly disagree* with this statement.

_____   1.   At a person's deepest core is a socialized, forward-moving being striving to become a fully functioning self.

_____   2.   People have the capacity for understanding their problems and the resources for resolving them.

_____   3.   The basic goal of therapy is to create a psychological climate of safety wherein clients will not feel threatened and will thus be able to drop their pretenses and defenses.

_____   4.   The therapist's function is rooted not primarily in techniques but in his or her ways of being and attitudes.

_____   5.   Effective therapists use themselves as instruments of change, for they must encounter the client on a person-to-person level.

_____   6.   The client uses the therapeutic relationship to build new ways of relating to others in the outside world.

_____   7.   The client can make progress in therapy without the therapist's interpretations, diagnoses, evaluations, and directives.

_____   8.   The relationship between the therapist and the client is the crux of progress in therapy.

_____   9.   The therapist's genuineness, accurate empathy, and unconditional positive regard are essential qualities of effective therapy.

_____  10.   When people are free, they will be able to find their own way.

_____  11.   Forming a diagnosis and developing a case history are not important prerequisites for therapy.

_____  12.   It is important that a therapist avoid being judgmental about the client's feelings.

_____  13.   Therapeutic change depends on clients' perceptions, both of their own experience in therapy and of the counselor's basic attitudes.

# OVERVIEW OF PERSON-CENTERED THERAPY

## KEY FIGURE AND MAJOR FOCUS

Founder: Carl Rogers. As a branch of humanistic psychology that stresses a phenomenological approach, person-centered therapy was originally developed in the late 1940s as a reaction against psychoanalytic therapy. Based on a subjective view of human experience, it emphasizes the client's resources for becoming aware and for resolving blocks to personal growth. It puts the client, not the therapist, at the center of therapy.

## PHILOSOPHY AND BASIC ASSUMPTIONS

The approach is grounded on a positive view of humanity that sees the personal as innately striving toward becoming fully functioning. The basic assumption is that in the context of a personal relationship with a caring therapist, the client experiences previously denied or distorted feelings and increases self-awareness. Clients are empowered by their participation in a therapeutic relationship. They actualize their potential for growth, wholeness, spontaneity, and inner-directedness.

## KEY CONCEPTS

One can direct one's own life. The client has the capacity for resolving life problems effectively without interpretation and direction from an expert therapist. This approach focuses on fully experiencing the present moment, learning to accept oneself, and deciding on ways to change. It views mental health as a congruence between what one wants to become and what one actually is.

## THERAPEUTIC GOALS

A major goal is to provide a climate of safety and trust in the therapeutic setting so that the client, by using the therapeutic relationship for self-exploration, can become aware of blocks to growth. The client tends to move toward more openness, greater self-trust, more willingness to evolve as opposed to being a fixed product, and more living by internal standards as opposed to taking external cues for what he or she should or ought to become.

## THERAPEUTIC RELATIONSHIP

Rogers emphasizes the attitudes and personal characteristics of the therapist and the quality of the client/therapist relationship as the prime determinants of the outcomes of therapy. The qualities of the therapist that determine the relationship include genuineness, nonpossessive warmth, accurate empathy, unconditional acceptance of and respect for the client, permissiveness, caring, and the communication of those attitudes to the client. The client is able to translate his or her learning in therapy to outside relationships with others.

## TECHNIQUES AND PROCEDURES

Because the approach stresses the client/therapist relationship, it specifies few techniques. Techniques are secondary to the therapist's attitudes. The approach minimizes directive techniques, interpretation, questioning, probing, diagnosis, and collecting history. It maximizes active listening and hearing, reflection of feelings, and clarification. The full participation of the therapist as a person in the therapeutic relationship is currently being emphasized.

## APPLICATIONS

The approach has wide applicability to many person-to-person situations, in both therapy and learning. It is a useful model for individual therapy, group counseling, student-centered teaching and learning, parent/child relations, and human-relations-training labs. It is especially well suited for the initial phases of crisis-intervention work. Its principles have been applied to administration and management and to working with systems and institutions.

## CONTRIBUTIONS

One of the first therapies to break from traditional psychoanalysis, it stresses the active role and responsibility of the client. It is a positive and optimistic view and calls attention to the need to account for a person's inner and subjective experiences. It makes the therapeutic process relationship-centered rather than technique-centered. It focuses on the crucial role of the therapist's attitudes. The model has generated a great deal of clinical research into both the process and the outcomes of therapy, which in turn has led to refining the tentative hypotheses. This approach has been applied to bringing people from diverse cultures together. The concepts have value in working within a multicultural context.

## LIMITATIONS

A possible danger is the therapist who, by merely reflecting content, brings little of his or her personhood into the therapeutic relationship. The approach has limited use with nonverbal clients. As an ahistorical approach it tends to discount the significance of the past. Some of the main limitations are due not to the theory itself but to some counselors' misunderstanding of the basic concepts and to their dogmatic practical applications.

# GLOSSARY OF KEY TERMS

**Accurate empathic understanding.** The act of perceiving the internal frame of reference of another, of grasping the person's subjective world, without losing one's own identity.

**Congruence.** The state in which self-experiences are accurately symbolized in the self-concept. As applied to the therapist, congruence is a matching of one's inner experiencing with external expressions.

**Self-actualizing tendency.** A growth force within us; an actualizing tendency leading to the full development of one's potential; the basis on which people can be trusted to identify and resolve their own problems in a therapeutic relationship.

**Humanistic psychology.** A movement, often referred to as the "third force," that emphasizes freedom, choice, values, growth, self-actualization, becoming, spontaneity, creativity, play, humor, peak experiences, and psychological health. (Although some of these overlap existential concepts, there are significant differences in accent between existential and humanistic psychology.)

**Therapeutic conditions.** The necessary and sufficient characteristics of the therapeutic relationship for client change to occur. These core conditions include therapist congruence (or genuineness), unconditional positive regard (acceptance and respect), and accurate empathic understanding.

**Unconditional positive regard.** The nonjudgmental expression of a fundamental respect for the person as a human; acceptance of a person's right to his or her feelings.

# QUESTIONS FOR DISCUSSION AND EVALUATION

1. Do you believe that most clients have the capacity to understand the resolve their own problems without directive intervention by the therapist? Why or why not?

2. The person-centered view of human nature is grounded on the assumption that people have the tendency to develop in a positive and constructive manner *if* a climate of respect

and trust is established. To what degree do you accept this premise? What are the implications of such a view for the practice of counseling?

3. What do you consider to be the strengths and the weaknesses of this approach in a multicultural context? What concepts might build effective bonds with clients from diverse cultural backgrounds? Do you see any shortcomings in staying with this orientation?

4. Are the client's goals and decisions influenced in a subtle way by the therapist's behavior and attitudes? Discuss.

5. Do you think that the client/therapist relationship advocated by the person-centered model is *alone* enough to bring about behavioral and personality changes in the client? Why or why not? If not, what else do you think is needed?

## PRACTICAL APPLICATION: REFLECTING CLIENT'S FEELINGS

*Directions*: The person-centered approach to counseling emphasizes understanding clients from an internal frame of reference. To do that, the therapist must be able to discriminate clients' feelings, hear accurately what messages they are sending, and reflect the deeper meanings that they are attempting to communicate. A common mistake that counselors make is to give a superficial reflection by merely repeating almost the same words the client used. The following exercises are designed to help you learn to grasp the more subtle messages of clients and to reflect feelings as well as content. First, write down a few key words or phrases that describe what the client is *feeling*. Second, write down what your response would be if you were to *reflect* to the client what you heard.

*Example*: Woman, 42, tells you: "So often I feel that I'm alone, that nobody cares about me. My husband doesn't seem to notice me, my kids only demand from me, and I just dread getting up in the morning."

    a. What is this person feeling? *Ignored. Unappreciated. Taken advantage of. Unloved.*

       *A sense of futility.*

    b. Respond by reflecting what you heard. *I sense a lot of loneliness and desperation, a*

       *feeling of "What's the use of going on this way?"*

1. Boy, 17, tells you: "I can't stand this school anymore. It doesn't mean anything. I'm bored and frustrated, and I hate school. I feel like dropping out today, but that's stupid because I'm graduating in two months."

    a. What is this person feeling?

    _____

    b. Respond by reflecting what you heard. _____

2. Girl, 14, tells you: "I feel like running away from home. My stepfather always criticizes me, and he puts me on restriction for things he claims I do that I don't do. My mother doesn't ever listen to me and always sides with him. They don't trust me at all."

    a. What is this person feeling? _____

    b. Respond by reflecting what you heard. _____

3.  A fifth-grader tells you: "None of the other kids like me. They always pick on me and tease me. I try real hard to make friends, but everyone hates me."

    a.  What is this person feeling? _____

    _____

    b.  Respond by reflecting what you heard. _____

    _____

    _____

4.  Woman teacher, 33, tells you: "I have really noticed a tremendous difference since I've been coming here for counseling. I'm a lot more open with my kids, and they are really noticing a change in me and like it, too! I am even able to talk to my principal without feeling like a scared little kid!"

    a.  What is this person feeling? _____

    _____

    b.  Respond by reflecting what you heard. _____

    _____

    _____

5.  Man, 45, tells you: "Damn, I'm so preoccupied since my wife left me that I can't think of anything but her. I keep going over in my head what I could and should have done so she would have stayed. It pisses me off that I can't get her out of my mind and go about my living!"

    a.  What is this person feeling? _____

    b.  Respond by reflecting what you heard. _____

    _____

    _____

6.  Man, 27, tells you: "Here I am, still in college and not a damn thing to show for my life. My wife is supporting me, and I know she resents me for not getting out and getting a job before this. But, you know, now I know what I want, and before I was just in school because my parents wanted me to be there."

    a.  What is this person feeling? _____

    _____

    b.  Respond by reflecting what you heard. _____

    _____

    _____

# CASE EXAMPLES

### MY WAY OF WORKING WITH STAN
### FROM THE PERSON-CENTERED PERSPECTIVE

The one central concept I value most from the person-centered perspective is the importance of therapists' using themselves and their relationship with the client as the major force for change. Thus, I would share with Stan my perceptions of him and the reactions I was having to being with him in these sessions. And I would let him know how I was affected by being in this relationship with him. In many ways I would let him point the direction he wanted to travel; he relates a lot of rich material, and I believe that he does have the capacity to understand himself and move in a constructive direction.

From this model I would also draw on the factor of trust as a major attribute of a productive relationship. One way I would attempt to build this trust is to be honest with Stan in these sessions. I would also encourage him to talk openly about feelings that he has felt the need to tuck away and keep secret. Furthermore, I assume that the best way to create trust in the therapeutic relationship is by modeling the very behaviors and attitudes that I hope he will acquire. Thus, if I am genuine in the session and do not hide behind pretenses and roles, he will drop his masks and be genuine with me. If I can *really* listen to him in a nonjudgmental way, I have the basis to come to now him and thus to care for him. If I am able to hear, appreciate, respect, and care for him, the chances are increased that he will be able to do these things for himself.

As you review Stan's case and think about him from a person-centered perspective, consider these questions:

1. The therapeutic relationship is the core of this approach. Knowing what you do of Stan, how would it be for you to develop a relationship with him? Is there anything that might get in your way with him?

2. Might you feel restricted in working with Stan without any techniques? Or might you feel a sense of freedom in meeting him in this way?

3. Assume that Stan complains to you that he feels he is getting nowhere in counseling, that he wants you to be more directive, and that he doesn't feel that you are active enough. What might your response be, and what might you do?

## HELGA: A DEPRESSED CLIENT WITH SUICIDAL IMPULSES

Helga has spent time in mental institutions because of deep depression, marked feelings of worthlessness, and several attempts to kill herself. She was born and reared in Germany and came to live in New Jersey in her late teens. She relates that she has never felt at home since she left Germany but that there is now nothing there for her to return to. She frequently mentions how lonely and isolated she feels. There are no friends in her life, no intimate relationships, and she feels a deep sense of rejection. Although she has been out of the last institution for over a year, she is an outpatient and has come to the day-treatment center on a regular basis. Assume that you are a new counselor and are seeing her for the first time. Think about how you might deal with her in the first five minutes of your initial session. At this first session Helga relates:

> I just dread getting up every morning. Everything seems like such a chore. I'm afraid that anything I do will turn to failure. I see no real sense in going on. I have constant thoughts of ending my life. I'm surely no use to anyone around me. I couldn't hold a husband or any job, and then I lost my kids. I just feel so worthless and rotten and full of guilt and hate for myself. No matter what I do or try, I just can't see any light at the end of that long, dark, cold, scary tunnel. I look forward to death, because then I won't have to suffer anymore.

1. What are your personal reactions to what Helga is saying? How does it affect you? What are you feeling as you listen to her?

2. What do you mainly hear Helga saying?

3. Given the way Helga presents herself, do you see much hope? Do you believe that there is a positive, trustworthy, and actualizing tendency within her?

4. In what ways might you use yourself as a person to create a relationship with Helga so that she might work through her depression? Do you think that your relationship with her by itself is sufficient, or would you see a need for interpretation, direction, and active techniques?

5. Would you be able to accept any direction or decision that Helga chose for herself, including suicide? What are the ethical and legal ramifications of accepting her choice to end her life? How would you deal with her suicidal ideation and threats?

6. To what extent would you want to explore her German background with her, especially since she does not feel at home in either culture?

7. Have you had enough life experiences similar to Helga's to enable you to empathize with her and enter her experiential world? How would you respond to her if she said: "You can't understand how uprooted I feel. I don't belong anywhere. But I just don't think you can know what this is like for me."

**A SUGGESTION**

Now that you have attempted to stay within the person-centered framework in working with both Stan and Helga, form small groups in class. One person can volunteer to "become" the client (Stan or Helga) while another volunteer shows how he or she would approach this client within the spirit of the person-centered approach. I recommend that you do this type of role playing in small groups for most of the cases presented in this manual. If you experience the roles of *both* client and counselor, you will be in a good position to discuss meaningfully what you like and don't like about each of the theoretical approaches. And you may learn a good bit about yourself by assuming the identity of the clients presented here, even briefly.

# REVIEWING THE HIGHLIGHTS

1. Person-centered therapy views human nature as _____

   _____

2. The unique feature that distinguishes this approach is _____

   _____

3. The therapeutic goals are _____

   _____

4. The central role of the therapist is _____

   _____

5. In the therapy process clients are expected to _____

   _____

6. The relationship between the client and the therapist is characterized by_____

   _____

7. Some of the major techniques are _____

   _____

8. I think this approach is most applicable to clients who _____

   _____

9. One aspect of the person-centered approach I like most is _____

   _____

10. One aspect of the person-centered approach I like least is _____

   _____

# QUIZ ON PERSON-CENTERED THERAPY: A COMPREHENSION CHECK

Score _____ %

*Note*: Refer to Appendix 1 for the scoring key.

*True/false items*: Decide if the following statements are "more true" or "more false" as they apply to person-centered therapy.

T  F  1. Person-centered therapy is best described as a completed and fixed "school," or model, of therapy.

T  F  2. Diagnosis of clients is seen as an important beginning point for therapy.

T  F  3. A major contribution of this approach has been the willingness of Rogers to state his formulations as testable hypotheses and submit them to research.

T  F  4. *Accurate empathic understanding* implies an objective understanding of a client and some form of diagnosis.

T  F  5. Directive procedures are called for when clients feel that they are "stuck" in therapy.

T  F  6. Free association is a basic part of this therapy.

T  F  7. This approach holds that the direction of therapy is the primary responsibility of the client, not the therapist.

T  F  8. A limitation of this approach is that it is a long-term process.

T  F  9. Transference is seen as the core of this therapy.

T  F  10. Interpretations by the therapist typically tend to interfere with client growth, according to Rogers.

*Multiple-choice items*: Select the *one best answer* of those alternatives given. Consider each question within the framework of person-centered therapy.

_____ 11. The founder of person-centered therapy is

a. Rollo May
b. Frederick Perls.
c. Abraham Maslow.

d. B. F. Skinner
e. none of the above.

_____ 12. Person-centered therapy is a form of

a. psychoanalysis
b. humanistic therapy.
c. behavioral therapy.

d. cognitive-oriented therapy.
e. both (c) and (d).

_____ 13. Which of the following is(are) considered important in person-centered therapy?

a. accurate diagnosis
b. accurate therapist interpretation
c. analysis of the transference relationship
d. all of the above
e. none of the above

_____ 14. Congruence refers to the therapist's

a. genuineness.
b. empathy for clients.
c. positive regard.

d. respect for clients.
e. judgmental attitude.

_____ 15. In person-centered therapy transference is

    a. a necessary, but not sufficient, condition of therapy.
    b. a core part of the therapeutic process.
    c. a neurotic distortion.
    d. a result of ineptness on the therapist's part.
    e. not an essential or significant factor in the therapy process.

_____ 16. Unconditional positive regard implies

    a. the therapist's acceptance of the client's right to all his or her feelings.
    b. the therapist's acceptance of the client as a person of worth.
    c. acceptance of all the client's past behavior.
    d. both (a) and (b).

_____ 17. Accurate empathic understanding refers to the therapist's ability to

    a. accurately diagnose the client's central problem.
    b. objectively understand the dynamics of a client.
    c. like and care for the client.
    d. sense the inner world of the client's subjective experience.

_____ 18. Which technique(s) is(are) most often used in the person-centered approach?

    a. questioning and probing
    b. analysis of resistance
    c. free association
    d. active listening and reflection
    e. interpretation

_____ 19. Which statement is most true of person-centered theory?

    a. Therapists should be judgmental at times.
    b. Therapists should direct the session when clients are silent.
    c. The skill a therapist possesses is more important than his or her attitude toward a client.
    d. The techniques a therapist uses are less important than are his or her attitudes.
    e. Both (a) and (b) are true.

_____ 20. Which of the following is(are) a contribution(s) of the person-centered viewpoint?

    a. It calls attention to the need to account for a person's inner experience.
    b. It relies on research to validate the concepts and practices of the approach.
    c. It provides the therapist with a variety of therapeutic techniques.
    d. It focuses on an objective view of behavior.
    e. Both (a) and (b) are contributions.

_____ 21. One of the strengths of the person-centered approach is that

    a. it offers a wide range of cognitive techniques to change behavior.
    b. it teaches clients ways to explore the meaning of dreams.
    c. it emphasizes reliving one's early childhood memories.
    d. therapists have the latitude to develop their own counseling style.
    e. clients are given a concrete plan to follow.

_____ 22. A limitation of the person-centered approach is

    a. a lack of research conducted on key concepts.
    b. a tendency for practitioners to give support without challenging clients sufficiently.
    c. a lack of attention to the therapeutic relationship.
    d. a failure to allow clients to choose for themselves.

_____ 23. Carl Rogers made a contribution to

    a.  developing the humanistic movement in psychotherapy.
    b.  pioneering research in the process and outcomes of therapy.
    c.  fostering world peace.
    d.  pioneering the encounter-group movement.
    e.  all of the above.

_____ 24. As a result of experiencing person-centered therapy, it is hypothesized, the client will move toward

    a.  self-trust.
    b.  an internal source of evaluation.
    c.  being more open to experience.
    d.  a willingness to continue growing.
    e.  all of the above.

_____ 25. Unconditional positive regard refers to

    a.  feeling a sense of liking for clients.
    b.  accepting clients as worthy persons.
    c.  approving of clients' behavior.
    d.  agreeing with with clients' values.
    e.  accepting clients if they meet the therapist's expectations.

# 8

# GESTALT THERAPY

## PRECHAPTER SELF-INVENTORY

*Directions*: Refer to page 46 for general directions. Use the following code:

5 = I *strongly agree* with this statement.

4 = I *agree*, in most respects, with this statement.

3 = I am *undecided* in my opinion about this statement.

2 = I *disagree*, in most respects, with this statement.

1 = I *strongly disagree* with this statement.

_____ 1. People must find their own way in life and must accept personal responsibility if they hope to achieve maturity.

_____ 2. In therapy it is more important to work on integration than on analysis.

_____ 3. The here-and-now focus of therapy is more important than a focus on the past or on the future.

_____ 4. It is far more fruitful for the therapist to ask "what" and "how" questions than to ask "why" questions.

_____ 5. Rather than merely talking about feelings and experiences, it is more productive in therapy to attempt to relive and reexperience those feelings as though they were happening now.

_____ 6. One's past is important to the degree that it is related to significant themes in one's present functioning.

_____ 7. Some people hang on to the past in order to justify their unwillingness to take responsibility for their own actions or growth.

_____ 8. A primary aim of therapy is to expand a person's capacity for self-awareness.

_____ 9. Neurosis is the result of blocking off threatening feelings and pushing them into the background.

_____ 10. Unfinished business from the past usually manifests itself in present problems with functioning effectively.

_____ 11. Catastrophic expectations and fantasies prevent one from taking risks that are necessary for living fully in the present.

_____ 12. A basic aim of therapy is to challenge the client to move from environmental support to self-support.

_____ 13. Awareness, in itself, is a curative factor in therapy.

_____ 14. Therapy should focus on the client's feelings, present awareness, body messages, and blocks to awareness.

_____ 15. The therapist's main function is to assist the client in gaining awareness of the "what" and "how" of experiencing in the here and now.

_____ 16. The therapist should avoid diagnosing, interpreting, and explaining at length the client's behavior.

_____ 17. In therapy it is extremely important to pay attention to the client's body language and other nonverbal cues.

_____ 18. As therapy progresses, the client should be expected to assume increasing responsibility for his or her own thoughts, feelings, and behavior.

_____ 19. It is important that therapists actively share their own present perceptions and experiences as they encounter clients in the here and now.

_____ 20. The techniques of therapy should be designed to help clients gain more awareness of fragmented and disowned aspects of themselves.

# OVERVIEW OF GESTALT THERAPY

## KEY FIGURES AND MAJOR FOCUS

Founder: Frederick ("Fritz") Perls. Key figures: Erving Polster and Miriam Polster. The approach is an experiential therapy that stresses here-and-now awareness and integration of the fragmented parts of personality. It focuses on the "what" and "how" of behavior and on the role of unfinished business from the past in preventing effective functioning in the present.

## PHILOSOPHY AND BASIC ASSUMPTIONS

Gestalt philosophy is rooted in existential philosophy and psychology. It stresses the unity of mind, body, and feelings. The basic assumption is that individuals are responsible for their own behavior and experiencing. The approach is designed to help people experience the present moment more fully and gain awareness of what they are doing. The approach is _experiential_ in that clients come to grips with what they are thinking, feeling, and doing as they interact with the therapist. The assumption is that growth occurs through personal contact rather than through the therapist's techniques or interpretations. A basic assumption is that clients have the capacity to do their own seeing, feeling, sensing, and interpreting. Thus, client autonomy is fostered, and clients are expected to be active in therapy.

## KEY CONCEPTS

Key concepts are acceptance of responsibility, the here and now, direct (as opposed to talked-about) experiencing, awareness, avoidance, bringing unfinished business from the past into the present, and dealing with impasses. Other concepts include energy and blocks to energy; contact and resistances to contact; body work and nonverbal clues; and levels of neurotic defensiveness. Five major channels of resistance are challenged in Gestalt therapy: introjection, projection, retroflection, confluence, and deflection.

## THERAPEUTIC GOALS

The goal is challenging the client to move from environmental support toward self-support and to gain increased and enriched awareness of moment-to-moment experiencing, which by itself is curative. With awareness the client is able to recognize denied aspects of the self and thus proceed toward reintegration of all its parts.

## THERAPEUTIC RELATIONSHIP

This approach stresses the I/thou relationship. The focus is not on the techniques employed by the therapist but on who the therapist is as a person and what the therapist is doing. The therapist assists clients in experiencing all feelings more fully and lets them make their own interpretations. The therapist does not interpret for clients but focuses on the "what" and "how" of their behavior. Clients identify their own unfinished business from the past that is interfering with their present functioning by reexperiencing past situations as thought they were happening at the present moment.

## TECHNIQUES AND PROCEDURES

Many techniques are designed to intensify direct experiencing and to integrate conflicting feelings. Ideally, techniques grow out of the dialogue between the therapist and client. These experiments are the cornerstone of experiential learning. The approach stresses confronting discrepancies and the ways in which clients are avoiding responsibility for their feelings. Clients engage in role playing but, by playing out all the various parts and polarities alone, gain greater awareness of the conflicts within themselves. For effective application of Gestalt procedures, it is essential that clients be prepared for such experiments. If clients manifest resistance, this is fertile material for exploration. It is essential that therapists respect the client's resistance and not force participation in any experiment.

## APPLICATIONS

The approach is well suited to group work, but it can also be used for individual counseling. It is applicable to elementary and secondary classrooms. In deciding the appropriateness of employing Gestalt techniques, questions of *when*, *with whom*, and *in what situation* should be raised. The techniques are most effectively applied to overly socialized, restrained, and constricted individuals. These techniques are less applicable to more severely disturbed individuals. But they can be useful in working with couples and families. The methods are powerful catalysts for opening up feelings and getting clients into contact with their present-centered experience.

## CONTRIBUTIONS

By encouraging direct contact and the expression of feelings, the approach deemphasizes abstract intellectualization of one's problems. Intense experiencing can occur quickly so therapy can be relatively brief. The approach recognizes the value of working with the past as it is important to the here and now. Its focus is on the recognition of one's own projections and the refusal to accept helplessness. Gestalt therapy gives attention to nonverbal and body messages. Its emphasis is on doing and experiencing, as opposed to merely talking about problems in a detached way. It provides a perspective on growth and enhancement, not merely a treatment of disorders. The method of working with dreams is a creative pathway to increased awareness of key existential messages in life.

## LIMITATIONS

The approach can be antiintellectual to the point that cognitive factors are discounted. In the hands of an ineffective therapist Gestalt procedures can become a series of mechanical exercises behind which the therapist as a person can stay hidden. The theoretical grounds of Gestalt therapy leave something to be desired. Moreover, there is a potential for the therapist to manipulate the client with powerful techniques. To offset some basic limitations training and supervision in Gestalt therapy are essential, as well as introspection on the therapist's part.

# GLOSSARY OF KEY TERMS

**Awareness.** The process of attending to and observing one's own sensing, thinking, feelings, and actions; paying attention to the flowing nature of one's present-centered experience.

**Confluence.** A disturbance in which the sense of the boundary between self and environment is lost.

**Confrontation.** An invitation for the client to become aware of discrepancies between verbal and nonverbal expressions, between feelings and actions, or between thoughts and feelings.

**Deflection.** A way of avoiding contact and awareness by being vague and indirect.

**Dichotomy.** A split by which a person experiences or sees opposing forces; a polarity (weak/strong, dependent/independent).

**Experiments.** Techniques designed to enhance here-and-now awareness; activities that clients try out as a way of testing new ways of thinking, feelings, and behaving.

**Introjection.** The uncritical acceptance of others' beliefs and standards without assimilating them into one's own personality.

**Modes of defense.** The five layers of neurotic ways of avoiding: the phony, the phobic, the impasse, the implosive, and the explosive.

**Projection.** The process by which we disown certain aspects of ourselves by ascribing them to the environment; the opposite of introjection.

**Retroflection.** The act of turning back onto ourselves something we would like to do (or have done) to someone else.

**Unfinished business.** Unexpressed feelings ( such as resentment, guilt, anger, grief) dating back to childhood that now interfere with effective psychological functioning. Needless emotional debris that clutters present-centered awareness.

# QUESTIONS FOR DISCUSSION AND EVALUATION

1. In Gestalt therapy the *past* is dealt with by asking the client to bring it into the present and to confront significant people as though they were present. The emphasis is on having clients embody some conflict *now*, as opposed to merely talking about an issue. What are your reactions to such an approach?

2. How can unfinished business from the past affect current functioning? Can you think of any unfinished business in your life that has a significant influence on you today? How might Gestalt methods work for you in these areas?

3. Gestalt therapy uses confrontational techniques. What does confrontation mean to you? What would it be like for you to employ action-oriented techniques as a counselor? What are the possibilities, if any, of Gestalt therapists' abusing power by confronting inappropriately?

4. Gestalt therapists accept the premise that clients can make their own interpretations by merely becoming aware of the "how" and "what" of their current behavior and that this awareness is in itself curative. What are your thoughts on this matter?

5. Consider that you might work with a wide array of ethnic minority clients in a community agency. Given the challenges of meeting the needs of this diverse population, what promises do you see in employing certain Gestalt techniques? What are potential pitfalls in using Gestalt experiments with culturally diverse clients?

# ISSUES AND QUESTIONS FOR PERSONAL APPLICATION

1. When a person talks about a problem in the past, he or she is asked to reenact the drama as though it were occurring *now* by "being there" in fantasy and reliving the experience psychologically. Following are two brief examples, one of a client's talking about a problem with his father and the other of a client's talking directly (in fantasy) to his father.

*Example 1*: When I was a kid, my father was never around. I wanted him to give me some approval and recognize that I existed. Instead, he was always doing other things. I know I was scared of him and hated him a bit for not being more of a father, but I just kept on feeling rejected by him. I guess that's why I have such a hell of a time showing affection to my own kids—I never really got any love from him. Do you suppose that's why I can't get *really* close to my own kids now?

Assume that you are a Gestalt therapist and that instead of answering the client's last question in the example above, you ask him to *talk directly* to his father—that is, to be 16 years old again and to say in fantasy what he was not able to say then to his father. Ask him to relive his feelings of rejection as though they were happening *now* and to tell his father what he is experiencing.

*Example 2*: You know, Dad, I hurt so much because all I really want is for you just to say that I mean something to you. I keep trying to please you, and no matter how hard I try, you never notice me. Damn it, I don't think there's anything I could ever do to make you care for me. I get so scared of you, because I'm afraid you'll beat me up if I let you know what I'm feeling. If I only knew what it would take to please you!

Do you see any qualitative difference between the two examples? Do you think the latter could lead the client to experience his feelings of rejection more fully than by merely talking about the rejection more fully than by merely talking about the rejection in an intellectual way? Now select a problem or concern that *you* have, and do two things: (1) deliberately talk about your problem, and (2) attempt, through fantasy, to put the problem into the here and now. What differences do you notice between the two approaches?

2. In Gestalt therapy a key concept is unfinished business, which generally involves unexpressed feelings such as resentment, rage, hatred, pain, anxiety, grief, guilt, rejection, and so on. Because those feelings are unexpressed, they are carried into the present in ways that interfere with effective contact with oneself and with others. Below are some statements indicative of unfinished business. Place a check (√) in front of each statement that you think fits you.

_____ a. "The nuns made me feel ashamed of my body."

_____ b. "I wasn't able to get to my father before he died."

_____ c. "Every time I think of my ex-husband I feel rage because of the way I let him treat me for so long."

_____ d. "I still don't think I've been able to forgive my father for the way he treated my mother."

_____ e. "It's hard for me to feel any liking for my wife when I think of all the ways she threw our money away on gambling."

_____ f. "I feel guilty when I think of how little I gave as a parent because of the fact that I went to school full time when my kids were growing up."

List some other statements that would reflect unfinished business in your life now. How do you think this unfinished business might affect you in your work as a counselor? Do you see any potential conflicts in working with your clients' unfinished business if you have the same kind of unfinished business in your life?

3. According to Perls, it is imperative to express resentments, for unexpressed resentment is converted into guilt. Try this experiment: Make a spontaneous list of all your conscious guilt feelings. Then, change the word *guilt* to *resentment* and see if it is appropriate. For example, you might say "I feel *guilty* because I don't make enough money to support my wife and kids in elegant style." Now, change the word *guilty* to *resentful*. Do this for every item on your list of things that you feel guilty about.

4. Gestalt therapists speak about "catastrophic expectations" that lead us to feel stuck. We imagine some terrible thing will happen if ____. List some threatening feelings or catastrophic fantasies that keep you from taking certain risks. What *are* some of your unreasonable fears? What risks do you avoid taking because of those expectations? How might you attempt to help a client deal with his or her catastrophic expectations?

# Suggested Activities and Exercises

*Directions*: Some Gestalt techniques lend themselves to being experienced in a classroom setting. Before you do the following exercises, review the description of the Gestalt exercises in the textbook. Experiment with the use of the techniques by applying them to yourself in the classroom setting. The example provided for the first exercise will help you get into focus.

## THE DIALOGUE EXERCISE

A person is engaged in a struggle between wanting to remain married and longing for the freedom of not being committed to anyone. The person is asked to sit in the center of the room, where two pillows are placed, and he carries on a dialogue between the two conflicting parts: the "committed side" and the "uncommitted side."

*Committed*: "It feels great to feel special and to feel loved by a woman, and I like being married to my wife most of the time."

*Uncommmitted*: "Sure, but some of the time marriage is a drag. It gets old and stale living with just one woman. Think of all the fun you're missing by limiting yourself."

*Committed*: "But think of all the possible risks of getting rejected. Besides I *do* like what I have now. It could get awfully lonely trying to meet new people."

*Uncommitted*: "And it could also be very exciting. Now you're not free, so even though you aren't lonely, you aren't excited."

*Committed*: "But it's not worth the price of putting my marriage in danger in the hope of finding more excitement."

*Uncommitted*: "Is your marriage worth that much if you won't challenge it? Think of all the things you could do as a single person!"

Now consider some type of polarity, or inner conflict, that you are struggling with, and carry on a dialogue between both parts. For example, your conflicts might be between your need to be loved and your need to tell yourself that you don't need anything from anybody, between your need to be tender and gentle and your need for aggression or toughness, or between your fighting side and your side that wants to resign.

## I TAKE RESPONSIBILITY FOR . . .

The purpose of this exercise is to help you accept personal responsibility for your own feelings. Out loud, make a statement describing your own feelings, and then add "and I take responsibility for it." For example, if you often feel helpless, you might say "I feel helpless, and I take responsibility for it." Other feelings that can be the objects of this exercise are boredom, isolation, rejection, stupidity, feeling unloved, and so on.

## I HAVE A SECRET

This exercise can be a method to explore fears, guilt feelings, and catastrophic expectations. Think of some personal secret. Do not actually share the secret with others, but imagine yourself revealing the secret. What fears do you have about people's knowing your secret? How do you imagine others might respond to you?

## REVERSAL TECHNIQUE

This exercise is sometimes useful when a person has attempted to deny or disown a side of his or her personality. For example, one who plays the role of "tough guy" might be covering up a gentle side. Or one who is always excessively nice might be trying to deny or disown negative feelings toward others. Select one of your traits, and then assume the opposite characteristic as fully as possible. What is the experience like for you? What value or limitations, or both, do you see in this technique?

## THE REHEARSAL EXERCISE

Much of our thinking is rehearsing. It is almost as though we rehearse, in fantasy, performances we think we are expected to play. In this exercise select some situation where you might typically be rehearsing all kinds of pros and cons. Then "rehearse" out loud. Act out all the things that you might experience inwardly. Ham it up a bit. Try to get the feel of the exercise. For example, you might consider such situations as volunteering for something, asking a person for a date, applying for a job, or facing someone you are afraid of.

## THE EXAGGERATION EXERCISE

This exercise is designed to call attention to body language and nonverbal cues. For this exercise, *exaggerate* some movement—a mannerism or a gesture—repeatedly. For example, if you habitually smile (even when you feel hurt or angry), exaggerate this smile. Really get into it, smiling as broadly as you can before each group member. Another example is to exaggerate a frown if you habitually tend to frown. Go around to each person and intensify your frowning. What do you experience as you exaggerate certain of your behaviors? What therapeutic value do you see in this technique? What limitations?

Other examples of behavior that are used for the exaggeration technique are pointing a finger at people, crossing arms tightly, nervous tapping of feet, clenching of fists, and shaking of hands.

## GESTALT APPROACH TO DREAM WORK

Consider taking one of your dreams and working with it by applying Gestalt methods. As an illustration of how to do this, I will provide a dream of my own and briefly work on parts of it.

### The Dream

I am talking with the principal of Whittier High School (the school where I used to teach). He is telling me that he is annoyed with me because I expected a private office and a three-day teaching schedule. I reply: "I didn't *demand* a private office, I merely requested one. I wonder why you seem so irritated?" He keeps telling me that he is put off by my demanding tone of voice and that he sees me as being unreasonable. I tell him that I also want to do more than teach standard courses; I would like to offer therapy groups for adolescents in the school. He immediately seems closed to the idea and tells me that it cannot be done. I continue to argue with him, and I say: "I don't enjoy arguing with you, but I won't be a 'yes man' either. After all, I've written a lot of books and I think that ought to count for something." Then a car hits his car (the one we are riding in together), and I want to pursue our conversation. He says "Now is not a good time for me to talk." I reply: "Well, let me see if I hear what you are saying. You really seem to object to my tone and manner." He is obviously preoccupied with his smashed fender and the other driver, who is taking off after hitting his car. At the same time, I am insisting on finishing this discussion!

An approach to exploring the messages of the dream is to "become" each of the various parts of the dream. Let me illustrate:

*Be the principal*:  "I wish you'd get off my back. You're continually asking for special treatment, and after all I have a lot of other teachers. I have to treat everyone the same."

*Be Jerry Corey*:  "Look, if I don't at least tell you what I'd like, then you'll never know, and I'll never get it. I can contribute in some special ways, and I'd like the chance to do this."

*Be the principal's gray hair* (he had gray hair in the dream):  "I'm older and wiser than you are. It's not your place to argue with me. Listen to me, and don't come at me with special requests."

*Be Jerry Corey's books* (I was trying to tell him of my writing):  "Notice me as important, dammit! I am special! I'm read and appreciated by many students in many places. Don't shove me aside!"

*Be the smashed fender, and talk to the principal*:  "I'm hurt and need immediate attention. The woman who hit me is speeding away. I'll push in against the tire and cut the tire, and then you can't move."

*Be the principal talking to the bent fender*:  "This is an important matter. I need to catch the woman who hit my car. Look at what she did to you, and she's just running off without telling me."

*Be Jerry Corey, and talk to the fender*:  "Gee, it's a shame that you're all bent that way and that she's speeding away. Maybe I can see her license plate. Nope, it's too faint. Oh well, what's the big deal, you're only a fender—one of many."

## Commentary

This can go on for some time, with dialogue between various parts of the dream. It's important that I avoid intellectualizing about the dream or merely reporting *about* the dream in the past tense. As much as possible, it is useful to really relive my dream, fully "get into" each role, and let uncensored reactions flow. It helps me to change voices and inflections as I become each part of my dream. Once this process is done, it is useful for me to ask:  "What is the main feeling I get from my dream? What is my dream telling me?" One of the messages I get from my dream is that I won't settle for being ignored or brushed away. I want the freedom to work in my own way, yet I have some fear that an "authority figure" will tell me what to do and won't take me seriously. I feel that I have to fight at times to keep my identity and not get lost in the shuffle.

## Recording and Working with Your Dreams

Attempt for a period to recall (or, even better, write down) your dreams. Practice reliving your dreams via here-and-now Gestalt procedures. Try to let yourself go, censoring as little as possible. Make your dreams come alive! Don't worry about being appropriate or correct. Just create a script with the material provided in your dream, and let interactions happen with these parts of your dream. It would be ideal for you to report your dreams in the present tense into a tape recorder and to actually "Gestalt" these dreams on tape. Make comments and observations *after* you have done this. You may become aware of certain patterns and clear messages. It could be an interesting class exercise to at least share in small groups what this process is like for you.

# CASE EXAMPLES

## MY WAY OF WORKING WITH STAN FROM THE GESTALT PERSPECTIVE

I especially like the action-oriented techniques that I can use from Gestalt therapy. With them, I can challenge Stan to relive unfinished situations from his past that are cluttering up his ability to live fully in the present. For example, one area that is unfinished (and begs for closure) is his feelings toward women. Stan allows himself to feel weak, ineffectual, intimidated, and impotent when he even *thinks* about being in the presence of a strong woman. Because he has mentioned his feelings of resentment (and guilt) toward his former wife and his mother, I would be inclined to have him bring both of them to a session now—in a symbolic way—and speak to them.

I might say: "Stan, in this chair sits your mother, and next to her sits your ex-wife. You've talked about them and all the terrible things you imagine they've done to you, and in doing so you've rendered yourself helpless. Here is a chance to take for yourself some of that power you continue to give to them. Are you willing to talk to each of these women, telling them now some of the things that you've been carrying around inside of you, yet keeping from them?" If Stan agreed, I would ask him to pick which woman he wanted to address first and to speak to her as though she were present. At some point I might also ask him to sit in "mother's chair" and "speak to Stan"; then he could sit in "ex-wife's chair" and "reply" as he imagines she would. The possibilities are many for lively exchanges and for following any leads of a verbal or nonverbal nature that Stan might provide. I would attempt to stay with him and focus him on whatever he was feeling at the moment, using this material as the basis of where to proceed with him.

As you review Stan's case and think about him from a Gestalt perspective, consider these questions:

1. What are some areas in Stan's life that you would be most inclined to focus on? What might you do if you thought there were significant issues to address that Stan had not brought up?

2. Assume that you invited Stan to "bring your mother into the now" and talk directly to her and that he replied that talking to an empty chair seemed dumb and phony. What might you say? If he persisted in "talking about" his mother, would you allow this direction to continue?

3. Can you think of some ways to blend the emotional work of Gestalt therapy with the cognitive focus of Adlerian therapy?

## KAREN: ANXIETY OVER CHOOSING FOR HERSELF

Assume the perspective of a Gestalt therapist, and show how you would proceed with Karen, a 27-year-old Asian American who is struggling with value conflicts pertaining to her religion, culture, and sex-role expectations. Here is what she has related to you during the first session.

Up to now in her life Karen has identified herself as a "good Catholic" who has not questioned much of her upbringing. She has never really seen herself as an independent woman; in many ways she feels like a child, one who is strongly seeking approval and directions from those whom she consider authorities. Karen tells you that in her culture she was taught to respect and honor her parents, teachers, priests, and other elders. Whenever she tries to assert her own will, if it differs from the expectations of any authority figure, she experiences guilt and self-doubt. She went to Catholic schools, including college, and she has followed the morals and teachings of her church very closely. She has not been married, nor has she even had a long-term relationship with a man. Karen has not had sexual intercourse, not because she has not wanted to but because she is afraid that she could not live with herself and her guilt. She feels very restricted by the codes she lives by, and in many ways she sees them as rigid and unrealistic. Yet she is frightened of breaking away from what she was taught, even though she is seriously questioning much of its validity and is aware that *her* views on morality are growing more and more divergent from those that she at one time accepted. Basically, Karen asks:

What if I am wrong? Who am I to decide what is moral and immoral? I've always been taught that morals are clear-cut and do not allow for individual conveniences. I find it difficult to accept many of the teachings of my church, but I'm not able to really leave behind those notions that I don't accept. What if there is a hell, and I'll be damned forever if I follow my own path? What if I discover that I "go wild" and thus lose any measure of self-respect? Will I be able to live with my guilt if I don't follow the morality I've been taught?

Karen is also struggling with the impact of cultural restraints on her view of what it means to be a woman. Generally, she sees herself as being dependent, unassertive, fearful of those in authority, emotionally reserved, socially inhibited, and unable to make decisions about her life. Although she thinks that she would like to be more assertive and would like to feel freer to be herself around people, she is highly self-conscious and "hears voices in her head" that tell her how she should and should not be. She wishes she could be different in some important respects, but she wonders if she is strong enough to swim against what she has learned from her culture, her parents, and her church.

Assume that Karen is coming for a series of counseling sessions in a community clinic. You know the above information about her, and what she wants from you is help in sorting out what she really believes about living a moral life versus what she has been told is the moral way to be. She says that she would like to learn how to trust herself and, in essence, have the courage to know her convictions and live by them. At the same time, she feels unable to act on her values, for fear that she will be wrong. How would you proceed with her?

1.  What do you see as Karen's basic conflict? How would you summarize the nature of her struggle?

2.  Do you think that in some ways she might be looking to you as another authority figure to tell her that it is all right for her to reject some of the moral codes she was taught and to follow her own? How might you test out this possibility? How could you help her without becoming another source of either approval or disapproval for her?

3.  This case raises a number of key issues for you to consider, a few of which are:

    a.  Can you respect her cultural values and at the same time help her make the changes she wants, even if they go against some of her traditions?

    b.  Perhaps the values of her culture specify that women should be somewhat reserved, unassertive, emotionally restrained, and deferential to authority. Would you attempt to help her adjust to these cultural norms, or would you encourage her to live by a new set of standards?

    c.  Would you be able to avoid imposing your own views or values on Karen? In what direction would you encourage her to move, if any?

    d.  What are your views pertaining to sex-role and gender issues that are apparent in this case? How would your values here affect the interventions you make with Karen?

4.  Below are some Gestalt techniques that you might consider using with Karen. Check those that you think you would use:

    _____ Ask her to carry on a dialogue between different parts or sides of a conflict.

    _____ Invite her to have a dialogue between the Asian side of her and the American side of her.

    _____ Suggest that she write an uncensored letter (that she does not mail) to one of her parents in which she tells them the ways in which she would like to be different than she is expected to be.

    _____ Invite her to create a dialogue between an assertive woman and an unassertive woman.

    _____ Ask her to rehearse out loud whatever she is thinking.

_____ Ask her to "become" a significant authority and then lecture to "Karen" in an empty chair.

_____ Ask her to carry on a fantasy dialogue with her boyfriend and say to him everything that she has not yet told him.

_____ Ask her to imagine herself being as wild as possible, along with the worst things that could happen if she were to lose all control.

5. List some other Gestalt-oriented techniques that you might use in your session with Karen: _____

_____

_____

6. Karen says that she feels very restricted by her morals and sees them as rigid and unrealistic. At the same time, she is frightened of breaking away from what she was taught. Thinking in a Gestalt framework, how might you proceed with helping her sort through her values and clarify them for herself?

7. What are your values as they pertain to the issues that Karen has brought up, and how do you think they will affect the way in which you counsel her? Explain.

## REVIEWING THE HIGHLIGHTS

1. Gestalt therapy views human nature as _____

_____

2. The unique feature that distinguishes this approach is _____

_____

3. The therapeutic goals are _____

_____

4. The central role of the therapist is _____

_____

5. In the therapy process clients are expected to _____

_____

6. The relationship between the client and the therapist is characterized by _____

_____

7. Some of the major techniques are _____

_____

8. I think this approach is most applicable to clients who _____

_____

9. One aspect of the Gestalt approach I like most is _____

_____

10. One aspect of the Gestalt approach I like least is _____

_____

# QUIZ ON GESTALT THERAPY:
## A COMPREHENSION CHECK

Score _____ %

*Note*: Refer to Appendix 1 for the scoring key.

*True/false items*: Decide if the following statements are "more true" or "more false" as they apply to Gestalt therapy.

T  F  1. Resistance refers to defenses we develop that prevent us from experiencing the present in a full and real way.

T  F  2. Blocked energy can be considered a form of resistance.

T  F  3. The basic goal of Gestalt therapy is adjustment to society.

T  F  4. Recent trends in Gestalt practice include more emphasis on confrontation, more anonymity of the therapist, and increased reliance on techniques.

T  F  5. Dreams contain existential messages, and each piece of dream work leads to assimilation of disowned aspects of the self.

T  F  6. According to Perls, therapeutic skill and knowledge of techniques are *the* crucial ingredients in successful therapy.

T  F  7. One of the functions of the therapist is to pay attention to the client's body language.

T  F  8. Gestalt techniques are primarily aimed at teaching clients to think rationally.

T  F  9. A major function of the therapist is to make interpretations of clients' behavior so that they can begin to think of their patterns.

T  F  10. Perls contends that the most frequent source of unfinished business is resentment.

*Multiple-choice items*: Select the *one best answer* of those alternatives given. Consider each question within the framework of Gestalt therapy.

_____ 11. The founder of Gestalt therapy is

    a. Carl Rogers.
    b. Sidney Jourard.
    c. Albert Ellis.
    d. William Glasser.
    e. none of the above.

_____ 12. Which is not true of Gestalt therapy?

    a. The focus is on the "what" and "how" of behavior.
    b. The focus is on the here and now.
    c. The focus is on integrating fragmented parts of the personality.
    d. The focus is on unfinished business from the past.
    e. The focus is on the "why" of behavior.

_____ 13. Which of the following is not a key concept of Gestalt therapy?

    a. acceptance of personal responsibility
    b. intellectual understanding of one's problems
    c. awareness
    d. unfinished business
    e. dealing with the impasse

_____ 14. According to the Gestalt view,

    a. awareness is by itself therapeutic.
    b. awareness is a necessary, but not sufficient, condition for change.
    c. awareness without specific behavioral change is useless.
    d. awareness consists of understanding the causes of one's problems.

_____ 15. The basic goal of Gestalt therapy is to help clients

    a. move from environmental support to self-support.
    b. recognize which ego state they are functioning in.
    c. uncover unconscious motivations.
    d. work through the transference relationship with the therapist.
    e. challenge their philosophy of life.

_____ 16. The impasse is the point in therapy at which clients

    a. avoid experiencing threatening feelings.
    b. experience a sense of "being stuck."
    c. imagine that something terrible will happen.
    d. do all of the above.
    e. do none of the above.

_____ 17. Gestalt therapy can _best_ be characterized as

    a. an insight therapy.
    b. an experiential therapy
    c. an action-oriented therapy.
    d. all of the above.
    e. none of the above.

_____ 18. Gestalt therapy encourages clients to

    a. experience feelings intensely.
    b. stay in the here and now.
    c. work through the impasse.
    d. pay attention to their own nonverbal messages.
    e. do all of the above.

_____ 19. The focus of Gestalt therapy is on

    a. the relationship between client and counselor.
    b. free-associating to the client's dreams.
    c. recognizing one's own projections and refusing to accept helplessness.
    d. understanding why we feel as we do.
    e. all of the above.

_____ 20. A contribution of this therapeutic approach is that

    a. it enables intense experiencing to occur quickly.
    b. it can be a relatively brief therapy.
    c. it stresses doing and experiencing, as opposed to talking about problems.
    d. All of the above are contributions.
    e. None of the above is a contribution.

_____ 21. The process of distraction, which makes it difficult to maintain sustained contact, is

    a. introjection.        d. confluence.
    b. projection.         e. deflection.
    c. retroflection.

_____ 22. The process of turning back to ourselves what we would like to do to someone else is

    a. introjection.        d. confluence.
    b. projection.         e. deflection.
    c. retroflection.

_____ 23. The tendency to uncritically accept others' beliefs without assimilating or internalizing them is

a. introjection.
b. projection.
c. retroflection.
d. confluence.
e. deflection.

_____ 24. The process of the blurring of awareness of differentiation between the self and the environment is

a. introjection.
b. projection.
c. retroflection.
d. confluence.
e. deflection.

_____ 25. What is a limitation (or limitations) of Gestalt therapy as it is applied to working with culturally diverse populations?

a. Clients who have been culturally conditioned to be emotionally reserved may not see value in experiential techniques.
b. Clients may be "put off" by a focus on catharsis.
c. Clients may be looking for specific advice on solving practical problems.
d. Clients may believe that showing one's vulnerability is being weak.
e. All of the above are limitations.

# 9

# TRANSACTIONAL ANALYSIS

## PRECHAPTER SELF-INVENTORY

*Directions*: Refer to page 46 for general directions. Use the following code:

5 = I *strongly agree* with this statement.

4 = I *agree*, in most respects, with this statement.

3 = I am *undecided* in my opinion about this statement.

2 = I *disagree*, in most respects, with this statement.

1 = I *strongly disagree* with this statement.

_____ 1. It is the client's responsibility to decide what specific changes he or she desires.

_____ 2. All people can learn to trust themselves, to think and decide for themselves, and to express their feelings.

_____ 3. Humans are capable of going beyond the limits of their conditioning and early programming.

_____ 4. Personality structure can be adequately explained by the ego states of Parent, Adult, and Child.

_____ 5. One's parents' verbal and nonverbal messages are highly influential in the formation of one's self-concept.

_____ 6. Games (indirect interactions with a payoff) are by their very nature manipulative, and they prevent authenticity.

_____ 7. The basic goal of therapy is to help clients make new decisions about their present behavior and the direction of their life.

_____ 8. As children we make basic decisions about ourselves and others in response to messages we receive.

_____ 9. Once early decisions have been made, they are *not* irreversible.

_____ 10. An appropriate role for the therapist is to function as a teacher, trainer, and resource person.

_____ 11. It is both desirable and important that client and therapist become equal partners in the therapeutic process.

_____ 12. The therapist's basic task is to help the client acquire the tools necessary for change.

_____ 13. A requisite for effective therapy is the client's capacity and willingness to understand and accept a therapeutic contract.

_____ 14. For therapy to be effective, it is essential that the client *act* and complete contracts, not merely talk about problems and gain insights into them.

_____ 15. The essence of therapy is to teach clients how to "write their own scripts" rather than being passively "scripted."

_____ 16. Because psychotherapy is largely a cognitive matter, it should emphasize the didactic (teaching/learning) process.

_____ 17. It is desirable that clients be weaned away from dependence on a therapist as soon as possible so that they can become their own therapist and deal effectively with future problems.

_____ 18. Clients should be taught the basic concepts of personal and interpersonal functioning so that they can better understand their transactions.

_____ 19. It is important for people to ask for the strokes they need and want.

_____ 20. It is not important to explore unconscious dynamics in the therapy process.

# OVERVIEW OF TRANSACTIONAL ANALYSIS

## KEY FIGURES AND MAJOR FOCUS

Founder: Eric Berne. Key figures: Robert Goulding and Mary Goulding. The approach focuses on people's cognitive and behavioral aspects. It is designed to help clients evaluate early decisions and make new and more appropriate ones. Current trends include an integration of techniques such as body work, role playing, psychosynthesis, encounter, Gestalt, and other experiential and emotive techniques.

## PHILOSOPHY AND BASIC ASSUMPTIONS

Individuals have the potential for choice and for reshaping their destiny. Though past injunctions may have molded them, with awareness they are able to write a new script. Through confrontation, clients can be inspired to change certain ways of thinking, feeling, and behaving. They are not victims of past experiences, for through the redecision process they can change the course of their life.

## KEY CONCEPTS

Personality structure consists of three ego states: Parent, Adult, and Child. The client is taught to recognize which is operant and thus learns to choose a given ego state. The approach focuses on games played to avoid intimacy, rackets, early decisions, redecisions, life scripts, parental injunctions, stroking, and basic psychological positions.

## THERAPEUTIC GOALS

The goals of transactional analysis are to achieve a degree of awareness that enables the client to make new decisions regarding future behavior and to become autonomous—that is, to be a script-free and game-free person capable of choosing. The essence of redecision therapy consists of teaching people how to "write their own scripts" rather than being passively "scripted."

## THERAPEUTIC RELATIONSHIP

The approach emphasizes an equal relationship between the client and the therapist that is characterized by a joint sharing of responsibility structured by a contract. The client contracts with the therapist for specific, desired changes; when the contract is fulfilled, therapy is terminated. Contracts reduce the power differential between therapist and client and foster a therapeutic partnership in which both work for change.

## TECHNIQUES AND PROCEDURES

The contract is an essential technique. The use of a script checklist and questionnaire to detect injunctions, games, life positions, and early decisions is also an important technique. Questioning is often employed. Other procedures include structural analysis, family modeling, analysis of games and rackets, analysis of rituals and pastimes, and script analysis.

## APPLICATIONS

The approach can be applied to parent/child relations, classroom and institutional situations, marriage counseling, family therapy, and individual therapy. It is well suited to group methods. In a group situation clients understand the structure and functioning of their individual personality, and they learn how they transact with others. TA can be used with all ages and for many types of problems: delinquent and criminal behavior, alcoholism, "reparenting" of schizophrenics, and interpersonal problems.

## CONTRIBUTIONS

Major contributions of the approach are the contract method, the active role of the client, and the emphasis on the client's doing, not merely "trying." The concepts are concrete, specific, and easily grasped. It is a brief therapy with wide applicability. It decreases the chance of dependence on the therapist. It emphasizes transactions and choice, recognizes key aspects of the past as related to present behavior, and gives a rationale for explaining self-defeating behavior in terms of the payoffs of games. People with any type of related professional training can make use of the principles and procedures. TA practitioners are open to integrating techniques from other orientations. In working with culturally diverse client populations, a value lies in exploring cultural injunctions such as "Don't talk about your problems with people outside your family."

## LIMITATIONS

The approach carries with it the chance of analyzing the self at a distance and thus of making the self a mechanical thing. The use of intellectual concepts can become a defense against feeling and experiencing, and people can be placed in artificial categories. TA terminology can also blur the therapist's creativity. It is possible for the approach to become a game in itself; one can master the technical style and thus leave out oneself as a person. The model does not include transference. There is little empirical research to support the theoretical concepts that form the basis of TA.

# GLOSSARY OF KEY TERMS

**Adult.** An ego state that is the processor of information. It is the analytical, rational, and objective part of personality.

**Child.** An ego state that consists of feelings, impulses, and spontaneous acts. This part of personality can manifest itself in several ways: the "Natural Child," the "Little Professor," and the "Adapted Child."

**Contamination.** The state that exists when the contents of one ego state are mixed with those of another. (Either the Parent, the Child, or both intrude within the boundaries of the Adult ego state and interfere with the clear thinking and functioning of the Adult.)

**Critical Parent.** An ego state that is fault-finding and harsh.

**Ego state.** One of the three distinct patterns of behavior and independent levels of psychological functioning: Parent, Adult, and Child.

**Exclusion.** The boundary problem that exists when one or more ego states are effectively prevented from functioning.

**Game.** A series of stereotyped and predictable patterns of behavior that ends with surprise bad feelings for at least one player.

**Injunction.** Parental message telling children what they have to do and be in order to get recognition. These messages, which are usually couched in some form of *don't*, may be either verbal or nonverbal.

**Karpman Drama Triangle.** A triadic interaction in which one person acts as persecutor, another as rescuer, and the third as victim. A useful device to help people understand the nature of games.

**Life position.** A stance that people assume in early childhood regarding their own intrinsic worth and that of others.

**Natural Child.** A form of the Child ego state that is impulsive, untrained, spontaneous, and expressive.

**Nurturing Parent.** An ego state that is supportive and caring.

**Parent.** An ego state that is an introject of parents and parent substitutes. Contains the "shoulds" and "oughts" that individuals collect from significant people in their life.

**Racket.** A habitual feeling (depression, guilt, anger, sadness) that people chronically cling to after a game.

**Redecision.** The process of reexperiencing early situations in which we made basic decisions about life, evaluating these decisions, and making new and more appropriate choices about life.

**Script.** A personal life plan, which individuals create by a series of early decisions regarding themselves, others, and their place in the world.

**Script analysis.** That part of the therapeutic process by which the life patterns of clients are identified, allowing them to take steps toward changing their programming.

**Stroke.** A form of recognition. Strokes may be positive or negative, conditional or unconditional.

**Structural analysis.** A tool by which clients become aware of the content and functioning of their ego states of Parent, Adult, and Child. Helps clients resolve patterns that they feel stuck with.

**Transaction.** An exchange of strokes between two or more people; the basic unit of human communication. Transactions may be complementary, crossed, or ulterior.

## QUESTIONS FOR DISCUSSION AND EVALUATION

1. Is awareness of early decisions sufficient to effect changes in personality and behavior? If not, what additional factors are needed to bring about change? Explain.

2. Do you believe that people are passively "scripted," or programmed, by the injunctions they are fed at an early age? Or do you believe that people choose to accept or reject these parental messages, make early *decisions*, and have the power to redecide and thus change their life plan? What are the implications of your view for the practice of counseling?

3. What are some of the advantages and disadvantages of contracts?

4. If you wanted to challenge your clients' early decisions and help them work toward redecisions, how might you do this? Provide an example of an early decision that you made and that you have either struggled with or changed.

5.  Gestalt techniques can be merged with TA theory. Discuss some of the possible values of such a combination, giving examples of how you might combine these two approaches. What other techniques (from other therapy schools) might you integrate with TA theory?

# PERSONAL APPLICATION: BECOMING AWARE OF INJUNCTIONS, EARLY DECISIONS, AND POSSIBILITIES FOR REDECISIONS

This exercise is designed to focus your thinking on the possible early decisions that your clients (and you) made in response to a series of parental injunctions. It is also designed to help you think about possible redecisions that your clients (and you) might make. In the blanks write down a possible decision and a redecision for each of the injunctions listed below, drawing on your own experience when applicable. The first two items are examples.

1.  *Don't think.*

    a.  Possible decision: *I'm stupid, so I'll let others think for me.*

    b.  Possible redecision: *I'll start trusting myself and doing my own thinking, even if this isn't what my parents wanted of me.*

2.  *Don't be.*

    a.  Possible decision: *It is best to keep myself invisible.*

    b.  Possible redecision: *Even though it is scary to be seen and heard, I prefer that to being a nonentity.*

3.  *Don't be close.*

    a.  Possible decision: _____

    b.  Possible redecision: _____

4.  *Don't be important.*

    a.  Possible decision: _____

    b.  Possible redecision: _____

5.  *Don't be a child.*

    a.  Possible decision: _____

    b.  Possible redecision: _____

6.  *Don't grow.*

    a.  Possible decision: _____

    b.  Possible redecision: _____

114

7. *Don't succeed.*

    a.  Possible decision: _____

    _____

    b.  Possible redecision: _____

    _____

8. *Don't be you.*

    a.  Possible decision: _____

    _____

    b.  Possible redecision: _____

    _____

9. *Don't be sane, and don't be well.*

    a.  Possible decision: _____

    _____

    b.  Possible redecision: _____

    _____

10. *Don't belong.*

    a.  Possible decision: _____

    _____

    b.  Possible redecision: _____

    _____

In small groups discuss the various decisions and redecisions. What are some of the injunctions that you "bought" as a child? What were some of your early decisions? Have you made any significant redecisions? Are you considering other new decisions?

In small groups free-associate with and explore freely as many injunctions as you can. Each person can take turns saying aloud the "shoulds" and the "should nots" that he or she accepted.

## YOUR PERSONAL LIFE-SCRIPT QUESTIONNAIRE

*Directions*: Write a concise answer to each question. Attempt to give your initial response, and then later go over all the questions with more reflection. One suggestion for classroom use is to have students form into dyads and then share *selected* portions of the questionnaire. It is important that each student choose what he or she will share with another person and that subtle coercion be carefully avoided.

1.  How do you see yourself now? _____

    _____

2.  What are *three* things that you'd most like to change about yourself? _____

    _____

3.  What has been preventing you from changing those things? _____

    _____

4. Are you your "own person," or are you living up to others' expectations of what you "should" be? _____

_____

5. How do you see your mother? _____

_____

6. How are you like your mother? _____

_____

7. How are you unlike your mother?_____

_____

8. What does your mother say when she compliments you? _____

_____

9. What does your mother say when she criticizes you?_____

_____

10. What is her main advice to you? _____

_____

11. What could you do to make her happy? _____

_____

12. What could you do to disappoint her? _____

_____

13. How do you see your father? _____

_____

14. How are you like your father? _____

_____

15. How are you unlike your father? _____

_____

16. What does your father say when he compliments you? _____

_____

17. What does your father say when he criticizes you? _____

_____

18. What is his main advice to you? _____

_____

19. What could you do to disappoint him? _____

_____

20. What are some of the main *dos* that you have learned and accepted? _____
    _____

21. What were some of the main *don'ts* that were programmed into you? _____
    _____

22. What is *one* important early decision you made as a child? _____
    _____

23. What is *one* early decision you made about yourself that you feel you have since *changed* by making a new decision? _____
    _____

24. What is one new decision that you would like to make? _____
    _____

25. What do you most like about yourself? _____
    _____

26. What do you least like about yourself? _____
    _____

27. What did your mother tell you (either directly or indirectly) about

    you? _____

    life? _____

    death? _____

    love? _____

    sex? _____

    marriage? _____

    men? _____

    women? _____

    your birth? _____

28. What did your father tell you (either directly or indirectly) about

    you? _____

    life? _____

    death? _____

    love? _____

    sex? _____

    marriage? _____

    men? _____

    women? _____

    your birth? _____

29. How did you see yourself as a child? _____

_____

30. How did you see yourself as an adolescent? _____

_____

31. What manipulative games did you play as a child to get what you wanted?_____

_____

_____

32. What were the payoffs (rewards) of those manipulative games? _____

_____

33. What games do you still play that you played as a child? _____

_____

34. If you were to give up those games, what do you suppose it would be like? _____

_____

_____

35. How did you see yourself five years ago? _____

_____

36. How would you like to see yourself five years from now? _____

_____

37. What are you doing now to make that ideal become real? _____

_____

38. If you were to write your own epitaph, what would it say? _____

_____

_____

39. What words do you fear might appear on your tombstone? _____

_____

40. What do you wish your mother had done differently? _____

_____

41. What do you wish your father had done differently? _____

_____

42. What do you most want out of life? _____

_____

43. If you could have three wishes, what would they be? _____

_____

44. What was a critical turning point in your life? _____

_____

45. When do you feel most "alive"? _____

_____

46. When do you feel all right about yourself? _____

_____

47. When do you feel not all right about yourself? _____

_____

48. When was the best time or period in your life? _____

_____

49. What risks have you taken lately? _____

_____

50. What new script would you like to write for yourself? _____

_____

_____

Now that you have finished this TA questionnaire, review your responses and address the following questions:

1. What patterns do you see? What possible injunctions and decisions are evident?

2. Look over the lifestyle-assessment questionnaire in Chapter 5 and compare some of your responses with the ones above. How do the two fit together?

3. If you were getting involved in your own counseling *as a client*, what main themes could you productively work on? What personal struggles did you become aware of by taking these two questionnaires? What kind of unfinished business might you be carrying around?

4. If you are willing, you might consider bringing your completed questionnaire to class and using the results as a basis for class discussion. Forming small groups to share what it was like for you to complete this inventory could be a learning experience.

## SUGGESTED ACTIVITIES AND EXERCISES

The following exercises can be done outside class and brought to class for discussion and demonstration. Most of the exercises are adaptable to group activities, and they form a good way for you to grasp experientially, for your own personal growth, the practical applications of TA.

1. This exercise is designed to help you determine whether you function in a rigid manner by operating too frequently or inappropriately from any *one* ego state. Take this self-inventory to help you decide whether you function principally in one ego state almost to the exclusion of the others.

   a. Are you a "Constant Parent"? Does your Parent exclude your Adult and Child? Check yourself against the following questions:

      (1) Do you frequently tell other people what to do?
      (2) Do you have a "strong will," to the point of maneuvering others to do things your way?
      (3) Do you often appear to others as a "helpful mother" or a "helpful father"?
      (4) Do you frequently use words like *should*, *ought*, and *must*?
      (5) Are you critical of others when they fall short of your standards or expectations?

   b. Are you a "Constant Adult"? Does your Adult exclude your Parent and Child? Check yourself against the following questions:

      (1) Do you typically deal with reality and emphasize the importance of being objective?
      (2) Do you focus on data processing to the point that you rarely express parental concern or childlike playfulness?
      (3) Are you overly rational, objective, and analytical?
      (4) Are you nonspontaneous, machinelike, and much like a computer that merely grinds out information and decisions based on data?
      (5) Do you have much time for recreation or for simply doing nothing?

   c. Are you a "Constant Child"? Does your Child exclude your Parent and Adult? Check yourself against the following questions:

      (1) Do you find yourself often seeking fun and excitement?
      (2) Do you look to others for constant approval or criticism?
      (3) Are you able to involve yourself fully in whatever you are doing at the moment?
      (4) Are you able to be impulsive and spontaneous and do what you feel like doing without being overly analytical or worried about what people might think?
      (5) Do you play helpless by saying "I can't" when you really mean "I won't"?

   After you have taken the self-inventory to determine whether you are functioning mainly in one ego state, answer the following questions:

   d. In which ego state do you function most of the time?

   e. Are you satisfied with being that way? Would you like to have more Parent and Adult and less Child, more Child and less Parent and Adult, or what?

   f. What can you do to function more fully in an ego state of your choice?

   g. Do you have a favorite ego state?

   h. Do you see your ego state as changing as you enter the various social situations at home? at work? at school? elsewhere?

   i. Does your ego state change as you are with different people such as your friends? your supervisor or employer? your parents? your children? your wife or husband? others?

   j. What does seeing your ego state as changing with different situations and people tell you about yourself?

   k. Do other people see you as you see yourself? What are the similarities and differences?

   l. If you become aware of any changes that you'd like to make, what specific *contracts* can you develop for yourself?

2. Here is a group exercise in role reversal designed to help us "become" our parents—that is, crawl inside their psychological worlds. Each class member decides whether he or she

wants to become his or her mother or father. After the roles are assumed, the group talks about life. What do I have in life? What do I treasure? How do I feel about living? What are the joys of my life? What hurt do I experience? How close do I feel to my children and to my spouse? Do I like myself? What conflicts do I experience? The idea is to become the parent of your choice and to speak in the manner you fantasize the parent would speak in expressing his or her views of life. The exercise can be done for as little as ten minutes, or it can be extended to an hour or several hours.

3. A variation of this group exercise is to assume the identity and role of one of your parents and talk about you. How, as your parent, do you see yourself? Consider factors such as expectations, proud feelings, disappointments, and so on. Also, group members can interview one another to find out how they see their "son" or "daughter" and to ascertain his or her feelings.

4. This exercise can be done in dyads or in a group. The purpose is to encourage us to look at the quality of life we perceive our parents experiencing, to get a clear focus on what our parents value, to understand more fully their lifestyles, and to decide what modifications we might want to make in our own values and behavior. For this exercise close your eyes, and visualize your parents at their present ages in a typical setting. Imagine what their marriage is like, how they relate to their children, what they have in their life, and so on. Now imagine yourself at their ages in the same setting. Imagine yourself to be just as they are: you are copies of them, you value what they value, your marriage is like theirs, and so on. What is the experience like? In what ways would you want to modify the outcomes of this fantasy?

5. A useful concept in TA is that of stroking. All folks need strokes. One's behavior as a child is shaped by the kinds of strokes received. Strokes can be either positive or negative, and both types are effective in molding persistent behavior that extends into adulthood. As a group experience, explore with one another the ways in which you were stroked as children. How did it work? What kinds of strokes do you receive now? What strokes do you seek out? What happens when you don't get the strokes you desire?

6. Write down through the course of a week some of your most pleasant memories as a child. Try to recapture some of the feelings you had then. Attempt to be various ages, from preschool to high school. Discuss in a group the results of your recollections and writings.

7. Follow the general directions for the preceding exercise, and recollect some of the most painful experiences of your childhood. Try to allow yourself to reexperience some of those times. Write down what you feel.

8. Pictures frequently say a lot more than words. What do your pictures tell about you? For the use of pictures in group sessions, bring to class some pictures of you taken during childhood and adolescence, or bring any pictures of you with your family. Have other group members tell you what they think, by viewing your pictures, that you experienced. You might also develop a chronological approach to some crucial decisions that you made during those years.


# CASE EXAMPLES

## MY WAY OF WORKING WITH STAN FROM THE TA PERSPECTIVE

Early in our sessions I would work with Stan in formulating a clear contract to provide the direction for his therapy. From transactional analysis one of the aspects that I find exceptionally meaningful is the exploration of injunctions and the early decisions that were made in relationship to these parental messages. Surely Stan heard messages such as "Don't be," "Don't be you," "Don't succeed," "Don't feel," "Don't be important," "Don't get close," and "Don't trust." On the basis of these injunctions, Stan may have made a number of *early decisions*:

- "I won't let myself get close to women, because if I do they will dominate me and take away any power I have."

- "I don't have what it takes to be as successful as my brothers and sisters, so I will settle for being a failure."

- "I really don't deserve to feel important, so if I begin feeling important, I'll do something to make sure that I mess things up."

Rather than merely talking with Stan about his early decisions in an intellectual manner, I would be inclined to ask him to recreate a situation as a child in which he remembers telling himself that he had better keep his distance from women. Using some of the experiential techniques of Gestalt therapy, I would ask him to relive this scene and create a dialogue for everyone in it. I would hope that the direction I was pursuing with him would give him a chance to make a new, more appropriate decision, but on an emotional level as well as a cognitive level. I would also explore what he has gotten from buying into these injunctions and the price he is paying for still striving to live by parental expectations.

As you review Stan's case and think about him from a TA perspective, consider these questions:

1. Compare the TA life-script questionnaire in this chapter with the lifestyle-assessment questionnaire in Chapter 5 ("Adlerian Therapy") of this manual. What similarities and differences do you notice?

2. Do you see any similarities between Stan's injunctions and early decisions (TA) and his "basic mistakes" (Adlerian)? Can you think of ways to combine an Adlerian and a TA perspective as you explore the major themes in Stan's life?

3. Do you see any of Stan's injunctions in yourself? To what degree might you be limited in challenging him if you have not challenged your own injunctions and made new decisions yourself?


## MARRIAGE COUNSELING WITH SEYMOUR AND MARTHA

Martha and Seymour, who have been married for 52 years, come to you for marriage counseling. Seymour has been retired for several years, and although he generally enjoys his life, he would like to feel the excitement that he felt when he was younger. He is particularly concerned about his aging. Martha has some concerns over not having more time with her sons, daughters, and grandchildren. She would like more family time. For many years she has not felt a real zest for living and now she realizes that if her life is going to change, she will have to take some active steps. She is tired of "just waiting" for good things in life to happen.

You've not met either before, and you have an initial session with them together. After they leave, you make the following notes to yourself about the intake session:

1. Seymour appears overly nice and extremely eager to please Martha. He feels guilty if he does something that displeases her.

2. Seymour keeps saying that all he really wants to do is make Martha happy and that when she is "up," he also is "up." When she is "down," he also is "down."

3. Seymour did not initiate marriage counseling, but he agreed to accompany Martha because he is willing to do "anything that might help the situation."

4. Martha pouts a lot and feels a sense of boredom and restlessness. In many ways she expects Seymour to make her "unbored," initiate new directions in their marriage, make her decisions for her, and make her feel important and special.

5. Martha complains continually about how dull her life is and how she feels trapped, yet she herself does very little to change anything. She feels abandoned by her children and grandchildren, and this troubles her because her family is her main priority. She expects Seymour to take this responsibility *for her* happiness.

6. Martha is aware that she controls Seymour and manipulates him with guilt. She admits that she likes having him in the palm of her hand, yet at the same time this style is "getting old." After all, she has been using this style for over 50 years! She'd like to change it, but at the same time she's afraid.

7. This couple has a great deal going for them, however. The fact that they have remained a couple for 52 years says something about them individually and as a couple. This fact could be a departure for the discussions in the therapy sessions.

8. Each of them can be challenged to formulate a clearer picture of what they want for themselves, from each other, and as a couple.

## How Would You Work with Seymour and Martha?

Assume that you are working within a TA frame of reference. If you were to have six marriage-counseling sessions with this couple, how would you answer the following questions?

1. What possible payoffs do you see in both Martha's and Seymour's games?

2. What kinds of transactions are *now* occurring between this couple?

3. What *early decisions* do you think Seymour made? Martha made? What decisions did each of them make about the *position* they would play with each other?

4. Who is playing the role of victim? persecutor? rescuer? Is there a shift in who is playing which roles?

5. Do you have any ideas concerning Martha's parental injunctions? Seymour's parental injunctions?

6. What kind of contract would you find applicable? How would you determine when this couple had met their contract?

7. What specific plans or procedures might you carry out in your six sessions with them?

8. Would the fact that this is an elderly couple, married for over 50 years, influence your direction in therapy? Do you think that you'd be able to relate to them? If there is a large age gap between you and this couple, could it cause them to hesitate to work with you? If they questioned your ability to relate to their situation because of age differences, how would you respond?

# REVIEWING THE HIGHLIGHTS

1. Transactional analysis views human nature as _____

_____

2. The unique feature that distinguishes this approach is _____

_____

3. The therapeutic goals are _____

_____

4. The central role of the therapist is _____

_____

5. In the therapy process clients are expected to _____

_____

6.  The relationship between the client and the therapist is characterized by _____

    _____

7.  Some of the major techniques are _____

    _____

8.  I think this approach is most applicable to clients who _____

    _____

9.  One aspect of transactional analysis I like most is _____

    _____

10. One aspect of transactional analysis I like least is _____

    _____


# QUIZ ON TRANSACTIONAL ANALYSIS: A COMPREHENSION CHECK                Score ____ %

*Note*:  Refer to Appendix 1 for the scoring key.

*True/false items*:  Decide if the following statements are "more true" or "more false" as they apply to transactional analysis.

T F  1. The technique of family modeling is an approach to working with a Constant Parent, a Constant Adult, or a Constant Child.

T F  2. Structural analysis is a tool by which clients become aware of the content and functioning of their Parent, Adult, and Child.

T F  3. TA places emphasis on working through the transference relationship.

T F  4. A useful technique to help people work through their ego states is the use of free association to their dreams.

T F  5. In TA therapy resistance is seen as an inevitable phenomenon and as a manifestation of one's unconscious; TA techniques are designed to uncover unconscious conflicts.

T F  6. The role of the TA therapist includes paying attention to didactic and cognitive issues.

T F  7. TA therapists stress the value of equal relationships in the therapy process.

T F  8. Rackets consist of one's life plan, and they include injunctions and decisions.

T F  9. The use of contracts is a basic part of TA therapy.

T F  10. TA assumes that clients can make new and more appropriate decisions to replace earlier archaic decisions.

*Multiple-choice items*:  Select the *one best answer* of those alternatives given.  Consider each question within the TA framework.

_____ 11. Which of the following is *not* a key concept in TA?

       a.  rackets          d.  free association
       b.  strokes          e.  games
       c.  scripts

_____ 12. Which ego state is the "processor of data and information" and works with facts and external reality?

   a. Parent
   b. Adult
   c. Child

_____ 13. The Karpman Drama Triangle is a useful device for helping people understand

   a. early decisions.          d. their ego states.
   b. games.                    e. none of the above.
   c. early childhood.

_____ 14. The basic goal of TA is to help clients

   a. uncover unconscious material.
   b. learn to live with existential anxiety.
   d. rid themselves of emotional disorders.
   d. change their irrational beliefs.
   e. make new decisions regarding their present behavior and the direction of their life.

_____ 15. The ultimate goal of TA is

   a. achieving autonomy.
   b. learning to understand games.
   c. working through the transference relationship.
   d. developing a better "racket."
   e. living by the rule of the Parent ego state.

_____ 16. TA tends to stress

   a. an equal relationship in which client and therapist become partners in the therapeutic process.
   b. a superior and aloof stand by the therapist.
   c. therapy in which the client/therapist relationship is not an important ingredient.
   d. a relationship similar to that between friends.
   e. none of the above.

_____ 17. A basic requisite for effective therapy is the client's capacity for and willingness to

   a. keep a daily journal of thoughts and feelings.
   b. accept the judgments of his or her therapist.
   c. develop a contract.
   d. free-associate during the therapy sessions.

_____ 18. The process by which a person becomes aware of the content and functioning of his or her ego states of Parent, Adult, and Child is known as

   a. transactional analysis.
   b. functional analysis.
   c. dream analysis.
   d. structural analysis.

_____ 19. What transactions can occur between people?

   a. complementary          d. all of the above
   b. crossed                e. none of the above
   c. ulterior

_____ 20. TA tends to stress

   a. cognitive factors.
   b. getting in touch with feelings.

c. control of aggressive impulses.

d. dealing with our existential aloneness.

_____ 21. Redecisional therapy, as practiced by the Gouldings, is done primarily in the context of

a. individual therapy.         c. family therapy.

b. couples therapy.         d. group therapy.

_____ 22. In their redecision therapy the Gouldings integrate TA concepts with techniques drawn from

a. psychodrama.         d. Gestalt therapy.

b. family therapy.         e. all of the above.

c. fantasy and imagery.

_____ 23. A contribution of TA to counseling with ethnic-minority clients is

a. its focus on dreams.

b. its structure, which helps clients understand how their culture has influenced them.

c. the abundance of research on TA theory as it is applied to working with culturally diverse client populations.

d. the fact that TA always begins by exploring the client's cultural background.

_____ 24. The unpleasant feelings that people experience after a game are called

a. injunctions.         d. rackets.

b. parental messages.         e. life positions.

c. script analysis.

_____ 25. In looking at the future of TA, this approach seems to be

a. getting more and more complex.

b. going back to its psychoanalytic roots in therapeutic practice.

c. moving toward becoming more and more cognitive.

d. focusing more on encouraging clients to emotionally reexperience crucial experiences when early decisions were made.

e. merging with Adlerian concepts.

# 10

# BEHAVIOR THERAPY

## PRECHAPTER SELF-INVENTORY

*Directions*:  Refer to page 46 for general directions.  Use the following code:

5 = I *strongly agree* with this statement.

4 = I *agree*, in most respects, with this statement.

3 = I am *undecided* in my opinion about this statement.

2 = I *disagree*, in most respects, with this statement.

1 = I *strongly disagree* with this statement.

_____  1.  A system of counseling and psychotherapy should rest on experimental results of its therapeutic claims so that the concepts and practice of the approach can be refined and developed.

_____  2.  It is important that the client be fully informed about the therapy process and have the major say in setting treatment goals.

_____  3.  In therapy the client controls *what* behavior is to be changed, and the therapist controls *how* behavior is changed.

_____  4.  Our behavior is influenced by our thinking processes, such as self-talk and inner dialogue.

_____  5.  Understanding the origins of personal problems is not essential for producing behavior change.

_____  6.  It is important that therapists identify their values and explain how such values might influence their evaluation of the client's goals.

_____  7.  Past history should be the focus of therapy only to the degree to which such factors are actively and directly contributing to a client's current difficulties.

_____  8.  Therapy should focus primarily on overt and specific behavior rather than on a client's feelings about a situation.

_____  9.  It is essential that the outcomes of therapy be evaluated to assess the degree of success or failure of treatment.

_____  10.  Maladaptive cognitions lead to maladaptive behaviors; adaptive behaviors can be induced if the client learns to generate positive, self-enhancing thoughts.

_____  11.  Clients are both the producer and the product of their environment.

_____  12.  The therapist should provide positive reinforcement for clients so that learning can be enhanced.

_____  13.  The proper role of the therapist is to serve as teacher, consultant, facilitator, coach, model, director, and problem solver.

_____ 14. The therapist's interest, attention, and approval are powerful reinforcers of client behavior.

_____ 15. It is important that clients be actively involved in the analysis, planning, process, and evaluation of a treatment program.

_____ 16. Specific techniques of therapy or a behavioral-management program must be suited to the requirements and needs of each individual client.

_____ 17. Therapeutic procedures should be aimed at behavior change.

_____ 18. A good working relationship between the client and the therapist is a necessary but not sufficient condition for behavior change to occur.

_____ 19. Because real-life problems must be solved with new behaviors outside therapy, the process is not complete unless actions follow verbalizations.

_____ 20. Any program of behavioral change should begin with a comprehensive assessment of the individual.

# OVERVIEW OF BEHAVIOR THERAPY

## KEY FIGURES AND MAJOR FOCUS

Key figures: Arnold Lazarus, Albert Bandura, Joseph Wolpe, and Alan Kazdin. Historically, the behavioral trend developed in the 1950s and early 1960s as a radical departure from the psychoanalytic perspective. Three major phases in the development of behavior therapy are (1) the classical-conditioning trend, (2) the operant-conditioning model, and (3) the cognitive trend.

## PHILOSOPHY AND BASIC ASSUMPTIONS

Behavior is the product of learning. We are both the product and the producer of our environment. No set of unifying assumptions about behavior can incorporate all the existing procedures in the behavioral field. Due to the diversity of views and strategies it is more accurate to think of _behavioral therapies_ rather than a unified approach. Contemporary behavior therapy encompasses a variety of conceptualizations, research methods, and treatment procedures to explain and change behavior.

## KEY CONCEPTS

The approach emphasizes current behavior as opposed to historical antecedents, precise treatment goals, diverse therapeutic strategies tailored to these goals, and objective evaluation of therapeutic outcomes. Therapy focuses on behavior change in the present and on action programs.

## THERAPEUTIC GOALS

The general goal is eliminating maladaptive behaviors and learning more effective behavior patterns. Therapy aims at changing problematic behavior through learning experiences. Generally, client and therapist collaboratively specify treatment goals in concrete and objective terms.

## THERAPEUTIC RELATIONSHIP

Although the approach does not assign an all-important role to the client/therapist relationship, a good working relationship is seen as an essential precondition for effective therapy. The skilled therapist is one who can conceptualize problems behaviorally and make use of the therapeutic relationship in bringing about change. The therapist's role is primarily exploring alternative courses of action and their possible consequences. Clients must be actively involved in the therapeutic process from beginning to end, and they must be willing to experiment with new behaviors both in the sessions and outside of therapy.

## TECHNIQUES AND PROCEDURES

Behavioral procedures are tailored to fit the unique needs of each client. Any technique that can be demonstrated to change behavior may be incorporated into a treatment plan. A strength of the approach lies in the many and varied techniques aimed at producing behavior change, a few of which are relaxation methods, systematic desensitization, reinforcement techniques, modeling, assertion training, self-management programs, and multimodal therapy.

## APPLICATIONS

The approach has wide applicability to a range of clients desiring specific behavioral changes. A few problem areas for which behavior therapy appears to be effective include phobic disorders, depression, sexual disorders, children's disorders, and the prevention and treatment of cardiovascular disease. Going beyond the usual areas of clinical practice, behavioral approaches are deeply enmeshed in geriatrics, pediatrics, stress management, behavioral medicine, business and management, and education, to mention only a few.

## CONTRIBUTIONS

Behavior therapy is a short-term approach that yields results and has wide applicability. It emphasizes research into and assessment of the techniques used, thus providing accountability. Specific problems are identified and attacked, and clients are kept informed about the therapeutic process and about what gains are being made. The approach has demonstrated effectiveness in many areas of human functioning. The concepts and procedures are easily grasped. The therapist is an explicit reinforcer, consultant, model, teacher, and expert in behavioral change. The approach has undergone tremendous development and expansion over the past two decades, and the literature continues to expand at a phenomenal rate. Behavioral approaches can be appropriately integrated into counseling with culturally diverse client populations, particularly because of their emphasis on teaching clients about the therapeutic process and the structure that is provided by the model.

## LIMITATIONS

The success of the approach is in proportion to the ability to control environmental variables. In institutional settings (schools, psychiatric hospitals, mental-health outpatient clinics) the danger exists of imposing conforming behavior. Therapists can manipulate clients toward ends they have not chosen. A basic criticism leveled at this approach is that it does not address broader human problems—such as meaning, the search for values, and identity issues—but focuses instead on very specific and narrow behavioral problems.

# GLOSSARY OF KEY TERMS

**Assertion training.** A set of techniques that involves behavioral rehearsal, coaching, and learning more effective social skills. Teaches people to express both positive and negative feelings openly and directly.

**BASIC ID.** The conceptual framework of multimodal therapy that is based on the premise that human personality can be understood by assessment of seven major areas of functioning: behavior, affective responses, sensations, images, cognitions, interpersonal relationships, and drugs/biological functions.

**Behavior rehearsal.** A technique consisting of trying out in therapy new behaviors that are to be used in everyday situations.

**Modeling.** Learning through observation and imitation.

**Multimodal therapy.** A model endorsing technical eclecticism. Uses procedures drawn from various sources without necessarily subscribing to the theory behind these techniques. Developed by Arnold Lazarus.

**Negative reinforcement.** The termination of or withdrawal of an unpleasant stimulus as a result of performing some desired behavior.

**Positive reinforcement.** A form of conditioning whereby the individual receives something desirable as a consequence of his or her behavior. A reward that increases the probability of its recurrence.

**Reinforcement.** A specified event that strengthens the tendency for a response to be repeated.

**Self-management.** A collection of strategies based on the idea that change can be brought about by teaching people to use coping skills in problematic situations such as anxiety, depression, and pain.

**Self-monitoring.** The process of observing one's own behavior patterns as well as one's interactions in various social situations.

**Social-learning theory.** A perspective holding that behavior is best understood by taking into consideration the social conditions under which learning occurs. Developed primarily by Albert Bandura.

**Systematic desensitization.** A procedure based on the principles of classical conditioning. The client is taught to relax while imagining a graded series of progressively anxiety-arousing situations. Eventually, the client reaches a point at which the anxiety-producing stimulus no longer brings about the anxious response.

## QUESTIONS FOR DISCUSSION AND EVALUATION

1. Advocates of the psychoanalytic approach, which emphasizes identifying and resolving underlying causes of behavioral problems, challenge behavior therapists by predicting that other symptoms will be substituted for the ones treated unless the underlying causes are also treated. Where do you stand with respect to this challenge?

2. In some ways it may seem that the behavioral approach and the existential approach are diametrically opposed. Yet some writers contend that combining *behavioral methods* with *humanistic values* leads to a synthesis of the best attributes of both approaches. What do you think?

3. An increasing emphasis in current behavior therapy is on teaching clients self-control procedures and self-management skills. The assumption is that learning coping skills can increase the range of self-directed behavior. What are the possibilities of behavior therapy, as you see them, for enhancing a client's choosing, planning, and self-direction?

4. Considering the counseling of culturally diverse client populations, what are some of the merits of the behavioral approach? What specific aspects of behavior therapy, both concepts and techniques, would you want to apply in your work in a multicultural setting?

5. A person's behavior can be controlled with or without the person's awareness. Do you think that clients in programs utilizing operant-conditioning procedures should be informed and given advance explanations of the treatment program? Would your answer depend on the type of clientele and the type of setting? What guidelines can you formulate regarding when you would or would not inform your clients?

130

# ISSUES FOR PERSONAL APPLICATION: DESIGNING A SELF-MANAGEMENT PROGRAM

As you know from reading the textbook, there is an increased use of self-management strategies. These include self-monitoring, self-reward, self-contracting, and stimulus control. Select some behavior you might like to change (stopping excessive eating, drinking, or smoking; teaching yourself relaxation skills in the face of tense situations you must encounter; developing a regular program of physical exercising or meditating; and so forth). Show how you would specifically design, implement, and evaluate your self-change program. Ideally, you will consider actually trying out such a program for some behavior changes you want to make in your everyday life.

- What specific behavior do you want to change?

- What specific actions will help you to reach the above goal?

- What self-monitoring devices can you use to keep a record of your progress?

- What reinforcements (self-rewards) can you use as a way of carrying out your plans?

- How well is your plan for change working? What revisions are necessary in order for your plan to work more effectively?

# PRACTICAL APPLICATIONS

## TRANSLATING BROAD GOALS INTO SPECIFIC GOALS

*Directions*:   An area of major concern in behavior therapy is the formulation of *concrete* and *specific* goals for counseling. Clients often approach the first counseling session with vague, generalized, abstract goals. A task for the therapist is to help the client formulate clear, concrete goals. The following exercises are designed to give you practice in that task. For each general statement in items 4–7 write a concrete goal, as illustrated in the three examples:

1. Broad goal:  *"I would like to be happier. I suppose I want to become self-actualized."*

   Specific goal:  *"I want to learn to know what I want and to have the courage to get this. I want to feel that I am doing what I really want to be doing."*

2. Broad goal:  *"I'd like to work on improving my relationship with people."*

   Specific goal:  *"I want to be able to ask those I'm close to for what I want and need. So often I keep my desires unknown, and thus I feel cheated with those people."*

3. Broad goal:  *"I suppose I need to work on my communication with my wife."*

   Specific goal:  *"I need to learn how to tell my wife what I'm thinking and feeling and not bury all this and expect her to guess if I'm pleased or not."*

4. Broad goal:  *"I want to know why I play all these stupid games with myself in my head."*

   Specific goal: _____

   _____

   _____

5. Broad goal:  *"I need to get in touch with my values and my philosophy of life."*

   Specific goal: _____

   _____

6.  Broad goal: _"It's awfully hard for me to be an autonomous and assertive individual."_

Specific goal: _____

_____

_____

7.  Broad goal: _"I have all sorts of fears and worries, and just about everything gets me_

_uptight."_ _____

Specific goal: _____

_____

_____

## LEARNING HOW TO BE CONCRETE

One way to help clients become more specific in clarifying broad goals is to do it for yourself. Make a list of specific behaviors that you would like to change in your own life. For example, your list might look like this:

1.  I want to say no when I really mean no, instead of saying yes and feeling guilty.

2.  I would like to spend less time studying and more time playing tennis and skiing.

3.  I want to respond to my kids without shouting.

4.  I want to lessen my fears about taking examinations.

List concrete goals in terms of specific _behavioral changes_ that you want for yourself:

1.  _____

2.  _____

3.  _____

4.  _____

5.  _____

6.  _____

# SUGGESTED ACTIVITIES AND EXERCISES

1.  Here is an exercise that you can do by yourself. For a period of at least a week, engage in relaxation training for approximately 20 to 30 minutes daily. The purpose of the exercise is to teach you to become more aware of the distinction between tension states and relaxation states. A further objective is to provide you with self-control procedures designed to reduce unnecessary anxiety and tension and to induce bodily relaxation. Self-relaxation is best learned in a quiet setting and in a prone position. The strategy for achieving muscular relaxation is the repeated tensing and relaxing of various muscular groups. Begin by tensing a specific set of muscles for several seconds and then relaxing those muscles for several seconds. In using this procedure, you should cover all the major muscular groups by using about two tension/release cycles per muscular group. For the purpose of deepening your relaxation, auxiliary techniques such as concentrating on your breathing and imagining yourself in peaceful and personally relaxing situations can eventually be added to the self-relaxation procedure.

a. *Hands and arms.* Begin by sitting back or lying down in a relaxed position with your arms at your sides. Take several deep breaths in order to become relaxed, and hold each breath for at least five seconds. Keep your eyes closed during the exercise. Now hold out your dominant arm, and make a fist with the dominant hand. Clench your fist tightly, and feel the tension in the forearm and the hand. Now let go. Now feel the relaxation, and feel the difference from before. After 15 to 20 seconds repeat the procedure, this time concentrating on the differences between relaxation and tension.

b. *Biceps.* Flex your dominant bicep, and notice the tension. Then, relax, tense, and relax again. Notice the warm feelings of relaxation.

c. *Fists.* Next, do the same for the nondominant fist. Hold the fist tightly, relax, and study the differences. Then repeat the tension/relaxation procedure, making sure to take your time.

d. *Biceps.* Flex the nondominant bicep. Be aware of the tension, and then release. Repeat the tension/relaxation pattern. Take several deep breaths, hold them, and notice the relaxation in your arms.

e. *Upper face.* Tense up the muscles of your forehead by raising your eyebrows as high as possible. Hold this for five seconds, and feel the tension building up. Relax and notice the difference. Then repeat this procedure.

f. *Eyes.* Now close your eyes tightly. Feel the tension around your eyes. Now relax those muscles, noting the difference between the tension and the relaxation. Repeat this process.

g. *Tongue and jaws.* Next clench your jaws by biting your teeth together. Pull the corners of your mouth back, and make an exaggerated smile, Release and let go, noticing the difference.

h. *Pressing the lips together.* Now press your lips together tightly, and notice the tension. Now relax the muscles around your mouth. Repeat.

i. *Breathing.* Take a few deep breaths, and notice how relaxed your arms, head, and mouth feel. Enjoy these feelings of relaxation.

j. *Neck.* Try to touch your chin to your chest, and at the same time apply counterpressure to keep it from touching. Release, note the difference, and then repeat. Pull your head back, and try to touch your back, but push back the opposite way with the opposing muscles. Notice the tension, release, and relax. Then repeat this procedure.

k. *Chest and shoulders.* Next pull back your shoulders until the blades almost touch, and then relax. Repeat. Then try to touch your shoulders by pushing them forward as far as you can. Then release, and feel the difference. Repeat. Now shrug your shoulders, and try to touch them to your ears. Hold, release, and repeat.

l. *Breathing.* Take a deep breath, hold it for seven seconds, and then exhale quickly. Do this again. Note the feelings of relaxation.

m. *Stomach muscles.* Tighten up your stomach muscles; make your stomach tight and hard like a knot. Relax those muscles. Repeat.

n. *Buttocks.* Now tighten your buttocks by pulling them together. Hold. Release. Repeat.

o. *Thighs.* Tense your thighs. Release the muscles quickly, and then repeat. Study the difference between the tension in the thighs and the relaxation you feel now.

p. *Toes.* Point your toes toward your head, and note the tension. Relax. Repeat. Then point your feet outward, and notice the tension. Release quickly and repeat. Point your feet inward and hold, and then relax. Repeat.

After each of the above muscle groups has been tensed and relaxed twice, the therapist typically concludes the relaxation training with a summary and review. This review consists of listing each muscle group and asking the client to let go of any tension. This is done for each of the above muscle groups, with the suggestion of becoming completely relaxed. The client is asked to notice the good feelings of relaxation, warmth, and calmness over the entire body. It's useful to have this relaxation exercise on tape, so that you can follow the procedure easily.

2. Review the section in Chapter 10 of the textbook describing *systematic desensitization*. Select some anxiety-provoking experience for you, and then set up a systematic-desensitization program to lessen your anxiety or fear. Follow your program privately as an out-of-class assignment. Class members may bring their results into class a week later to describe and share their experiences with the procedure. Following are a few guidelines for setting up a systematic-desensitization program for yourself:

   a. Begin by using the relaxation procedure described in the previous exercise.

   b. Decide what specific behavior or situations evoke anxiety reactions for you. For example, speaking in front of others may be anxiety producing for you.

   c. Construct a hierarchy, which should be arranged from the worst situation you can imagine to a situation that evokes the least anxiety. For example, the greatest anxiety for you might result from the thought of delivering a lecture to hundreds of people in an auditorium. The least-anxiety-provoking situation might be talking with a fellow student you know well.

   d. Apply the relaxation procedures that you have learned; keep your eyes closed, and begin by imagining yourself in the least anxiety-arousing situation on your hierarchy. Then, while imagining a peaceful and pleasant scene, allow yourself also to imagine yourself in the next most anxiety-arousing situation. At the moment you experience anxiety as you imagine the more threatening situation, switch off that scene, put yourself back into the pleasant scene, and relax again.

   e. The idea is to move progressively up the hierarchy until you can imagine the scene that produces the greatest degree of anxiety and still be able to induce relaxation again. This procedure ends when you can remain in a relaxed state even while you are imagining a particular scene that formerly was the most disturbing to you.

3. Assume that your client expresses a desire to lose 20 pounds and then keep his weight down. Using learning principles and behavioral techniques, show the specific steps for *weight control* that you might take with your client. As guidelines you might consider the following questions:

   a. Has the client consulted a physician about his weight problem? If he has not, would you undertake a therapy program without having him first visit a physician?

   b. What is his motivation for losing weight? What specific reinforcements might help him stick with his weight-reduction program?

   c. What kind of self-observation and charting behavior would you suggest? Would you ask him to keep a record of when he eats, what he eats, and so on?

   d. How would you deal with him if he went on eating binges and failed to follow through with his program? What might you say or do?

   e. What are the specific learning concepts involved in the weight-control program?

   Now assume that your client is a chain smoker and expresses a real interest in quitting. Having tried before, she stopped smoking but resumed the practice when she felt pressure in her daily life. With that information develop a program of *smoking control* designed to eliminate her smoking behavior by using the principles of learning theory. Describe the steps that you would take in designing specific procedures of the program.

4. *Multimodal therapy* begins with a comprehensive assessment of the various modalities of human functioning. For practice in thinking assessment terms within this framework,

look at the case of Stan, and attempt an initial assessment of him on the dimensions listed below:

a. *Behavior*. How active is Stan? What are some of his main strengths? What specific behaviors keep him from getting what he says he wants?

b. *Affect*. How emotional does Stan seem? What are some problematic emotions for him?

c. *Sensation*. How aware of his senses is Stan? Does he appear to be making full use of all his senses?

d. *Imagery*. How would you describe Stan's self-image? How does he describe himself now? How does he see himself?

e. *Cognition*. What are some of the main "shoulds," "oughts," and "musts" that appear to be in Stan's life now? How do they get in the way of effective living for him? How do his thoughts affect the way he feels and acts?

f. *Interpersonal relationships*. How much of a social being is Stan? How capable does he appear to be of handling intimate relationships? What does he expect from others in his life?

g. *Drugs/biology*. What do you know about Stan's health? Does he have any concerns about his health? Does he use any drugs?

Based on this initial assessment of Stan, what kind of treatment program would you outline for him as a behavior therapist?

# CASE EXAMPLES

## MY WAY OF WORKING WITH STAN
## FROM THE BEHAVIOR-THERAPY PERSPECTIVE

I value the action-oriented methods of behavior therapy, for insight alone is not considered enough to cause behavior change. If Stan hopes to change, he will have to take specific action in the real world, and this approach provides many techniques for helping him gain this needed practice. For example, he wants to resolve his inferiority feelings when dealing with professors and be able to approach them and talk with them about how is doing in the course.

I might ask Stan to approach me as though I were his professor and role-play his typical approach. I would ask him to talk out loud about whatever he is telling himself, so that we could both hear his self-talk. Initially, I would want to show him how his cognitions affect his behavior—how the things he is telling himself cement his feelings of worthlessness and stupidity, which have a direct effect on his behavior around professors. It would be important to help Stan approach his professors with new self-talk and a new set of expectations, such as "I am worth asking for my professor's time, and if I ask, I'll be able to work out some problems I've been having."

After we role-played more positive approaches in the session itself, I would encourage Stan to keep a record (in a spiral notebook that he could carry around in his pocket) of his negative self-statements when he is near professors. Also, he would be encouraged to seek out one of his professors and talk with him or her, actually implementing some of the ideas that we discussed in this session. Next week at the session, we would follow up and see how well he was changing behavior in his everyday world.

As you review Stan's case and think about him from a behavioral perspective, consider these questions:

1. Assume that it is next week and that Stan has done nothing by way of homework or follow-up to work on his self-talk. What might be your response? Where would you proceed from there?

2. This perspective assumes that as a counselor your technical skills are essential in therapy. What reactions do you have to this assumption in light of those approaches that hold that a therapeutic relationship itself is a sufficient condition for change?

3. Do you see any possibilities of integrating some of the feeling dimensions from the experiential therapies (Gestalt, person-centered, and existential therapy) with the focus on behavior and cognition in this approach? How might you integrate several of these approaches?

## EDDIE: AN ATTENTION-GETTING CHILD

A third-grade teacher seeks your professional help with an 8-year-old boy in her class. She tells you that Eddie's behavior is highly disruptive because he is continually acting out his problems in a hostile or aggressive manner. He punches other children for no apparent reason, tears up others' work, rarely follows instructions, continually talks at times that are disruptive, and draws attention to himself through negative behavior. He seems to take delight in seeing other children get angry.

The teacher tells you that she is at a loss to know how to deal with Eddie's behavior. She considered asking that he be removed from her classroom, but she hesitated because she believes that he has many pressing conflicts and is a deeply troubled child. She asks you to see him for a session and give her some guidance in dealing with his behavior.

You see Eddie for an individual session, during which you discover that his father is both verbally and physically abusive. Without provocation his father calls him names and beats him up. One time, Eddie was beaten so badly that he had severe cuts and bruises, and his father threatened him with a "real beating" if he did not agree to say that he had had a bicycle accident. You also discover that Eddie comes from a single-parent family. His father had custody since his parents divorced when he was in preschool. Eddie tells you that he would feel really lost if he didn't have his father. He thinks that maybe he has done many wrong things to deserve the treatment he gets.

Working within a behavioral framework, show how you would proceed in this session with Eddie so that you might be in a better position to make recommendations to his teacher and might offer him some direct help yourself.

1. What goals would you have in mind during this session? How would you attempt to meet them? What questions would you ask of Eddie? How might you approach the issue of his disruptive behavior in class? What might you want to tell him? What would you tell his teacher?

2. What speculations can you offer about the reasons for Eddie's disruptive behavior? Where might he have learned his aggressive behaviors?

3. How do you expect that you would handle the issue of Eddie's beatings by his father? How would you deal with Eddie on this matter? Might you approach his father? If so, what would you say, and what would you hope to accomplish? Might you consult the authorities? What are your legal obligations in this case?

4. During your session what behaviors would you most want to observe? What would you do with your observations as far as Eddie is concerned? How much would you share with him of what you know from his teacher and of what you actually observe?

5. Would the fact that Eddie comes from a single-parent home influence your interventions? How would you deal with him when he told you that he would be lost without his father?

6. If you were to continue working with Eddie as his counselor, what *specific behavioral procedures* might you employ, and toward what end?

7. In terms of suggestions to the teacher, what behavioral principles might you recommend that she be aware of in dealing with Eddie? How might she extinguish his negative behavior? And how could she give positive reinforcement?

# REVIEWING THE HIGHLIGHTS

1. Behavior therapy views human nature as _____

   _____

2. The unique feature that distinguishes this approach is _____

   _____

3. The therapeutic goals are _____

   _____

4. The central role of the therapist is _____

   _____

5. In the therapy process clients are expected to _____

   _____

6. The relationship between the client and the therapist is characterized by _____

   _____

7. Some of the major techniques are _____

   _____

8. I think this approach is most applicable to those clients who _____

   _____

9. One aspect of behavior therapy I like most is _____

   _____

10. One aspect of behavior therapy I like least is _____

   _____

# QUIZ ON BEHAVIOR THERAPY: A COMPREHENSION CHECK

Score _____%

*Note:* Refer to Appendix 1 for the scoring key.

*True/false items:* Decide if the following statements are "more true" or "more false" as they apply to behavior therapy.

T  F  1. Multimodal therapy was developed by Albert Bandura.

T  F  2. Multimodal therapy endorses technical eclecticism.

T  F  3. Behavior therapy has gone well beyond the usual areas of clinical practice, for behavioral principles are applied to areas such as pediatrics, business, and education.

T  F  4. There is no unifying set of assumptions about behavior that can incorporate all the existing procedures in the behavioral field.

T  F  5. The newest trend in the development of behavior therapy is the focus on cognitive factors that are related to behavior.

T  F  6. Typically, the goals of the therapeutic process are determined by the therapist.

T  F  7. Behavior therapists tend to be active and directive, and they function as consultants and problems solvers.

T  F  8. Multimodal therapy consists of a series of techniques that are used with all clients in much the same way.

T  F  9. There is a growing trend toward integrating cognitive and behavioral methods to help clients manage their own problems.

T  F  10. A program of behavioral change should begin with a comprehensive assessment of the client.

*Multiple-choice items*:  Select the *one best answer* of those alternatives given.  Consider each question within the framework of behavior therapy.

_____ 11. Behavior therapy is grounded on

   a. the psychodynamic aspects of a person.
   b. the principles of learning.
   c. a philosophical view of the human condition.
   d. the events of the first five years of life.

_____ 12. Behavior therapy is based on

   a. applying the experimental method to the therapeutic process.
   b. a systematic set of concepts.
   c. a well-developed theory of personality.
   d. the principle of self-actualization.
   e. both (b) and (c).

_____ 13. In behavior therapy it is generally agreed that

   a. the therapist should decide the treatment goals.
   b. the client should decide the treatment goals.
   c. goals of therapy are the same for all clients.
   d. goals are not necessary.

_____ 14. Which is not true as it is applied to behavior therapy?

   a. Insight is necessary for behavior change to occur.
   b. Therapy should focus on behavior change and not attitude change.
   c. Therapy is not complete unless actions follow verbalizations.
   d. A good working relationship between client and therapist is necessary for behavior change to occur.

_____ 15. According to most behavior therapists, a good working relationship between the client and therapist is

   a. a necessary and sufficient condition for behavior change to occur.
   b. a necessary, but not sufficient, condition for behavior change to occur.
   c. neither a necessary nor a sufficient condition for behavior change to occur.

_____ 16. Which of the following is not true regarding behavior therapy?

   a. The client must be an active participant.
   b. The client is merely passive while the therapist uses techniques.
   c. Therapy cannot be imposed on unwilling clients.
   d. Therapist and client need to work together for common goals.

_____ 17. Which of the following is *not* a key concept of behavior therapy?

   a. Behavior is learned through reinforcement.
   b. Present behavior is stressed more than past behavior.
   c. Emphasis is on cognitive factors.
   d. Emphasis is on action and experimenting with new behaviors.
   e. Emphasis is on the role of insight in treatment.

____ 18. An appropriate technique for people who have difficulty in expressing anger or irritation is

    a. systematic desensitization.
    b. assertion training.
    c. time out from reinforcement.
    d. modeling.
    e. none of the above.

____ 19. Behavior-therapy techniques

    a. must be suited to the client's problems.
    b. are assessed to determine their value.
    c. are geared toward behavior change.
    d. All of the above are true.
    e. None of the above is true.

____ 20. What is(are) the contribution(s) of behavior therapy?

    a. It gives a psychodynamic explanation of behavior disorders.
    b. It intensifies the client's feelings and subjective experiencing.
    c. It makes explicit the role of the therapist as a reinforcer.
    d. The client is clearly informed of specific procedures used.
    e. Both (c) and (d) are contributions.

____ 21. Who is the developer of multimodal therapy?

    a. Albert Bandura
    b. B. F. Skinner
    c. Joseph Wolpe
    d. Arnold Lazarus
    e. none of the above

____ 22. A limitation of behavior therapy is

    a. its lack of research to evaluate the effectiveness of techniques.
    b. its deemphasis on the role of feelings in therapy.
    c. its lack of clear concepts on which to base practice.
    d. its lack of attention paid to a good client/therapist relationship.
    e. its overemphasis on early childhood experiences.

____ 23. Contemporary behavior therapy places emphasis on

    a. the interplay between the individual and the environment.
    b. helping clients acquire insight into the causes of their problems.
    c. a phenomenological approach to understanding the person.
    d. encouraging clients to reexperience unfinished business with significant others by role playing with them in the present.
    e. working through the transference relationship with the therapist.

____ 24. Which is *not* true as it applies to multimodal therapy?

    a. Therapeutic flexibility and versatility are valued highly.
    b. Therapists adjust their procedures to effectively achieve the client's goals in therapy.
    c. Great care is taken to fit the client to a predetermined type of treatment.
    d. The approach encourages technical eclecticism.
    e. The therapist makes a comprehensive assessment of the client's level of functioning at the outset of therapy.

____ 25. Which of the following is *not* considered one of the modalities of human functioning in multimodal therapy?

    a. sensation           d. unfinished business
    b. affect             e. drugs/biology
    c. interpersonal relationships

# 11

# RATIONAL-EMOTIVE THERAPY AND OTHER COGNITIVE-BEHAVIORAL APPROACHES

## PRECHAPTER SELF-INVENTORY

*Directions*: Refer to page 46 for general directions. Use the following code:

5 = I *strongly agree* with this statement.

4 = I *agree*, in most respects, with this statement.

3 = I am *undecided* in my opinion about this statement.

2 = I *disagree*, in most respects, with this statement.

1 = I *strongly disagree* with this statement.

_____ 1. Humans are born with the potential for both rational thinking and irrational thinking.

_____ 2. Blame is the core of most emotional disturbances.

_____ 3. Emotions are the product of human thinking.

_____ 4. Even though it is desirable to be loved and accepted, it is not necessary.

_____ 5. We tend to accept irrational ideas, with which we unthinkingly keep reindoctrinating ourselves.

_____ 6. Because they continue to accept and perpetuate irrational beliefs, human beings are largely responsible for creating their own emotional disturbances.

_____ 7. Therapy is largely a teaching/learning process.

_____ 8. The main goal of therapy should be to reduce clients' self-defeating outlook and help them acquire a more rational philosophy of life.

_____ 9. Central functions of the therapist should include challenging clients' illogical ideas and teaching them how to think and evaluate in a rational way.

_____ 10. Therapy is essentially a cognitive, active, directive, behavioral process.

_____ 11. It is appropriate for a therapist to persuade, to be highly directive, to attack faulty thinking, and to serve as a counterpropagandist.

_____ 12. Therapy should focus on a reeducative process whereby the client learns how to apply logical thinking to problem solving.

_____ 13. Emotional and intellectual insight is not a crucial part of the therapeutic process.

_____ 14. A warm or deep personal relationship between client and therapist is neither a necessary nor a sufficient condition for psychotherapy.

_____ 15. Active homework assignments should be an integral part of the therapeutic process.

_____ 16. Translating learning into *action* outside the therapy session is essential for therapy to be effective.

_____ 17. Modeling and behavior reversal are key ways of learning in therapy.

_____ 18. A therapist should continue to challenge the illogical ideas that underlie a client's fears.

_____ 19. If we correct our faulty thinking, we will be likely to eliminate our bad feelings.

_____ 20. Therapy should focus on the present.

# OVERVIEW OF RATIONAL-EMOTIVE AND COGNITIVE-BEHAVIORAL THERAPY

## KEY FIGURES AND MAJOR FOCUS

Founder: Albert Ellis is the founder of RET and is the grandfather of the cognitive-behavioral approaches. Aaron Beck is the key spokesman for cognitive therapy. The approach grew out of Ellis's disenchantment with psychoanalytically oriented therapy. He found that insight and awareness of early childhood events did not result in the reduction of the client's emotional disturbances. A highly didactic, cognitive, behavior-oriented approach, rational emotive therapy stresses the role of action and practice in combating irrational, self-indoctrinated ideas. It focuses on the role of thinking and belief systems as the roots of personal problems. Other forms of cognitive-behavioral therapy include Beck's cognitive therapy and Donald Meichenbaum's cognitive behavior modification. Beck's model shares with RET the active, directive, time-limited, structured approach used to treat various disorders such as depression, anxiety, and phobias.

## PHILOSOPHY AND BASIC ASSUMPTIONS

Individuals are born with the potential for rational thinking but tend to fall victim to the uncritical acceptance of irrational beliefs that are perpetuated through self-reindoctrination. The assumption is that thinking, evaluating, analyzing, questioning, doing, practicing, and redeciding are at the base of behavior change. RET is a didactic and directive model. Therapy is a process of reeducation. The cognitive-behavioral approaches are based on the assumption that a reorganization of one's self-statements will result in a corresponding reorganization of one's behavior. Cognitive therapy rests on the premise that cognitions are the major determinants of how we feel and act.

## KEY CONCEPTS

RET holds that although emotional disturbance is rooted in childhood, people keep telling themselves irrational and illogical sentences. The approach is based on the A-B-C theory of personality: A = actual event; B = belief system; C = consequence. Emotional problems are the result of one's beliefs, which need to be challenged. The scientific method of logical and rational thought is applied to irrational beliefs. Cognitive therapy consists of changing dysfunctional emotions and behaviors by modifying inaccurate and dysfunctional thinking. The techniques are designed to identify and test the client's misconceptions and faulty assumptions.

## THERAPEUTIC GOALS

The goal of RET is to eliminate a self-defeating outlook on life and acquire a more rational and tolerant philosophy. Clients are taught that the events of life themselves do not disturb us; rather, our interpretation of these events is critical. Clients are taught how to identify and uproot their "shoulds," "musts," and "oughts." Further, they are taught how to substitute preferences for demands. The goal of cognitive therapy is to change the way the client thinks. Changes in beliefs and thought processes tend to result in changes in the way people feel and how they behave.

## THERAPEUTIC RELATIONSHIP

In RET a warm relationship between the client and the therapist is not essential. However, the client needs to feel unconditional positive regard from the therapist. The therapist does not blame or condemn clients; rather, he or she teaches them how to avoid rating and condemning themselves. The therapist functions as a teacher; the client functions as a student. As clients begin to understand how they are continuing to contribute to their problems, they need to actively practice changing their self-defeating behavior and converting it into rational behavior. In cognitive therapy a collaborative effort is emphasized. Together the therapist and client frame the client's conclusions in the form of a testable hypothesis. Cognitive therapists are continuously active and deliberately interactive with clients; they also strive to engage the client's active participation and collaboration throughout all phases of therapy.

## TECHNIQUES AND PROCEDURES

Rational-emotive therapists are eclectic in that they use a variety of cognitive, affective, and behavioral techniques, tailoring them to individual clients. The approach tends to use diverse techniques and borrows many from behavioral approaches. Cognitive techniques include disputing irrational beliefs, cognitive homework, changing one's language, and the use of humor. Emotive techniques include rational-emotive imagery, role playing, and shame-attacking exercises. Behavioral techniques include operant conditioning, self-management strategies, and modeling, to mention a few. Techniques are designed to induce clients to critically examine their present beliefs and behavior. With respect to techniques and therapeutic style, there are some differences between RET and cognitive therapy. RET is highly directive, persuasive, and confrontive. Beck's cognitive therapy emphasizes a Socratic dialogue and more emphasis on helping clients discover their misconceptions for themselves.

## APPLICATIONS

Applications of RET include individual therapy, ongoing group therapy, marathon encounter groups, brief therapy, marriage and family therapy, sex therapy, and classroom situations. RET is applicable to clients with moderate anxiety, neurotic disorders, character disorders, psychosomatic problems, eating disorders, poor interpersonal skills, marital problems, parenting skills, addictions, and sexual dysfunctions. It is most effective with those who can reason well and who are not seriously disturbed. The most common application of Beck's cognitive therapy is in the treatment of depression; cognitive methods have also been very useful in teaching people how to manage stress.

## CONTRIBUTIONS

These therapies have wide applicability. Counseling is brief and places value on active practice in experimenting with new behavior so that insight is carried into doing. It discourages dependence on the therapist and stresses the client's capacity to control his or her own destiny. RET has shed much light on how people can change their emotions by changing the content of their thinking. It is in many ways the forerunner of other increasingly popular cognitive-behavioral therapies. With respect to cognitive therapy, Beck has made pioneering efforts in the treatment of anxiety, phobias, and depression, and his approach has received a great deal of attention from clinical researchers.

## LIMITATIONS

RET does not provide a rationale for or clear explanation of why one tends to reindoctrinate oneself with irrational beliefs or why one clings to those beliefs. It does not apply to people with limited intelligence. Possible dangers are the imposition of the therapist's own philosophy on the client and the psychological harm done by the therapist who "beats down" clients with persuasion. In general, the cognitive-behavioral approaches have the limitation of not emphasizing the exploration of emotional issues. Their focus on the role of thinking can lead to an intellectualized approach to therapy.

# GLOSSARY OF KEY TERMS

**A-B-C model.** The theory that people's problems do not stem from activating events but, rather, from their beliefs about such events. Thus, the best route to changing negative emotions is the changing of one's beliefs about situations.

**Automatic thoughts.** Personal ideas that result from a particular stimulus and that lead to emotional responses.

**Cognitive errors.** In cognitive therapy, the client's misconceptions and faulty assumptions. (Examples include arbitrary inference, selective abstraction, overgeneralization, magnification, polarized thinking, and personalization.)

**Cognitive restructuring.** A process of actively altering maladaptive thought patterns and replacing them with constructive thoughts and beliefs.

**Cognitive structure.** The organizing aspect of thinking, which monitors and directs the choice of thoughts. Implies an "executive processor," one that determines when to continue, interrupt, or change thinking patterns.

**Cognitive therapy.** An approach and set of procedures that attempts to change feelings and behavior by modifying faulty thinking and believing.

**Collaborative empiricism.** A strategy of viewing the client as a scientist who is able to make objective interpretations.

**Coping-skills program.** A behavioral procedure for helping clients deal effectively with stressful situations by learning to modify their thinking patterns.

**Distortion of reality.** Erroneous thinking that disrupts one's life. Can be contradicted by the client's objective appraisal of the situation.

**Internal dialogue.** The sentences that people tell themselves and the debate that often goes on "inside their head." A form of self-talk, or inner speech.

**Irrational belief.** An unreasonable conviction that leads to emotional and behavioral problems.

**Musturbation.** A term coined by Albert Ellis to refer to behavior that is absolutist and rigid; we tell ourselves the we *must*, *should*, or *ought to* do or be something.

**Rationality.** The quality of thinking, feeling, and acting in ways that will help us attain our goals. Irrationality consists of thinking, feeling, and acting in ways that are self-defeating and that thwart our goals.

**Rational-emotive imagery.** A form of intense mental practice for learning new emotional and physical habits. Clients imagine themselves thinking, feeling, and behaving in exactly the way they would like to in everyday situations.

**Self-instructional therapy.** An approach to therapy based on the assumption that what people say to themselves directly influences the things they do. Training consists of learning new self-talk aimed at coping with problems.

**Shame-attacking exercises.** An RET strategy of encouraging people to do things despite a fear of feeling foolish or embarrassed. The aim of the exercise is to teach people that they can function effectively even if they might be perceived as doing foolish acts.

**Stress-inoculation training.** A form of cognitive behavior modification developed by Donald Meichenbaum that involves an educational, rehearsal, and application phase. Clients learn the role of thinking in creating stress, are given coping skills for dealing with stressful situations, and practice techniques aimed at changing behavior.

**Therapeutic collaboration.** A process whereby the therapist actively strives to engage the client's active participation in all phases of therapy.

## QUESTIONS FOR DISCUSSION AND EVALUATION

1.  Do you agree with the assumption of RET that the basis for emotional disturbance lies in irrational beliefs and thinking? To what degree do you accept the notion that events themselves do not cause emotional and behavioral problems but, rather, that it is our cognitive evaluation and beliefs about life events that lead to our problems?

2.  According to Ellis, effective psychotherapy can take place without personal warmth from the therapist. He contends that too much warmth and understanding can be counterproductive by fostering dependence on the therapist for approval. What are your reactions to this view of the client/therapist relationship?

3.  In Beck's cognitive therapy the assumption is that a client's internal dialogue plays a major role in behavior. How individuals monitor themselves, how they give themselves praise or criticism, how they interpret events, and how they make predictions of future behavior are directly related to emotional disorders. How could you apply Beck's ideas to counseling a depressed client? How might you teach such a client to challenge his or her own thinking and develop new thinking?

4.  In Meichenbaum's cognitive behavior modification, cognitive restructuring is vital in teaching people how to cope effectively with stress in their life. Part of his program involves teaching clients cognitive and behavioral strategies to cope with stressful situations. If you had a client who wanted to learn self-management techniques to reduce stress, what are some specific steps you would teach the client? How could you draw from Meichenbaum's stress-inoculation training in working with your client?

5.  Think of situations in which you might encounter clients with culturally diverse backgrounds. What aspects of RET and cognitive-behavioral therapy do you think might work well in multicultural counseling? How might you have to modify some of your techniques so that they would be appropriate for the client's cultural background?

## ISSUES AND QUESTIONS FOR PERSONAL APPLICATION

The following questions and some of the underlying issues can be applied personally to help you get a better grasp of RET. Bring the questions to class for discussion.

1.  Are you aware of reindoctrinating yourself with certain beliefs and values that you originally accepted from your parents or from society? Make a list of some of your beliefs and values. Do you want to keep them? Do you want to modify them?

2.  Are you able to accept yourself in spite of your limitations and imperfections? Do you blame yourself or others for your limitations?

3.  Review Ellis's list of irrational ideas. How many can you identify with? How do you think your life is affected by your irrational beliefs? How do you determine *for yourself* whether your beliefs are rational or irrational?

To help focus your thinking on the above issues, put a check (√) before each of the following irrational beliefs that you see as applying to yourself:

_____ a.  "I must be thoroughly competent in everything I do."

_____ b.  "Others must treat me fairly and in ways that I want them to."

_____ c.  "I must have universal approval, and if I don't get this approval from everyone, it's horrible and I feel depressed."

_____ d.  "Life must be the way I want it to be, and if it isn't, I can't tolerate it."

_____ e.  "If I fail at something, the results will be catastrophic."

_____ f.  "I should feel eternally guilty and rotten and continue to blame myself for all of my past mistakes."

_____ g.  "Because all of my miseries are caused by others, I have no control over my life, and I can't change things unless *they* change."

List a few other statements you tend to make that might pinpoint your core irrational ideas: _____

_____

_____

_____

_____

4.  Select one of your beliefs that causes you trouble.  Then review the A-B-C theory of personality, and attempt to apply that method to changing your irrational belief.  What is the experience like for you?  Do you think that the method holds promise for helping you lead a less troubled life?  How can you apply the approach to your daily life?

5.  How can you challenge your own irrational beliefs and attitudes? Once you are aware of some basic problems or difficulties, what do you see that you can do *for yourself* to change toward a more rational system?

6.  RET therapists are highly active and directive, and they often give their own views without hesitation.  Does that style fit you personally?  Could you adopt it and feel comfortable? Why or why not?

7.  The RET therapist acts as a model.  What implications do you see for self-development of the client?  Can the client grow to become his or her own person, or does he or she become a copy of the therapist?

8.  In being a model for clients, it is important that therapists not be highly emotionally disturbed, that they live rationally, that they not be worried about losing their clients' love and approval, and that they have the courage to confront clients directly.  Would you have any difficulty in being that type of model? Explain.

9.  Consider the applications of RET to school counseling or to counseling in community mental-health clinics.  Assume that a practitioner who employs the principles and methods of RET does not have a doctorate, has not had any supervised internship, and has not had extensive training in RET.  What cautions do you think need to be applied?  What are the potential misuses of the approach?  How can the approach have more potentially harmful results than, for example, the person-centered approach?

10.  If you were to be a client in counseling, which approach might you favor for yourself—Ellis's RET or Beck's cognitive therapy?  What specific features of rational emotive-therapy might be useful in helping you cope with your problems?  And what aspects of cognitive therapy could you use?

11. According to Meichenbaum's cognitive theory of behavior change, there are three relevant phases. Clients are asked to (1) observe and monitor their own behavior, identifying negative thoughts and feelings; (2) begin to create a new internal dialogue by substituting positive and constructive self-statements for negative ones; and (3) acquire more effective coping skills that they can practice both in the therapy session and in real-life situations. For at least one week, identify some behavior you would like to change, and apply this three-phase process. Can you think of ways to use this strategy with your clients? In what counseling situations might you use Meichenbaum's cognitive-restructuring techniques?

12. Assume that you are working with a small group of college students who have problems with test anxiety and fears relating to failure. If you were to employ *cognitive methods* to change their mental set and expectations, what are some things you might say to these students? In what ways might thoughts, self-talk, self-fulfilling prophecies, and attitudes of failure (all examples of cognitive processes) influence these students' *behavior* in test-taking situations?

   a. How would you set up your program?

   b. What cognitive techniques would you use? What other behavioral techniques would you employ to change these students' cognitive structures and their behavior?

   c. What are some ways by which you might evaluate the effectiveness of your program?

13. Complete the RET Self-Help Form on pages 147–148 by making it a homework assignment for a week. After you complete the form, look for patterns in your thinking. What connections do you see between your beliefs and the way you feel? Focus especially on creating *disputing* statements.

## PRACTICAL APPLICATIONS

RET is based on the assumption that people create their own emotional disturbances. It places the individual squarely in the center of the universe and gives him or her almost full responsibility for choosing to make or not to make himself or herself seriously disturbed. It follows logically that if people have the capacity to make themselves disturbed by foolishly and devoutly believing in irrational assumptions about themselves and others, they can generally make themselves undisturbed again. RET assumes that change can best be accomplished through rational-emotive procedures and that to effect behavioral change, hard work and active practice are essential.

The homework-assignment method is one good way of assisting clients in putting new behavior into practice. The method encourages clients to actively attack the irrational beliefs at the roots of their problems. In this exercise suggest what you consider might be an appropriate homework assignment for each situation described below. The purpose of the exercise is to help you think about the possibilities of using the homework-assignment method.

   1. The client, a college sophomore, wants to overcome his shyness around girls. He does not date and even does his best to keep away from girls, because he is afraid they will reject him. But he does want to change that pattern. What homework might you suggest? _____

_____

_____

   2. The client says that because she feels depressed much of the time, she tries to avoid facing life's difficulties or anything about her that might make her feel more depressed. She would like to feel happy, but she is afraid of doing much. What homework might you suggest?

_____

_____

# RET SELF-HELP FORM

Institute for Rational-Emotive Therapy
45 East 65th Street, New York, N.Y. 10021
(212) 535-0822

**(A) ACTIVATING EVENTS,** thoughts, or feelings that happened just before I felt emotionally disturbed or acted self-defeatingly: _____

_____

**(C) CONSEQUENCE or CONDITION**—disturbed feeling or self-defeating behavior—that I produced and would like to change: _____

_____

| **(B) BELIEFS—Irrational BELIEFS (IBs)** leading to my CONSEQUENCE (emotional disturbance or self-defeating behavior). Circle all that apply to these ACTIVATING EVENTS (A). | **(D) DISPUTES** for each circled IRRATIONAL BELIEF. Examples: *"Why* MUST I do very well?" *"Where is it written* that I am a BAD PERSON?" *"Where is the evidence* that I MUST be approved or accepted?" | **(E) EFFECTIVE RATIONAL BELIEFS (RBs)** to replace my IRRATIONAL BELIEFS (IBs). *Examples: "I'd* PREFER *to do very well but I don't* HAVE TO." *"I am a* PERSON WHO *acted badly, not a BAD PERSON." "There is no evidence that I* HAVE TO *be approved, though I would* LIKE *to be."* |
|---|---|---|
| 1. I MUST do well or very well! | | |
| 2. I am a BAD OR WORTHLESS PERSON when I act weakly or stupidly. | | |
| 3. I MUST be approved or accepted by people I find important! | | |
| 4. I NEED to be loved by someone who matters to me a lot! | | |
| 5. I am a BAD, UNLOVABLE PERSON if I get rejected. | | |
| 6. People MUST treat me fairly and give me what I NEED! | | |

**(OVER)**

147

7. People MUST live up to my expectations or it is TERRIBLE!

................................................................

................................................................

................................................................

8. People who act immorally are undeserving, ROTTEN PEOPLE!

................................................................

................................................................

................................................................

9. I CAN'T STAND really bad things or very difficult people!

................................................................

................................................................

................................................................

10. My life MUST have few major hassles or troubles.

................................................................

................................................................

................................................................

11. It's AWFUL or HORRIBLE when major things don't go my way!

................................................................

................................................................

................................................................

12. I CAN'T STAND IT when life is really unfair!

................................................................

................................................................

................................................................

13. I NEED a good deal of immediate gratification and HAVE to feel miserable when I don't get it!

................................................................

................................................................

Additional Irrational Beliefs:

................................................................

................................................................

**(F) FEELINGS and BEHAVIORS** I experienced after arriving at my EFFECTIVE RATIONAL BELIEFS: _____

**I WILL WORK HARD TO REPEAT MY EFFECTIVE RATIONAL BELIEFS FORCEFULLY TO MYSELF ON MANY OCCASIONS SO THAT I CAN MAKE MYSELF LESS DISTURBED NOW AND ACT LESS SELF-DEFEATINGLY IN THE FUTURE.**

3. The client feels that he must win everyone's approval. He has become a "super nice guy" who goes out of his way to please everyone. Rarely does he assert himself, for fear that he might displease someone who then would not like him. He says he would like to be less of a nice guy and more assertive. What homework might you suggest? _____

_____

_____

4. The client would like to take a course in creative writing, but she fears that she has no talent. She is afraid of failing, afraid of being told that she is dumb, and afraid to follow through with taking the course. What homework might you suggest? _____

_____

_____

5. The client continually blames himself by telling himself what a rotten louse he is because he does not give his wife enough attention. He feels totally to blame for the marital problems between him and his wife, and he says he cannot let go of his terrible guilt. What homework might you suggest? _____

_____

_____

6. Each week the client comes to his sessions with a new excuse for why he has not succeeded in following through with his homework assignments. Either he forgets, gets too busy, gets scared, or puts it off—anything but actually *doing* something to change what he *says* he wants to change. Instead of really doing much of anything, he whines each week about how rotten he feels and how he so much would like to change but just doesn't know how. What homework might you suggest? _____

_____

_____

_____

# CASE EXAMPLES

## MY WAY OF WORKING WITH STAN
## FROM THE RATIONAL-EMOTIVE PERSPECTIVE

One of the first things that I would draw on from the rational-emotive model is the value of teaching Stan that it is he who is keeping himself disturbed through the process of self-indoctrination of irrational ideas. Early in the session I would challenge him to see that only he can uproot his faulty thinking by difficult work, both in the session and out. A place where we might begin is a core irrational idea that he carries around: "If everyone doesn't approve of me and tell me that I am worth something, I am doomed to feel rotten, and in fact I *am not* worth much." This irrational belief seems especially strong as it relates to women, for he gives them the power to devastate him.

Because Stan continually rates himself silently, I would ask him to engage in a self-rating process out loud. I would have him mention all of the things he does and then follow up by asking him to assign himself a grade for each of these functions. I would focus on the self-destructive things he tells himself when he is with a woman. For example, he wants to approach an attractive woman, yet he stops himself, because he is convinced that if she turned him down, he simply could not stand this rejection. My work with him would be directed at having him learn that her rejection is not the cause of his feeling terrible but rather *his evaluation* of the situation and what he tells himself about rejection. Thus, I would get him to challenge his own fatalistic thinking and see that he has been living with untested assumptions. For homework, I would ask Stan to practice by approaching women, if that is something he wants to do, and to work actively toward learning to critically evaluate those beliefs that are self-defeating.

As you review Stan's case and think about him from both a rational-emotive and cognitive-behavioral perspective, consider these questions:

1.  Identify what Ellis would call Stan's central "irrational beliefs" or what Beck would call his "cognitive distortions" or "characteristic logical errors." Drawing from ideas from both Ellis's RET and Beck's cognitive therapy, how would you go about helping Stan challenge the erroneous beliefs that lead to his problem?

2.  What do you think Stan's RET Self-Help Form would look like?

3.  Using Meichenbaum's *stress-inoculation training*, how would you go about teaching Stan to cope with the stresses he says he experiences in daily situations?


## CAROL: "I'M TO BLAME FOR ALL THE PROBLEMS IN MY FAMILY"

As the oldest of three children, Carol (who is 29) berates herself for her family's tension and dissension. Her father is depressed most of the time (which Carol feels responsible for); her mother feels overburdened and ineffectual (Carol feels she contributes to this); and both her sisters are doing poorly in school and having other personal problems (Carol also assumes responsibility for this). Somehow she is convinced that if she were different and did what she *should do*, most of these problems would greatly diminish. Assume, as you listen to her, that you hear her saying some of the following things:

*   "My father looks to me to be the strong one in the family. I *must* be strong if I'm to gain his approval, which I feel I *must* have."

*   " Since my mother is overworked, I *should* take on more of the responsibility for taking care of my younger sisters. I *ought* to be able to talk with them and help them with their problems."

*   "My sisters both expect me to do their chores for them, to help them at school, and to live up to the image they have of me. I *ought* to meet their ideals, and it would be absolutely horrible of me to fail in this regard. Then if they grow up with problems, I'll have only myself to blame for the rest of my life."

1.  Rank the following in order of importance, from the perspective of rational-emotive therapy:

    _____ providing Carol with support and understanding

    _____ creating a warm and personal relationship with her

    _____ telling her that she should not think the way she does

    _____ confronting her with her irrational assumptions

    _____ asking her to question the origin of her beliefs

    _____ asking her what she most wants to change

    _____ teaching her how to identify her own faulty thinking and how to dispute it

    _____ providing her with reassurance

Are there some of the above things that you would *not* do? If so, what are they? Are there some things that you would stress that are not mentioned above? If so, what are they?

2. One of the things a rational-emotive therapist would do is teach Carol that her thinking and her evaluation of events are causing her problems (feelings of inadequacy, anxiety, and insecurity). What do you hear her saying to herself that is irrational?

3. As a rational-emotive therapist you would want to help her undermine her self-destructive thinking, once she had identified disturbance-creating beliefs. Check the therapeutic techniques that you might be inclined to use:

_____ active teaching methods

_____ readings

_____ relaxation exercises

_____ fantasy exercises in which she relives past experiences

_____ specific homework assignments

_____ therapist interpretation

_____ free-association exercises

_____ a journal of events, thoughts, feelings and outcomes

_____ behavioral rehearsal

_____ writing her autobiography

_____ writing a "letter" to her sisters and parents

_____ methods of disputing irrational beliefs

List some other procedures you would be inclined to use: _____

_____

_____

4. Discuss in greater length which of the above techniques you would expect to rely on the most. What might you expect to occur through the use of these procedures? What outcomes would you hope for?

5. Assume that Carol holds steadfastly to her beliefs and tries to convince you that they are *not* irrational? For example, she tells you: "I just *know* that if I were more adequate as a daughter, my father wouldn't be depressed. It's because I've let him down so that he feels useless as a father." How would you respond?

6. Assume that Carol tells you that she does try to question her belief system and has applied rational methods of disputation. Yet she says that no matter how many times she tells herself that a particular belief is irrational, she still *feels* guilty and inadequate. She does not think that just telling herself new things will work. Do you think that rational means alone are enough in Carols' case? How might you respond to her?

7. If Carol seems to hang on to the idea that she *must* have the approval of her father in order to feel adequate as a person, what direction might you take?

8. What value do you see in asking Carol to do a written RET Self-Help Form?

9. Apply the technique of rational-emotive imagery in Carol's case. How would you help her imagine herself thinking, feeling, and behaving in the way she would ideally like to?

10. What differences, if any, might there be between using Beck's cognitive therapy and using Ellis's RET?

# REVIEWING THE HIGHLIGHTS

1. Rational-emotive therapy views human nature as _____
   _____

2. The unique feature that distinguishes this approach is _____
   _____

3. The therapeutic goals are _____
   _____

4. The central role of the therapist is _____
   _____

5. In the therapy process clients are expected to _____
   _____

6. The relationship between the client and the therapist is characterized by _____
   _____

7. Some of the major techniques are _____
   _____

8. I think this approach is most applicable to those clients who _____
   _____

9. One aspect of the rational-emotive approach I like most is _____
   _____

10. One aspect of the rational-emotive approach I like least is _____
    _____

# QUIZ ON RATIONAL-EMOTIVE
# AND COGNITIVE-BEHAVIORAL THERAPY:
# A COMPREHENSION CHECK       Score ____%

*Note:* Refer to Appendix 1 for the scoring key.

*True/false items:* Decide if the following statements are "more true" or "more false" as they apply to rational-emotive or other cognitive-behavioral therapies.

T F 1. RET makes use of both cognitive and behavioral techniques, but it does not use emotive techniques.

T F 2. RET stresses the importance of the therapist's demonstrating unconditional positive regard for the client.

T F 3. Cognitive therapy for depression was developed by Meichenbaum.

T F 4. RET is a form of cognitive-behavioral therapy.

T F 5. Ellis shares Rogers's view of the client/therapist relationship as a condition for change to occur within clients.

T F 6. Beck developed a procedure known as stress-inoculation training.

T F 7. To feel worthwhile, human beings need love and acceptance from *significant* others.

T  F   8.  Ellis maintains that events themselves do not cause emotional disturbances; rather, it is our evaluation of and beliefs about these events that cause our problems.

T  F   9.  A difference between Beck's cognitive therapy and Ellis's RET is that Beck places more emphasis on helping clients discover their misconceptions for themselves than does Ellis.

T  F  10.  According to Beck, people become disturbed when they label and evaluate themselves by a set of rules that are unrealistic.

*Multiple-choice items*:   Select the *one best answer* of those alternatives given.  Consider each question within the framework of rational-emotive and cognitive-behavioral therapies.

_____  11.  Rational-emotive therapy stresses

   a.  support, understanding, warmth, and empathy.
   b.  awareness, unfinished business, impasse, and experiencing.
   c.  thinking, judging, analyzing, and doing.
   d.  subjectivity, existential anxiety, self-actualization, and being.
   e.  transference, dream analysis, uncovering the unconscious, and early experiences.

_____  12.  RET is based on the philosophical assumption that human beings are

   a.  innately striving for self-actualization.
   b.  determined by strong unconscious sexual and aggressive forces.
   c.  potentially able to think rationally but have a tendency toward irrational thinking.
   d.  trying to develop a lifestyle to overcome feelings of basic inferiority.
   e.  determined strictly by environmental conditioning.

_____  13.  RET stresses that human beings

   a.  think, emote, and behave simultaneously.
   b.  think without emoting.
   c.  emote without thinking.
   d.  behave without emoting or thinking.

_____  14.  RET views neurosis as the result of

   a.  inadequate mothering during infancy.
   b.  failure to fulfill our existential needs.
   c.  excessive feelings.
   d.  irrational thinking and behaving.

_____  15.  According to RET, what is the core of most emotional disturbance?

   a.  self-blame          d.  unfinished business
   b.  resentment          e.  depression
   c.  rage

_____  16.  RET contends that people

   a.  have a need to be loved and accepted by everyone.
   b.  need to be accepted by most people.
   c.  will become emotionally sick if they are rejected.
   d.  do not need to be accepted and loved.
   e.  both (b) and (c) are correct.

_____  17.  According to RET, we develop emotional disturbances because of

   a.  a traumatic event.
   b.  our beliefs about certain events.
   c.  abandonment by those we depend on for support.
   d.  withdrawal of love and acceptance.

_____ 18. According to RET, a personal client/therapist relationship is

    a. necessary, but not sufficient, for change to occur.
    b. necessary and sufficient for change to occur.
    c. neither necessary nor sufficient for change to occur.

_____ 19. RET includes all of the following methods except for

    a. persuasion.
    b. counterpropaganda.
    c. confrontation.
    d. logical analysis.
    e. analysis of the transference relationship.

_____ 20. Cognitive therapy is based on the assumption that

    a. our feelings determine our thoughts.
    b. our feelings determine our actions.
    c. cognitions are the major determinants of how we feel and act.
    d. the best way to change thinking is to reexperience past emotional traumas in the here and now.
    e. insight is essential for any type of change to occur.

_____ 21. In cognitive therapy techniques are designed to

    a. assist clients in substituting rational beliefs for irrational beliefs.
    b. help clients experience their feelings more intensely.
    c. identify and test clients' misconceptions and faulty assumptions.
    d. enable clients to deal with their existential loneliness.
    e. teach clients how to think only positive thoughts.

_____ 22. The type of cognitive error that involves thinking and interpreting in all-or-nothing terms or categorizing experiences in either/or extremes is known as

    a. magnification and exaggeration.
    b. polarized thinking.
    c. arbitrary inference.
    d. overgeneralization.
    e. none of the above.

_____ 23. Beck's cognitive therapy differs from Ellis's RET in that Beck emphasizes

    a. a Socratic dialogue.
    b. helping clients discover their misconceptions by themselves.
    c. working with the client in collaborative ways.
    d. more structure in the therapeutic process.
    e. all of the above.

_____ 24. Beck's cognitive therapy has been most widely applied to the treatment of

    a. stress symptoms.
    b. anxiety reactions.
    c. phobias.
    d. depression.
    e. cardiovascular disorders.

_____ 25. In Meichenbaum's self-instructional therapy, which of the following is given primary importance?

    a. detecting and debating irrational thoughts
    b. the role of inner speech
    c. learning the A-B-C theory of emotional disturbances
    d. identifying cognitive errors
    e. exploring feelings that are attached to early decisions

# 12

# REALITY THERAPY

## PRECHAPTER SELF-INVENTORY

*Directions*:   Refer to page 46 for general directions.  Use the following code:

5 = I *strongly agree* with this statement.

4 = I *agree*, in most respects, with this statement.

3 = I am *undecided* in my opinion about this statement.

2 = I *disagree*, in most respects, with this statement.

1 = I *strongly disagree* with this statement.

_____  1.   The core of counseling and therapy is the acceptance of personal responsibility.

_____  2.   Each person has a need for a success identity.

_____  3.   Responsibility implies meeting one's own needs in such a way that others are not deprived of fulfilling their needs.

_____  4.   Emphasis on factors such as unconscious motivation actually gives the client an excuse for avoiding reality.

_____  5.   Insight is not essential to producing change.

_____  6.   There can be no basic personal change unless the client makes an evaluation of his or her behavior and then decides that a change is important.

_____  7.   It is clients' responsibility, not the therapist's, to evaluate their current behavior.

_____  8.   What is important is not the way the real world exists but, rather, the way we perceive the world to exist.

_____  9.   We consciously choose most unsatisfactory behaviors, such as depression and anxiety.

_____  10.   The notion of transference is both false and misleading.  It can keep the therapist hidden, and it can be used to avoid discussing one's current behavior.

_____  11.   It is not the therapist's role to judge the client's behavior, because a therapist should not function as a moralist or the guardian of standards of any social or political group.

_____  12.   We attempt to control the world externally so that it comes as close as possible to our own subjective vision of the world.

_____  13.   The therapist should function much as a teacher does.

_____  14.   Unless the therapist creates an involvement with the client, no motivation for therapy exists.

_____  15.   Therapy should focus on *present behavior*, not on the past, not on attitudes, and not on feelings.

_____ 16. A therapist should get clients to make a value judgment regarding the quality of their behavior.

_____ 17. For therapy to be effective, it is essential that clients decide on a plan for action and that they make a commitment to implement this plan in daily life.

_____ 18. Clients should not be allowed to engage in making excuses, blaming, or explaining why a particular plan failed.

_____ 19. Therapy should focus on the client's potential and positive aspects.

_____ 20. Punishment aimed at changing behavior is ineffective and is harmful to the therapeutic relationship; therefore, it should be eliminated.

# OVERVIEW OF REALITY THERAPY

## KEY FIGURES AND MAJOR FOCUS

Founder: William Glasser. The approach was developed in the 1950s and 1960s. Originally it had no systematic theory but emphasized that individuals are responsible for what they do. In the 1980s Glasser began teaching control theory, which holds that all people have choices about what they are doing. It is based on the assumption that human behavior is purposeful and originates from within the individual. This behavior is our best attempt to get what we want.

## PHILOSOPHY AND BASIC ASSUMPTIONS

Glasser's approach is based on the assumption that people are self-determining and in charge of their lives. His premise is that all behavior is aimed at satisfying the human needs for survival, belonging, power, freedom, and fun. His theory describes how people attempt to control the world around them and teaches them ways to more effectively satisfy their needs and goals so that others do not suffer in the process.

## KEY CONCEPTS

The main idea of this approach is that behavior is the attempt to control our perceptions of the external world to fit the individual's internal and need-satisfying world. Reality therapy rejects many of the themes in psychoanalytic therapy such as the medical model, focus on the past, dwelling on feelings or insight, transference, and the unconscious. (For a more detailed summary of other key concepts, refer to the figure "The Basic Concepts of Reality Therapy," on page 160.)

## THERAPEUTIC GOALS

The overall goal of this approach is to help people find better ways of meeting their needs for belonging, power, freedom, and fun. Therapists help clients gain the psychological strength to accept personal responsibility for their life. Clients are assisted in learning ways to regain control of their lives and to live more effectively. They are challenged to examine what they are doing, thinking, and feeling to figure out if there is a better way for them to function.

## THERAPEUTIC RELATIONSHIP

To accomplish the above goals, the therapist initiates the therapeutic process by becoming involved with the client and creating a warm, supportive, and challenging relationship. Both _involvement_ with and concern for the client are demonstrated through the entire process. Once this involvement has been established, counselors confront clients with the reality and consequences of their actions. Throughout therapy the counselor avoids criticism, refuses to accept a client's excuses for not following through with an agreed-on plan, and does not easily give up on the client. (For more details on the nature of this relationship, review the description of the counseling environment in the charts on "The Basic Concepts of Reality Therapy," the "Cycle of Counseling Using Reality Therapy," and the "Summary Description of the Cycle of Counseling," pages 160–162.)

## TECHNIQUES AND PROCEDURES

Once a relationship is established, clients explore their total behavior (elements of doing, thinking, feeling, and physiology). They also evaluate for themselves how well what they are doing is working for them. There are specific procedures that lead to change, some of which are exploring wants, needs, and perceptions; focusing on what clients are currently doing and thinking; and getting clients to make a commitment to an action plan. Special procedures that are used include skillful use of questioning, self-help methods, and humor. (For a more detailed summary of the procedures that lead to change, see the charts "The Basic Concepts of Reality Therapy," "Cycle of Counseling Using Reality therapy," and "Summary Description of the Cycle of Counseling.")

## APPLICATIONS

Originally designed for working with youthful offenders in detention facilities, reality therapy is applicable to people with a variety of behavioral problems. It can be applied to individual, marital, family, and group therapy. It is widely used by educators on both the elementary and secondary levels. It has found wide application in military clinics that treat alcohol and drug abusers.

## CONTRIBUTIONS

As a short-term approach reality therapy can be applied to a wide range of clients. It provides a structure for both clients and therapists to evaluate the degree and nature of changes. It consists of simple and clear concepts that are easily understood by many in the human-services field, and the principles can be used by parents, teachers, ministers, educators, supervisors, social workers, and counselors. As a positive and action-oriented approach it appeals to a variety of clients who are typically viewed as "difficult to treat."

## LIMITATIONS

Reality therapy does not give enough emphasis to feelings, the unconscious, dreams, transference, early childhood traumas, and the past, and it may not be suitable for all cultural groups. There is a tendency to play down the crucial role of clients' social and cultural environment in the shaping of their behavior. This approach may foster a treatment that is symptom-oriented and discourage an exploration of deeper emotional issues.

# GLOSSARY OF KEY TERMS

**Autonomy.** The state that exists when individuals accept responsibility for what they do and take control of their life.

**Commitment.** The act of sticking to a realistic plan aimed at change.

**Control theory.** The view that humans are internally motivated and behave to control the world around them according to some purpose within them.

**Involvement.** A therapist's interest in and caring for the client.

**Paining behaviors.** Choosing misery by developing symptoms (such as headaching, depressing, and anxietying) because these seem like the best behaviors available at the time.

**Picture album.** The perceptions and images we have of how we can fulfill our basic psychological needs.

**Responsibility.** The act of satisfying one's needs in ways that do not interfere with others' fulfilling of their needs.

**Total behavior.** The integrated components of doing, thinking, feeling, and physiology.

**Value judgments.** Client evaluation of current behavior to decide whether it is working.

## QUESTIONS FOR DISCUSSION AND EVALUATION

1. Consider the major phases involved in the process of reality therapy. If you were a client, how do you imagine you would react to this approach?

2. Reality therapy emphasizes discussing what clients are *doing*—their current behavior—as well as what they are thinking. The assumption is that if they change what they are doing and thinking, they are likely to change their feelings and physiological symptoms. What do you think of this emphasis in counseling?

3. What are the values and the limitations of the strict emphasis on present behavior to the exclusion of exploring the client's past?

4. Assume that you were working with involuntary clients, mostly minority-group youths who were associated with gangs. Also assume that your clients were not particularly motivated to change their behavior but were motivated only to keep out of the courtroom. In what ways might you apply the principles of reality therapy?

5. In counseling a culturally diverse population what are some of the merits of using reality therapy?

## PROBLEM SITUATIONS:
## THE PRACTICE OF REALITY THERAPY

The following situations relate to the cycle of counseling using reality therapy. For each situation consider how you might respond to the client from a reality-therapy perspective.

1. *Create a relationship.* You meet a client whom for some reason you take a disliking to. You are aware that the first step in reality therapy is to make friends and develop a therapeutic relationship, yet you are finding it very difficult to care for this person, much less get involved and develop a friendship with him. (Think of *what* kind of person might be difficult for you to relate to in a counseling situation, and imagine that he is the client in question.) If he were sent to you by the court, what might you do or say? Before giving him a referral, can you think of anything you might do to challenge yourself on your dislike for the client?

2. *Focus on current behavior.* Another client whom you have been working with for several weeks seems to continually bring up her miserable home life. She complains that she was never loved by either her mother or father, that she feels stuck with these early memories and feelings and that she very much wants to get these feelings out now. In spite of your efforts to have her address the question "What are you doing now?" she insists that she needs to talk about her past and get her feelings out. What direction might you take? Would you allow her to focus on her miserable past, if that is what she wants? Why or why not? Do you see any value in permitting or even encouraging her to experience catharsis and relive these feelings from her childhood? Do you have any ideas how you might encourage her to look at and talk about what she is actually *doing* today?

3. *Help clients evaluate their behavior.* You have a third client, Debbie, who appears to have difficulty in making a value judgment about her behavior. Although she tells you that she does not like her life at this time, she has a tendency to blame others for her failures, and she is a bit defensive when it comes to making an honest appraisal of what she does. You have asked her a number of times: "Is what you are doing helping you? Is what you are doing now what you want to be doing? " In spite of your efforts she tends to sit at home and keeps herself depressed, hoping and waiting for others to change things for her. What do you do now? What might be your next move with Debbie? Do you have any idea of how you might help her take an honest look at her own part in her problems?

4. *Help clients make a plan.* Another of your clients, Rob, is moving along nicely. (At last—success!) Rob admits that his heavy drug use is not working for him. He is aware that when he sits around the house smoking pot or getting loaded with his friends, this behavior is not getting him where he wants to be. He would like to get into graduate school (in counseling!), yet he fears the workload and fears failing. But he is ready for a change. What plans might be realistic? How might you help him formulate a plan of action? Can you think of some short-range goals that he might pursue? What kind of contract would you want to establish with Rob? Any homework assignments you might suggest?

5. *Get a commitment.* Let's assume that Rob is still with you, that he has agreed to follow through with a written plan that the two of you have developed together, and that he has also made a commitment to you and to himself to follow through with his plans. He comes in the following week and admits that he has done absolutely nothing about making his plans a reality. Instead, his friends came over, and they "got high" and had fun and persuaded him to forget about working so hard. Rob is feeling guilty because he has not kept his commitment. What would you do? What can you imagine yourself saying to Rob at this juncture?

6. *Accept no excuses.* Let's say that Rob renews his commitment with you and agrees to stick with the written plan. He promises to go to at least two colleges before the next session and fill out the applications for admission. A week passes, and Rob returns with "good excuses" for not having done what he said he would do. He complains about not having a car to get to the colleges, and besides, he had to work overtime last week. How would you deal with his excuses? If you challenged him on his excuses and he became defensive, how might you react? Where would you go from here with Rob? (Do not give up and refer him yet!)

7. *Don't use punishment.* You are counseling parents about problems they are having with disciplining their child. The father asserts that the only real way to get his child to "shape up" is to use a variety of punishments. He maintains that his wife has been too lenient and that this is the cause of most of the child's problems. What would you be inclined to do in this situation? Where would you proceed if the father sharply disagreed with you on your stand not to use punishment, preferring to have his child see and accept reasonable consequences?

8. *Don't give up.* Rob comes back again after some success in following through with his plans. In fact, he tells you that he has been accepted into graduate school and has even signed up for nine units. As the semester comes closer, however, he is convinced that he does not have what it takes to succeed in graduate school. He tries to convince you that he is too dumb, that he does not have enough experience, and that if he failed a class, the situation would be unbearable. He is feeling *very* depressed, and he wants to give up on himself. He tells you that he is surprised that you have not given up on him by this time. Do you have any ideas on how you might challenge Rob not to give up on himself? Might there be a danger that you could feel like giving up on him? What might you do to keep your own faith in his ability to change and succeed? At this point, where might you go with Rob?

# THE BASIC CONCEPTS OF REALITY THERAPY

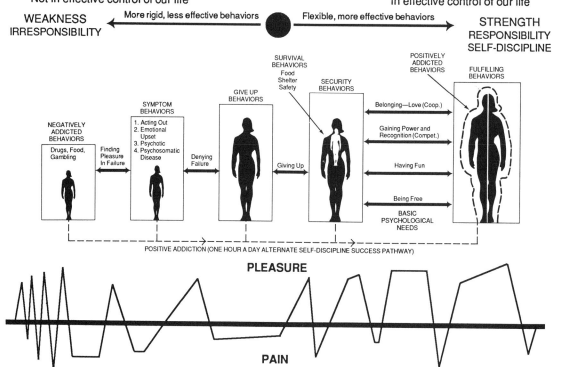

## THE PRACTICE OF REALITY THERAPY

Counselors should be aware that reality therapy is an ongoing process made up of two major components: (1) the counseling environment and (2) specific procedures that lead to changes in behavior. The art of counseling is to weave these components together in ways that lead clients to evaluate their lives and decide to move in more effective directions.

## THE COUNSELING ENVIRONMENT

The counselor should attempt to create a supportive environment within which clients can begin to make changes in their lives. To create this environment counselors should consistently:

Be friendly and listen to their clients' stories. It is important that counselors be perceived as people who are not overwhelmed by clients' situations and who have confidence that they can help their clients find more effective ways to fulfill their needs.

Try not to allow clients to talk about events in the past unless these events can be easily related to present situations.

Avoid discussing clients' feelings or physiology as though these were separate from their total behaviors. Always relate them to their concurrent actions and thoughts over which clients have more direct control.

Accept no excuses for irresponsible behavior. This relates particularly to clients not doing what they said they would do.

Avoid punishing, criticizing or attempting to protect clients from the reasonable consequences of their behavior.

## THE PROCEDURES THAT LEAD TO CHANGE

Counselors must be sure to use the following specific procedures:

Focus on clients' total behaviors, that is, how they are acting, thinking and feeling now. Help them to learn the difficult lesson that, painful and self-destructive as these may be, all total behaviors are chosen.

Ask clients what they want now, their present pictures. Then expand this to the directions they would like to take their lives. If they say they do not know, continue to focus on what they are doing now (total behaviors) to make sure that they realize they are choosing their present directions.

The core of reality therapy is to ask clients to make the following evaluation, "Does your present behavior have a reasonable chance of getting you what you want now and will it take you in the direction you want to go?"

Usually, clients answer "no", which means that where they want to go is reasonable but their present behaviors will not get them there. Counselors should then help them plan new behaviors. For example, "I want to improve my marriage but to do so I will have to treat my spouse differently."

Sometimes they answer "no", but then they seem unable to get where they want to go no matter how hard they try. Counselors should then ask them to consider changing directions. For example, "No matter how well I treat my spouse, he/she is still unloving. It looks like I have to consider divorce." In this case, the plan now becomes more to change the direction than the behavior.

In the rare situation in which they answer "yes", this means that they see nothing wrong with their present behavior or where they want to go. Counselors should then continue to focus on the clients' present behaviors and keep repeating the core question in a variety of ways. Be patient, with difficult clients this may take a while.

Before a plan is attempted, both client and counselor should agree that it has a good chance to succeed. Once a plan is agreed upon, ask the client to make a commitment to the counselor to follow through with the plan. Clients who make commitments tend to work harder. With young students, and others at times, a written commitment is generally more effective than a verbal one.

Do not give up on the client's ability to find a more responsible life, even if the client makes little effort to follow through on plans. If the counselor gives up, it tends to confirm the client's belief that no one cares enough to help.

# CYCLE OF COUNSELING USING REALITY THERAPY

**PROCEDURES**

**ENVIRONMENT**

Make Plans
(2 Types)

Commitment to Plans
(Involves Total Behavior)

Don't Accept Excuses

Don't Criticize or Argue

Don't Give Up Easily

DON'T

**EVALUATION**
(7 Types)

Explore Total Behavior: Direction
and "Doing" ("Acting") Aspect

C. Get Commitment to Counseling (5 levels)
B. Share wants and perceptions
A. Explore wants, needs, & perceptions

--------BE FRIENDS--------

A. Use "attending behaviors"
B. AB-CDEFG
C. Suspend Judgement
D. Do the Unexpected; Paradoxical Techniques
E. Use Humor
F. Be Yourself
G. Share Self
H. Listen for Metaphors
I. Listen for Themes
J. Summarize & Focus
K. Allow or Impose Consequences
L. Allow Silence
M. Be Ethical

DO

Follow Up,
Consultation,
Continuing
Education

**PROCEDURES**

**ENVIRONMENT**

Copyright 1986 Robert E. Wubbolding, EdD
Revised; 1987, 1988, 1989

Adapted by **Robert E. Wubbolding, EdD**
from Basic Concepts of Reality Therapy,
Institute for Reality Therapy, Los Angeles, 1986
Reproduced by Permission of Robert E. Wubbolding, EdD

# SUMMARY DESCRIPTION OF THE "CYCLE OF COUNSELING"
*(The Cycle of Counseling is explained in detail in a book by Robert E. Wubbolding, Using Reality Therapy, Harper & Row, 1988.)*

## Introduction:

The practice of Reality Therapy has been reformulated by Wm. Glasser, MD, from the classic "8 steps" to two general concepts: Environment conducive to counseling and Procedures leading to change. The "Cycle of Counseling" is an expression and an extension of these two general principles. This description is intended to provide a **brief** summary.

## Relationship between Environment & Procedures:

1. As indicated in the chart, the Environment is the foundation upon which the effective use of Procedures is based.

2. Though it is **usually** necessary to establish a safe, warm, friendly Environment before change can occur, the counselor can feel free to enter the "Cycle of Counseling" at any point. Thus, the Practice of Reality Therapy does not occur in lock step fashion.

3. Be Friends implies establishing and maintaining a professional relationship. Methods for accomplishing this comprise some efforts on the part of the therapist that are Environmental and others that are Procedural.

## ENVIRONMENT:

DO: Be Friends:

A. Use Attending Behaviors: Eye contact, posture, effective listening skills.

B. AB = "Always Be . . ." **C**onsistant, **C**ourteous & **C**alm, **D**etermined that there is hope for improvement, **E**nthusiastic (Think Positively), **F**irm & **F**air, **G**enuine.

C. Suspend Judgement: View client behaviors from a low level of perception, i.e., acceptance is crucial.

D. Do the Unexpected: Use paradoxical techniques as appropriate; Reframing and Positioning.

E. Use Humor: Help client to fulfill need for fun within therapy sessions.

F. Be Yourself: Adapt the Cycle to **your own** personality.

G. Share Self: Self-disclosure within limits is helpful.

H. Listen for Metaphors: Use client's figures of speech and provide other ones.

I. Listen to Themes: Listen for behaviors that have helped, value judgements, etc.

J. Summarize & Focus: Tie together what the client has said and focus on client rather than on "Real World."

K. Allow or Impose Consequences: Within reason, clients should be responsible for their own behavior.

L. Allow Silence: This allows client to think, as well as to take responsibility.

M. Be Ethical: Study Codes of Ethics and their applications, e.g., how to handle suicide threats, etc.

## DON'T:

Accept Excuses: Stress what client can control rather than "Real World".

Criticize or Argue: Accept client rather than "belittling" or trying to "convince".

Give Up Easily: Keep confidence that client can develop more effective behaviors. Also, continue to use the "Cycle of Counseling".

Follow Up, Consult, and Continue Education:

Determine a way for client to report back, talk to another professional person when necessary, and maintain ongoing program of professional growth.

## PROCEDURES:

"Radio Station **WDEP**"

Be Friends:

A. Explore **W**ants, Needs, & Perceptions: Discuss picture album, i.e., set goals for counseling, fulfilled & unfulfilled pictures, needs, viewpoints and "locus of control."

B. Share Wants & Perceptions: Tell what you want from clients and how you view their situations, behaviors, wants, etc. This procedure is secondary to A above.

C. Get a Commitment to Counseling: Help clients solidify their desire to find more effective behaviors.

Explore Total Behavior:
Help clients examine the **D**irection of lives, as well as specifics of how they spend their time.

**E**valuation - The Cornerstone of Procedures:
Help clients evaluate their behavioral direction, specific behaviors as well as wants, perceptions and commitment to counseling. Counselor evaluates own behavior through follow-up, counsultation and continued education.

Make **P**lans: Help clients change direction of their lives. There are 13 characteristics of a good plan.

Get Commitment to Plans:
Use written planning sheet, handshake, follow-up, etc.

**Note:** The "Cycle of Counseling" describes specific guidelines & skills. Effective implementation requires the artful integration of the guidelines & skills contained under Environment & Procedures in a spontaneous & natural manner geared to the personality of the counselor. This requires, training, practice & supervision.

**For more information contact:**
Robert E. Wubbolding, EdD, Director
Center for Reality Therapy
7777 Montgomery Road
Cincinnati, Ohio 45236
(513) 561-1911

The CENTER FOR REALITY THERAPY provides counseling consultation, training & supervision in Reality Therapy including applications to schools, agencies, hospitals, companies and other institutions. The Center is a provider for the National Board of Certified Counselors. The Center's sister organization, The Center for Counseling & Managing, Inc., provides psychological counseling and management training.

# CASE EXAMPLES

## MY WAY OF WORKING WITH STAN
## FROM THE REALITY-THERAPY PERSPECTIVE

The perspective of reality therapy teaches me the value of paying attention to what clients are saying by observing how they are actually behaving. Thus, if I am interested in really hearing and understanding Stan, one good way is to notice his behavior in the session and ask him to report what he has been doing the previous week about taking steps to change. It does not mean that I would avoid an exploration of feelings; nor would I avoid talking with him about attitudes that seem to be getting in his way. The focus, however, would be: "Stan, what do you want from these therapy sessions? What are some current behaviors that you most want to change? How can you go about doing so?"

From this perspective I also value the place of *planning* for change. Thus, I would work with Stan on specific steps that he can see are open to him to make the changes he has indicated he wants to make. In a kind and caring manner, yet with firmness, I would expect him to make some *commitments*—to state some specific things he *will* do, *how* he will go about doing them, and *when* he will do them. For example, he mentioned that he wanted to get involved in doing volunteer work in a mental-health agency. During the session we would go over the specifics of *how* he might proceed (with possibilities of role playing with feedback). I would seek a commitment on his part to actually *do something* before the next session to get a volunteer placement. He might agree to interview in one agency, or he might at least agree to write a resume and bring it to his next session. Each week we could assess his progress in terms of what he was actually doing or not doing to bring about changes. As needed, we could revise his action plan for change.

As you review Stan's case and think about him from a reality-therapy perspective, consider these questions:

1. Apply the cycle of counseling of reality therapy to what you know of Stan. Systematically show how you might get him to focus on what he is doing, to make an evaluation of his behavior, and to formulate realistic plans.

2. Stan continues to bring up his past with you, talking about the rotten things his parents did to him. He wants to really "get into his feelings," because he is convinced that until he can express his bottled-up emotions, he will not be able to change. What would be your course of action with him?

3. What do you think you would do or say if Stan made commitments and then did not follow through. Assume that he provided ready-made excuses for not completing agreed-on plans. Where would you go with him?

## CANDY: AN ADOLESCENT IN REBELLION

Fourteen-year-old Candy, her father, and her mother are sitting with you in your office for an initial counseling session. Her father begins:

> I'm just at the end of my rope with my daughter! I'm sick and tired of what I see her doing to disrupt our family life. I'm constantly wondering what she'll pull next in her long line of antics. She's gone to the Colorado River with some guys who are older than she is, in outright defiance of my order not to go. She's done any number of things she knows I disapprove of, and the result is that she's suspended from school for three weeks or until she gets some counseling. This was the last straw that broke my back. Her getting kicked out of school was just too much. It moved me to call you, so we can get to the bottom of Candy's problem and get her straightened out. God only knows she needs some straightening out. She's into drugs and dating older men, and I strongly suspect that she's been messing around. Candy knows what my values are, and she knows that what she's doing is wrong. I just don't know how to convince her that if she doesn't change, she'll come to a bad end.

Candy's mother is rather quiet and does not list complaints against Candy. She generally agrees that Candy does seem defiant and says she does not know how to handle her. She says she becomes very upset at seeing her husband get angry and worried over the situation, and she hopes that counseling will help Candy see some of what they see.

As for Candy she initially says very little other than "I guess I've got a problem." She appears very withdrawn, sullen, and not too eager to open up in this situation with her parents. She is in your office mainly because she was brought by her parents.

Show how you would proceed to use the cycle of counseling as a reality therapist if Candy were your client for three sessions.

1. What are your initial reactions, thoughts, and feelings about this situation? How willing would you be to work with Candy as your primary client if she had come in simply because her father said that she needed counseling?

2. Assume that in an individual session with Candy she does open up with you, and you find out that her father's presentation of the problems is correct. In fact, matters are worse than he imagined. Candy tells you that she had an abortion recently after a short affair with a married man in his early 30s. She also tells you that she has been experimenting with various drugs. How might you proceed in working with her if you found yourself being very concerned over where her behavior might lead her? What might you want to say to her? What would you hope that she would seriously consider?

3. Your central task as a reality therapist would be to guide Candy toward making an honest value judgment about her current behavior and to help her evaluate the results of her behavior. Show how you would attempt to do this. How might you respond if Candy resists looking at he own behavior, insisting that her problems stem from her demanding and moralistic father, who drives her to rebellion.

4. What are *your values* regarding drug usage, sexual experimentation, abortion, accepting parental values, attending school, and the other issues in Candy's case? How would your values affect your relationship with her? Might you be inclined to "straighten her out" by using persuasion, suggesting how she should change, or in other ways lecturing her? Might you instead attempt to influence her subtly to change her behavior in the way you think she should? Or do you think that you could accept her choices, *providing* that she made an evaluation of her behavior and decided that she did not really want to change?

5. Assume that you have a session with Candy, her father, and her mother after seeing Candy for three individual sessions. The purpose of this session is to talk about where to go from here and to make recommendations. What would you be inclined to tell the parents? What would you *not* tell the parents? What specific recommendations might you make?

6. The focus has been on Candy. Might you direct the focus to either or both of the parents? Might you want them to look at their actions and attitudes and to see their role in Candy's problem? If so, how might you go about doing this in a way that would not be likely to increase the parents' defensiveness?

7. What value do you see in counseling for a client such as Candy, who attends sessions mainly because of her father's orders? Can you think of ways in which you might get involved with her to the extent that she could find benefit from counseling for herself? What might you do and say to establish such a therapeutic involvement?

## REVIEWING THE HIGHLIGHTS

1. Reality therapy views human nature as _____

_____

2. The unique feature that distinguishes this approach is _____

   _____

3. The therapeutic goals are _____

   _____

4. The central role of the therapist is _____

   _____

5. In the therapeutic process clients are expected to _____

   _____

6. The relationship between the client and the therapist is characterized by _____

   _____

7. Some of the major techniques are _____

   _____

8. I think that this approach is most applicable to those clients who _____

   _____

9. One aspect of reality therapy I like most is _____

   _____

10. One aspect of reality therapy I like least is _____

    _____

# QUIZ ON REALITY THERAPY: A COMPREHENSION CHECK

Score _____ %

*Note*:  Refer to Appendix 1 for the scoring key.

*True/false items*:   Decide if the following statements are "more true" or "more false" as they apply to reality therapy.

T  F  1. What is important is not the way the real world exists but, rather, the way we perceive the world to exist.

T  F  2. A new development in reality therapy is known as control theory.

T  F  3. A good way to change behavior is for us to be self-critical.

T  F  4. It is important to explore the past as a way to change current behavior.

T  F  5. One of the therapist's functions is to make judgments about clients' present behavior.

T  F  6. The focus of reality therapy is on attitudes and feelings.

T  F  7. The use of contracts is a part of reality therapy.

T  F  8. Reality therapy is grounded on some existential concepts.

T  F  9. It is the client's responsibility to decide on the goals of therapy.

T  F  10. Appropriate punishment is an effective way to change behavior.

*Multiple-choice items*:  Select the *one best answer* of those alternatives given.  Consider each question within the framework of reality therapy.

_____ 11. The founder of reality therapy is

    a.  Albert Ellis.          d.  Eric Berne.
    b.  Albert Bandura.      e.  none of the above.
    c.  Joseph Wolpe.

_____ 12. According to this approach,

    a.  insight is necessary before behavior change can occur.
    b.  insight is not necessary for producing behavior change.
    c.  insight will come only with changed attitudes.
    d.  insight can be given to the client by the teachings of the therapist.
    e.  insight will be discovered by the client alone.

_____ 13. The view of human nature underlying reality therapy is

    a.  that we have a need for identity.
    b.  that we have the need to feel loved and to love others.
    c.  that we need to feel worthwhile to ourselves and others.
    d.  All of the above are true.
    e.  None of the above is true.

_____ 14. Which is *not* a key concept of reality therapy?

    a.  focus on the present
    b.  unconscious motivation
    c.  value judgments
    d.  involvement as part of the therapy process
    e.  responsibility

_____ 15. Which of the following is *not* true of reality therapy?

    a.  Punishment is eliminated.
    b.  Clients must make commitments.
    c.  Therapists do not accept excuses or blaming.
    d.  Therapy is a didactic process.
    e.  Working through the transference relationship is essential for therapy to occur.

_____ 16. Regarding the goals of reality therapy,

    a.  it is the therapist's responsibility to decide specific goals for clients.
    b.  it is the client's responsibility to decide goals.
    c.  the goals of therapy should be universal to all clients.
    d.  society must determine the proper goals for all clients.
    e.  both (c) and (d) are true.

_____ 17. Concerning the role and place of value judgments in reality therapy,

    a.  it is the therapist's function to make value judgments concerning the morality of the client's behavior.
    b.  clients should make value judgments concerning their behavior.
    c.  value judgments should not be a part of reality therapy.
    d.  value judgments should be made only when clients ask their therapists for such feedback.

_____ 18. Which statement is *not* true of reality therapy?

    a.  It is based on a personal relationship.
    b.  It focuses on attitude change as a prerequisite for behavior change.
    c.  Planning is essential.
    d.  The focus is on the client's strengths.

_____ 19. Reality therapy was designed originally for working with

    a. elementary schoolchildren.
    b. youthful offenders in detention facilities.
    c. alcoholics.
    d. drug addicts.
    e. people with marital conflicts.

_____ 20. Which of the following would _not_ be used by a reality therapist?

    a. drugs and medication
    b. hypnosis
    c. the analysis of dreams
    d. the search for causes of current problems
    e. all of the above

_____ 21. Which of the following statements is true as it applies to control theory?

    a. Behavior is the result of external forces.
    b. We are controlled by the events that occur in our lives.
    c. We can control the behavior of others by learning to actively listen to them.
    d. We are motivated completely by internal forces, and our behavior is our best attempt to get what we want.
    e. We can control our feelings more easily than our actions.

_____ 22. According to Glasser, all of the following are basic psychological needs except for

    a. competition.      d. freedom.
    b. belonging.      e. fun.
    c. power.

_____ 23. Control theory tends to focus on

    a. feeling and physiology.
    b. doing and thinking.
    c. coming to a fuller understanding of the past.
    d. the underlying causes for feeling depressed or anxious.
    e. how the family system controls our decisions.

_____ 24. Sometimes it seems as though people actually choose to be miserable (depressed). Glasser explains the dynamics of _depressing_ as being based on

    a. keeping anger under control.
    b. getting others to help us.
    c. excusing our unwillingness to do something more effective.
    d. all of the above.
    e. none of the above.

_____ 25. All of the following are procedures in reality therapy that are said to lead to change except for

    a. exploring wants, needs, and perceptions.
    b. focusing on current behavior.
    c. the therapist's evaluating of the client's behavior.
    d. the client's evaluating of his or her own behavior.
    e. the client's committing to a plan of action.

# 13

# CASE ILLUSTRATION: COMPARISON OF APPROACHES

## SUGGESTED ACTIVITIES AND EXERCISES

Review Chapter 13 of the textbook, which details Stan's case and demonstrates nine approaches to working with him. Some suggestions for class activities are as follows:

1. In class, discuss your views as you consider the following questions. Pay particular attention to Stan's current psychodynamics and the way in which each therapy deals with his problems. Use the questions as a guide to your critique of each of the therapeutic approaches.

   a. *Psychoanalytic therapy*

      (1) How would you link Stan's current difficulty with women to his experiences with his mother?

      (2) Did he identify with his father, whom he saw as weak? Explain.

      (3) What key influences in his early developmental years do you think contributed to many of his current problems?

   b. *Adlerian therapy*

      (1) What can be learned about Stan from a summary and interpretation of his *family constellation*?

      (2) What direction could you pursue with him based on his *early recollections*?

      (3) What are "basic mistakes"? How might you proceed in working with his mistaken assumptions about life? (*Note*: Refer to Chapter 5 of this manual, where there is a completed lifestyle questionnaire on Stan. This would be an excellent place for everyone to start, since you would have some common knowledge about his psychodynamics.)

   c. *Existential therapy*

      (1) What are some specific ways in which you see Stan avoiding his anxiety and running from his freedom?

      (2) How might you, as an existential therapist, work with his suicidal fears? What parts of his life may be "dead"?

      (3) Guilt is a dominant force in his life. What are some examples of his guilt that seem neurotic?

   d. *Person-centered therapy*

      (1) Do *you* believe that Stan has the capacity to make significant personality changes principally by means of the therapeutic relationship between you and him? Is that enough? Do you think more active and directive strategies would be needed for him? Why or why not?

(2) How do you think this approach would work if he were an ethnic-minority client?

(3) What chief differences do you notice between the psychoanalytic therapist's view and the person-centered therapist's view of him?

e. *Gestalt therapy*

(1) How does the Gestalt therapist work on Stan's unfinished business differently than does the psychoanalytic therapist? Which style of dealing with the past do you prefer? Why?

(2) What do you see as Stan's unfinished business that is obstructing his present functioning?

(3) What main differences do you notice between the Gestalt approach and the person-centered approach? In Stan's case which do you prefer? Why?

f. *Transactional analysis*

(1) If Stan were a member of an ethnic-minority group, what aspects of his culture would you want to explore with him? Can you think of some cultural injunctions that he might have accepted?

(2) How would you account for his investment in his many "bad" feelings? What is the payoff?

(3) What possible advantages do you see in combining Gestalt and TA techniques in his case?

g. *Behavior therapy*

(1) How does the existential therapist's view of Stan's anxiety and guilt differ from the behavior therapist's view?

(2) What is your evaluation of the specific techniques (modeling, role playing, behavior rehearsal, and systematic desensitization) that the behavior therapist used with him? How do you think this treatment plan might transfer to his outside life and lead to changes?

(3) On the issue of insight on Stan's part, the psychoanalyst and the behavior therapist differ. The first therapist sees it as essential, and the latter sees it as unimportant and thus focuses on behavior. Which view do you think is correct? Why?

h. *Rational-emotive therapy*

(1) What does RET have in common with TA and behavior therapy in the ways in which the therapists view Stan and their general styles of working with his problems?

(2) The rational-emotive therapist proceeded with Stan in three specific stages. What do you think about the *way* in which this therapist worked with him? What might you have done differently?

(3) Contrast the way the RET therapist approached Stan with that of the psychoanalytic therapist and that of the person-centered therapist. Which of the three do you prefer for Stan? Why?

i. *Reality therapy*

(1) What do you think about the fact that this therapist did not explore Stan's past, particularly when you contrast that approach with the Gestalt and psychoanalytic approaches?

(2) This therapist focused on Stan's successes. Do you think that emphasizing the client's strengths has some advantages over exploring problems? Explain.

(3) What similarities do you notice between reality therapy and behavior therapy in the ways in which the therapists worked with Stan?

2. Now show how you might proceed with Stan by combining concepts from various theories. Give some idea of how you would work with him if you could meet with him 6 to 12 times. Attempt to integrate techniques and concepts that suit your personal style, and show how you could draw on several of the models in a balanced way.

3. Describe how you might pay attention in working with Stan to factors of thinking, feeling, and doing. How could you develop a series of counseling sessions that would encourage him to explore his feelings, develop insight, put his problems into a cognitive perspective, and take action to make the changes he would most like to make?

4. In conceptualizing Stan's case and in thinking about a treatment plan (or approaches you might take with him), you might consider some of the following questions:

   a. How much direction and structuring do you see him as needing? To what degree would you take the responsibility for structuring his sessions?

   b. Would you be inclined toward short-term therapy or long-term therapy? Why?

   c. What major themes would you be likely to focus on in his life?

   d. How much might you be inclined to work toward major personality reconstruction? How inclined would you be to work toward specific skill development and problem-solving strategies?

   e. What values do you hold that are similar to Stan's? How do you expect that this similarity would either get in the way of or facilitate the therapeutic process?

   f. Assume that Stan is an ethnic-minority client. Think of the ways in which you might modify your techniques. What special issues would you want to explore with him if he were Black? Native American? Hispanic? Asian-American?

   g. What ethical issues do you think may be involved in working with Stan's case?

   h. How might you structure outside-of-therapy activities (homework, reading, journal writing, and so forth) for Stan? Thinking about his case, can you come up with suggestions of activity-oriented homework assignments for him?

   i. In working with Stan how much interest would you have in his *past experiences*? How might you work with some early childhood issues? What interest would you have in his *current* functioning? Would you have a concern about his *future* strivings and aspirations? How might you work with him on his expectations?

   j. Might you be inclined to focus on his thinking processes and his belief systems (cognitive dimension)? his *feelings* associated with his experiences (emotional dimension)? his ability and willingness to *do* something different and to *take action* (behavioral dimension)? Which dimension do you think you would make the focus of therapy? Why?

5. In thinking about termination of Stan's therapy, show what criteria you might use to determine when it would be appropriate. Consider a few of these issues:

   a. Would you, as Stan's counselor, suggest termination? Would you wait until he brought up the matter?

   b. Consider each of the various therapeutic approaches. When would he be ready to stop coming in for counseling? What are some different standards to determine his readiness for termination, depending on various theories of therapy?

   c. What might you do if you thought he was ready to terminate but *he* did not feel ready to quite yet? What if he wanted to stop coming to sessions and you were convinced that he had many more issues to explore that he was avoiding and that he was somewhat frightened about continuing therapy?

d.  What ideas do you have for evaluating overall therapy?  How might you assess his level of change?  How would you measure the outcomes of your work together?

When you have finished the above exercises, or those among them that you selected, I highly recommend that you devote some time in class to a discussion of what you have learned by getting involved in these exercises.  What did you learn about being a counselor? about being a client? about integrating the various therapeutic orientations?  What did you learn about yourself through this process?

# ADDITIONAL CASES FOR PRACTICE

Show how you would work, using an integrative approach with the situations presented in the following five brief cases.  These cases are designed to give you some additional practice in applying concepts and techniques from the various approaches to specific situations.  I suggest that you use the material I have provided merely as a point of departure.  You can flesh out each case yourself by creating additional data.  The following questions are useful to apply to each of the vignettes.

1.  What are the ethical, legal, and clinical issues that each case represents?  What is your assessment of each of these key issues?  What value issues arise in each case?  How might your values affect the way in which you intervene?

2.  Which theoretical approaches would be most helpful to you in counseling the clients involved in each case?  What specific concepts would be useful?  What are some specific techniques and procedures that you are likely to employ?

3.  What is your assessment of the core of the problem involved in each scenario?  Show how you would proceed, and give your rationale for the interventions you would expect to make.

4.  In each vignette, what are some special considerations relative to factors such as differences in ethnicity, cultural values, socioeconomic status, religious values, sexual orientation, lifestyle characteristics, and sex-role and gender expectations?

## 1.  A Husband Betrayed by His Wife

The Reverend Joshua Hunter, a Black Baptist minister in his late 30s lives with his wife and children in a small town in North Carolina.  About a month ago his wife told him that she had been having an affair for over a year and intended to ask for a divorce.  At first Joshua was totally shocked and went into denial.  He thought to himself that he must be having a horrible dream.  As reality hit him, he experienced a range of emotions.  He is seeking counseling because he says that he cannot cope with his feelings and is just not able to function and get through a day.  In counseling he tells you:

> I feel so humiliated and shamed in front of all those who respected me.  It's hard to face anyone.  With all this going on, I just don't know how I can continue in the ministry in my town.  It's hard to understand why this happened to me, because I've always tried to be the best husband and father that I could be.  I know I was gone a lot, with all the work that needed to be done in the parish, but it's so hard to understand why she is doing this to me.  As hard as I try to put this crazy thing out of my mind, it's just impossible to do so.  All day long, and even much of the night, I keep ruminating about all she told me.  As a God-fearing man I just don't know what to do next.

## 2.  A Lesbian Confronts Her Parents

Gail is seeking counseling because she feels a strong need to tell her parents about her true identity as a person and her lifestyle.  Her parents are strictly religious people who are highly intolerant of homosexuality.  For most of her life Gail struggled with hiding the feelings she had for other women. She tells you that she has been living a lie so as not to be disowned by her mother and father. She says, however, that from her adolescence she has known deep down that she is a lesbian but was not able to actually admit it to herself until her junior year at college. She then went on to graduate school and got a master's degree in social work. She has been involved in a long-term relationship with one woman, and they have been considering taking steps to adopt a child. If this happens, there will be no way that she can continue hiding her sexual orientation. Although she counsels others, she is coming to you for counseling because she wants to clarify her priorities and make some key decisions about taking the risk of confronting her parents. She wants their approval and acceptance of the person who she is, yet she finds herself resenting them when she thinks of how they are likely to relate to her decisions.

### 3. A Man with a Disability Searches for Meaning

Herb suffered a spinal-cord injury when he was cutting trees and one of them fell on him. For a time after the accident, he continually asked himself "Why did this have to happen to me?" He tells you that for the first two years after he became a paraplegic, he fantasized about suicide a great deal. He had been very physically active, and to be confined to a wheelchair for the rest of his life was more than he thought he could bear. It has been five years since his injury, and he says he has a better outlook on life than he had then, but he still goes into periods of depression and wonders what the meaning of his life is, especially when he considers all the physical activities that he loved so much that he cannot do any longer. A close friend urged Herb to get into counseling to work on his dissatisfaction and help him find a new direction in his life. He tells you that he would really like to discover a way to feel worthwhile again, and he seems somewhat inspired when he thinks of the accomplishments of some of his physically disabled friends. He says: "If they can overcome odds, even in sports, maybe I could, too. It's just that I get discouraged, and then it seems like such hard work to get myself into gear. I'm so much hoping that I can find this motivation in counseling."

### 4. A Woman Struggles with Her Cultural Background

Dr. Deborah Wong is from a second-generation Chinese family. She tells you that even though she has lived in the United States all of her life, her Chinese roots are deep, and she has many conflicts over whether she is Chinese or American. Sometimes she feels like neither. Deborah has distinguished herself in her profession, and she holds a highly responsible position as a pediatrician. She feels married to her work, which she says is the thing she can do best in life. She has not made the time to cultivate intimate relationships with either sex, and she tells you that she very much feels as if she is "missing out" on life. She has always felt tremendous pressure to excel and never to let her family down. She feels as if she is in a competitive race with her older brothers, with whom her parents have always compared her. No matter how hard she works or what she accomplishes, she always feels a sense of inadequacy and experiences "not being enough." With some mixed feelings she is seeking counseling because she wants to feel "sufficient as a person." Although she enjoys her profession, she'd also like to learn to take some time for herself. She also wants to develop a close relationship with a man. Yet whenever she is not working, she experiences guilt.

### 5. A Man Grieves over the Loss of His Wife

At age 74 Erving says he has been totally lost ever since his wife "left" him after a long battle with lung cancer. A hospice worker strongly encouraged him to participate in counseling to work through his grief reactions over the death of his wife, Amanda. During her illness the hospice group was of tremendous help to both Amanda and Erving. However, after her death, he felt strange when he'd go to a hospice group meeting. He tells you:

> Over 90 percent of the group members are widows, and I keep thinking that I wish it had been me who died instead of Amanda. Even though it has been over a year since her death, I still feel lost and struggle to get through each day. I'm so lonely and miss her so much. They say it takes time, but I don't seem to be getting any better.

Nothing seems very worthwhile anymore, and without her in my life I can't find anything I really like doing. I never had many friends. Amanda was really my only friend, and now that she's gone, it doesn't seem that there is any way to fill this huge gap in my life.

He would like to get over feeling regret at what he didn't say to her as well as what he didn't do with her when she was alive. He'd like to resolve feeling so guilty that he is alive while she is gone.

# 14

# An Integrative Perspective

In this chapter most of the exercises are designed to help you make some comparisons among the various therapy approaches, to help you see a basis for the integration of several approaches, to encourage you to think of the aspects you like and dislike about each therapy, and to give you some practice in applying specific therapies to various client populations.

## Applications of Theoretical Approaches to Specific Client Populations or Specific Problems

As a basis for review and to help you compare and integrate the approaches, I am presenting a list of specific clients, problems, or situations. Decide which of the approaches you would be likely to use in each case. It should be pointed out that there is no one "right approach" for these cases; rather, you are asked to select an approach and give your reasons for your selection. In some cases you might want to select more than one therapy, and you might want to employ several techniques. Keep in mind that the purpose of these exercises is to stimulate your thinking in applying the theories you have studied to specific cases. Thus, focus on the advantage you see of a particular approach for each of the following cases.

1. Roger, at age 33, is extremely inhibited. He finally seeks out therapy because he is in so much pain over his fears of talking to others or being in public. Roger is very nonverbal and gives only skimpy details; he obviously wants direction and help in conquering his severe inhibitions. During the initial interview he appears extremely uncomfortable and strains whenever he is expected to talk.

   a. Select an approach that you are likely to use in the above case. _____

   _____

   b. What are your reasons? _____

   _____

   c. What techniques from this approach might be most appropriate? _____

   _____

   _____

2. Jim is a 40-year-old engineer who says that he has gone to many encounter groups and has had a good deal of therapy. He says: "In spite of all this group stuff and head shrinking, I still don't seem to be able to get past the insight level. I see a lot of things I didn't see before, and I understand more why I'm the way I am, but I still don't seem to be able to use what I know to make changes in my life. I'm still troubled by the same old hang-ups, and so far I haven't been able to do much about resolving them."

   a. Select an approach that you are likely to use with Jim. _____

   _____

b. Your reasons? _____

_____

c. What techniques from this approach might you use? _____

_____

3. The client population is a group of drug addicts who are part of a federally funded detoxification center. The director of the center would like the clients to be seen occasionally on an individual basis, but for the most part she would like them in small groups for the therapy. She was awarded her grant on the basis that she had a program that could teach the clients interpersonal skills and could enhance their self-esteem while they were off of drugs.

a. Select an approach that you think is most appropriate for the above case. _____

_____

b. Reasons? _____

_____

c. What techniques from this approach might be most appropriate? _____

_____

4. An adolescent girl is having extreme difficulty in coping with stress and the demands of school. Penny has many fears of failing, of not being liked by other students, and of being seen as "different," and she suffers from headaches and physical tenseness. She says that she would like to lead a "normal life" and be able to go to school and function adequately. She is afraid that unless she can deal with these stresses, she will "go crazy."

a. Select an approach that you think is most appropriate for the above case. _____

_____

b. Reasons? _____

_____

c. What techniques from this approach might be most appropriate? _____

_____

5. A married couple, Diane and Scott, present themselves for marriage counseling. Scott did not particularly want to come in, but he is willing to give things a try. He basically feels that life is fine, the marriage is all right, and there are no major problems with their children. In short, he likes his life, except he wishes that *she* could be more at peace, and that she would stop bugging him! Diane feels pretty discouraged about life. Her kids do not appreciate her, and surely her husband does not recognize or appreciate her. She feels that she has to be both the mother and the father at home, that she has to make all the decisions, and that Scott will not listen to her. She wants to feel heard by him.

a. Select an approach that you think is most appropriate for the above case. _____

_____

b. Reasons? _____

_____

c. What techniques from this approach might be most appropriate? _____

_____

_____

6. Fran is returning to college now that her children are in high school. She says: "I feel as if I don't know who I am anymore. At one time I knew what my purpose was, and now I just feel confused (and scared) most of the time. I like going to college and doing something for myself, and at the same time I feel guilty. I ask myself what I'm trying to prove. The most recurring feeling I have is that it's wrong for me to be enjoying college and doing this just for me."

   a. Select an approach that you think is most appropriate for the above case. _____

   _____

   b. Reasons? _____

   _____

   c. What techniques from this approach might be most appropriate? _____

   _____

7. The setting is a state hospital for the mentally disordered sex offender. One ward is composed of a group of male sex offenders (mostly rapists and other violent types), and the program director wants them to be in some form of group therapy. She says about these men: "They are very verbal and pretty bright for the most part. They are diagnosed as *sociopathic personalities*, which means they are generally resistant to treatment, will con the therapist, and will learn the language and play the game—all so they can get a good report and get discharged. They do not feel much remorse or guilt for their offenses." She wants the group to focus on getting them to look at their offenses and learn something about themselves in terms of how poorly they dealt with their tensions and impulses. She hopes they can learn more constructive approaches to dealing with their feelings in the future.

   a. Select an approach that you think is most appropriate for the above case. _____

   _____

   b. Reasons? _____

   _____

   c. What techniques from this approach might be most appropriate? _____

   _____

8. The client, Yvonne, specifically wants to work on her dreams. She says that they are frequent and powerful and that she wants to learn what they are telling her about what is going on in her life.

   a. Select an approach that you think is most appropriate for the above case. _____

   _____

   b. Reasons? _____

   _____

   c. What techniques from this approach might be most appropriate? _____

   _____

9. Joan comes in for crisis counseling. This young woman complains of chronic depression and is frightened by the frequency of her suicidal thoughts and impulses. She attempted suicide several years ago and was committed to a state mental hospital for a time. She fears being "sent up" again, because she does not know how to cope with her bouts of depression.

   a. Select an approach that you think is most appropriate for the above case. _____

   _____

b.  Reasons? _____

_____

c.  What techniques from this approach might be most appropriate? _____

_____

10.  Sue's presenting problem is her perfectionistic tendencies.  She says that she makes herself sick by driving herself so hard.  As she puts it: "I can never do anything and feel that I've done it well enough.  No matter what I do, I keep telling myself that it doesn't come up to standard, and that I'm capable of so much more.  I can never enjoy anything, but instead I feel rotten and guilty most of the time.  How can I learn to accept myself and not be so driven?"

a.  Select an approach that you think is most appropriate for the above case. _____

_____

b.  Reasons? _____

_____

c.  What techniques from this approach might be most appropriate? _____

_____

11.  Ted, a grossly overweight but otherwise attractive young man, says that he wants help in losing his excess pounds.  No matter how many resolutions he has made, he keeps failing to stick to a diet and exercise program.  Ted says that he is willing to give therapy a try.

a.  Select an approach that you think is most appropriate for the above case. _____

_____

b.  Reasons? _____

_____

c.  What techniques from this approach might be most appropriate? _____

_____

12.  The parents bring Tim, a 7-year-old phobic child, for treatment of his fear of riding in cars.  When he was 6, he was in a serious auto accident, and he has developed phobic reactions to even getting close to cars.  His parents are anxious to know what can be done to help him work through his fears.

a.  Select an approach that you think is most appropriate for the above case. _____

_____

b.  Reasons? _____

_____

c.  What techniques from this approach might be most appropriate? _____

_____

13.  The clients are a group of elderly people in a ward of a state mental hospital.  Most of them are senile and have little capacity to relate to one another.  They are typically people who feel lost, abandoned, and depressed, and they have lost much of the meaning in their life.  The program director would like some form of therapy aimed at enabling these patients to learn to make contact with one another and to encourage them to talk about their feelings and their experiences.

a.  Select an approach that you think is most appropriate for the above case. _____

_____

b. Reasons? _____

_____

c. What techniques from this approach might be most appropriate? _____

_____

14. Herb comes to therapy to help him work through his feelings about his divorce. He feels that the divorce was his fault, and that if he had been different, his wife would not have left. He keeps bemoaning the fact that she left him. He feels devastated to the extent that he can hardly function. He is preoccupied with getting her back.

a. Select an approach that you think is most appropriate for the above case. _____

_____

b. Reasons? _____

_____

c. What techniques from this approach might be most appropriate? _____

_____

15. Jake, who is middle-aged, is seeking therapy because he wants to learn how to deal with his anger. As long as he can remember, he has felt anger toward someone: his mother, his wife, his children, his boss, and his few friends. He says that he is frightened of his anger and of what he might do, so he keeps it all bottled up. He reports that as a child he was always given the message that anger is a bad emotion and that you should surely never show angry feelings. Jake also realizes that he fears getting close to people, and he would like to explore his fear of intimacy as well as his fear of his anger.

a. Select an approach that you think is most appropriate for the above case. _____

_____

b. Reasons? _____

_____

c. What techniques from this approach might be most appropriate? _____

_____

The above exercises make good discussion material for small groups in class. In addition to comparing and discussing their selections, my own students have found it valuable in these small groups to get some practice in role playing. One of the students might assume the identity of a given client while another student functions as a counselor by using a particular technique that is a part of one of the theories. This activity may last about ten minutes; then others in the group give the "counselor" their reactions, and another student may work with the client using a different approach. This combination of practice and discussion typically works well.

## QUESTIONS AND ISSUES:
## GUIDELINES FOR STUDYING COUNSELING THEORIES

In reviewing the various approaches to psychotherapy, apply the following questions to each theory. Comparing your own thinking on the underlying issues with the positions of the various therapies can assist you in developing a frame of reference for your personal style of counseling. These questions, by serving as guidelines for organizing your views as you read, will at least help you evaluate each approach critically. Refer to the questions frequently as you read and study the textbook.

1. Are you drawn to a particular theory because it fits your own lifestyle, experiences, and value system? Does your theory provide you with confirmation of your views, or does it challenge you to think about the counseling process?

2. What aspects of each theory are most attractive to you? Why?

3. What aspects of each theory are least attractive to you? Why?

4. To what degree does each theory challenge your own previous frame of reference?

5. Does the theory account for differences in culture, gender, lifestyle, and socioeconomic status? How relevant is the theory when it is applied to working with culturally diverse client population?

6. What are the implications of each theory for multicultural counseling? Can you think of any ethnic or cultural groups that are likely to experience difficulties with any of the particular therapy approaches?

7. Are you using the methods and techniques of a particular approach in a flexible manner, especially in working with culturally diverse clients? Do you tailor your techniques to the needs of your clients, or do you fit your clients to your techniques?

8. To what degree does your acceptance or rejection of a particular theory indicate your own biases?

9. Examine the contemporary popularity of each theory, and attempt to identify factors that contribute to this popularity or lack of it. Consider issues such as efficiency, expense, population served, time involved, and so on.

10. What one theory best fits your view of counseling and therapy? What one therapy do you find most divergent from your own views?

11. What does each theoretical approach offer you that is most significant in terms of integrating it into your practice? What are the least significant and least applicable aspects of each approach?

12. What are the philosophical assumptions underlying each theory? How is the view of human nature of each theoretical approach reflected in the therapeutic goals? in the client/therapist relationship? in the techniques and procedures?

13. What are some unique features of each of the therapies presented? What is the central focus of each approach? What are the significant contributions?

14. What are the limitations of each approach in terms of its theoretical concepts, the therapeutic process, and the applications of techniques to various counseling situations? What are some other limitations with respect to practical aspects such as time involved, level of training necessary, kind of population for which the therapy is effective or ineffective, settings where it is appropriate or inappropriate, and cost? What are some limitations of the approach as applied to multicultural counseling?

15. What are some common denominators among the therapies? Do most approaches share some underlying areas of agreement with regard to goals, therapeutic process, and use of techniques?

16. What approaches can be combined to give a broader, deeper, and more useful way of working therapeutically with people? For example, what are the possible benefits of combining Gestalt therapy and transactional analysis? or combining the basic philosophy of existential therapies with Gestalt techniques? or transactional analysis with rational-emotive therapy? or rational-emotive therapy with reality therapy?

17. What are some contrasts between therapies? For example, what major differences exist between psychoanalysis and behavior therapy? between psychoanalysis and existential therapy and behavior therapy? between person-centered therapy and rational-emotive

therapy? between psychoanalysis and rational-emotive therapy? between reality therapy and person-centered therapy? between transactional analysis and psychoanalysis? between Adlerian therapy and each of the other approaches?

18. What criteria exist for determining the degree of "successful" outcomes of counseling and psychotherapy in each approach? How specific are the criteria? Can they be measured objectively or observed?

19. Most approaches emphasize the client/therapist relationship as a crucial determinant of the outcomes of the therapeutic process. How does each approach view the nature and importance of the therapeutic relationship? What constitutes a "good personal relationship"?

20. What time frame does each approach emphasize: the past? the present? the future? How do the therapies that focus on the here and now account for the client's past and future?

21. How do the various therapies view the issue of the balance of responsibility between the therapist and the client? To what degree is the client's behavior controlled in the counseling session? outside the sessions? What degree of structure is provided by the therapist?

22. What are the advantages and disadvantages of practicing within the framework of one specific theory as opposed to developing a more eclectic approach made up of several different therapies?

23. What is the position of each of the theoretical approaches on the following basic issue?

    a. the importance of the role of interpretation

    b. diagnosis as essential or detrimental

    c. the balance between the cognitive aspects and feeling aspects

    d. transference and countertransference

    e. insight as a crucial factor

    f. the orientation of therapy toward insight or action

    g. the degree to which therapy is viewed as a didactic and reeducative process

    h. the issue of reality

24. For each therapeutic model assume that you are a practitioner following that approach. How would you work with clients? How would you function? What would you focus on with respect to goals and therapeutic procedures?

25. For each approach cast yourself into the role of a client to get a sense of how you might respond to the approach. What would be your goals, role, and experience in the therapy process? How might you react to some of the techniques in each of the approaches?

## SUGGESTED ACTIVITIES AND EXERCISES: DEVELOPING YOUR PHILOSOPHY OF COUNSELING

During the first week in the semester I routinely ask my students to write their philosophy of life (and counseling). At that point their views and values toward counseling are fuzzy. The exercise helps them gain a clearer focus on the basic attitudes and issues underlying counseling practice, and it typically generates thoughtful reflection. The material also can provide a variety of resources for discussion in class.

During the final weeks of the course I ask them to write a *revision* of the earlier paper. This time I ask them to integrate what they have learned from their readings in the various theories with their own basic values related to counseling. A *comparison* of the two papers provides excellent summary and integration material at the conclusion of the course, and it allows students to determine what they have personally learned during the semester.

I recommend that you write your philosophy of counseling or, at the very least, develop a fairly comprehensive outline of your key ideas on that topic. What follows is offered as a guideline.

1. What is your view of human nature? How is your point of view significant in terms of your philosophy of counseling? What factors account for changes in behavior?

2. What is your definition of counseling? How would you explain to a prospective client what counseling is about?

3. What goals of counseling do you view as appropriate? What are some inappropriate goals?

4. What are the most important functions of a counselor or therapist? How would you define your own role as a helper?

5. What do you think are the essential characteristics of an effective relationship between the client and the therapist? How important is this relationship as a factor for change?

6. What makes for a therapist's excellence? What distinguishes a mediocre therapist from an outstanding one?

7. What are the main values you live by? How did those values become yours? How might those central values influence you as a helping person?

8. What are some of your beliefs and attitudes about

    a. religion?

    b. "the good life"?

    c. social change?

    d. oppression of minorities?

    e. women's rights (or men's rights) (or children's rights)?

    f. sex outside of marriage?

    g. abortion?

    h. marriage versus alternative lifestyles?

    i. freedom and responsibility?

    j. antisocial behavior?

    k. using drugs?

    l. education?

    m. counseling clients with a different cultural background from yours?

    n. counseling clients with a different value system from yours?

    o. neglect of the aged?

    p. welfare?

    Select a few of the issues about which you have the strongest convictions, and explain in what ways your attitudes are relevant to your work in a helping profession. Can you add some other areas that have significance for you? What predictions can you make about how your convictions might be either an asset or a liability in your working therapeutically with others?

9. What key ethical concerns do you have about the practice of counseling? How would you go about resolving an ethical dilemma that you might face?

10. What gives you a sense of meaning and purpose in life? How is your life's meaning potentially related to your need to help others?

11. Why are you selecting work in one of the helping professions? What is in it for you personally? What needs of yours are being met by being a "helping person"?

12. To what degree are you doing in your life what you would want for your clients? What are you doing in your own life that will enable you to be an agent of change for your clients?

13. Which theory of counseling comes closest to your way of seeing clients? What aspects of that theory are most appealing to you, and why? How do you think that your theory of counseling will affect the way you work with clients?

14. What life experiences of yours will help you work effectively with a wide range of clients? What struggles or crises have you effectively faced in your life, and how did you deal with them? What experiences have you had with people whose cultural values are different from your own?

15. Can you think of some limitations in your own life experience that might hinder your ability to understand and relate to certain clients? For example, are you aware of any prejudices toward ethnic and cultural groups that could interfere with your objectivity? Or do you hold rigid views pertaining to sex roles, including what is "proper" for women and for men? How might you overcome some of your personal limitations so that you could counsel a wider range of clients more effectively?

# Scoring Key for Chapter Quizzes

| Item Number | Chapter 4 Psychoanalytic Therapy | Chapter 5 Adlerian Therapy | Chapter 6 Existential Therapy | Chapter 7 Person-Centered Therapy | Chapter 8 Gestalt Therapy | Chapter 9 Transactional Analysis | Chapter 10 Behavior Therapy | Chapter 11 Rational-Emotive Therapy and Other Cognitive-Behavioral Approaches | Chapter 12 Reality Therapy |
|---|---|---|---|---|---|---|---|---|---|
| 1 | F | T | F | F | T | T | F | F | T |
| 2 | T | T | T | F | T | T | T | T | T |
| 3 | T | F | T | T | F | F | T | F | F |
| 4 | F | F | F | F | F | F | T | T | F |
| 5 | T | T | T | F | T | F | T | F | F |
| 6 | F | F | F | F | F | T | F | F | F |
| 7 | F | F | T | T | T | T | T | F | T |
| 8 | F | T | F | F | F | F | F | T | T |
| 9 | T | T | F | F | F | T | T | T | T |
| 10 | T | F | T | T | T | T | T | T | F |
| 11 | D | D | E | E | E | D | B | C | E |
| 12 | B | B | D | B | E | B | A | C | B |
| 13 | C | B | C | E | B | B | B | A | D |
| 14 | B | D | B | A | A | E | A | D | B |
| 15 | C | E | A | E | A | A | B | A | E |
| 16 | C | C | D | D | D | A | B | D | B |
| 17 | A | D | A | D | B | C | E | B | B |
| 18 | B | B | E | D | E | D | B | C | B |
| 19 | C | A | D | D | C | D | D | E | B |
| 20 | C | D | C | E | D | A | E | C | E |
| 21 | C | B | B | D | E | D | D | C | D |
| 22 | C | E | B | B | C | E | B | B | A |
| 23 | B | A | C | E | A | B | A | E | B |
| 24 | E | E | B | E | D | D | C | D | D |
| 25 | A | C | D | B | E | D | D | B | C |

# A GUIDE TO PROFESSIONAL ORGANIZATIONS

It is a good idea while you are a student to begin your identification with state, regional, and national professional associations. To assist you in learning about student memberships, eight major national professional organizations are listed, along with a summary of student membership benefits, if applicable. I suggest that you contact your local, state, and regional organizations and get involved in their activities, especially conventions and conferences.

## AMERICAN ASSOCIATION FOR COUNSELING AND DEVELOPMENT

The AACD has 56 state branches and four regional branch assemblies. Students qualify for a special annual membership rate of $32 and for half-rate membership in any of the 14 divisions. AACD membership provides many benefits, including a subscription to the *Journal of Counseling and Development*, eligibility for professional liability insurance, legal-defense services, and professional development through workshops and conventions. For further information, contact:

American Association for Counseling and Development
5999 Stevenson Avenue
Alexandria, VA 22304
Telephone: (703) 823-9800

## NATIONAL BOARD FOR CERTIFIED COUNSELORS

The NBCC offers a certification program for counselors. National Certified Counselors meet the generic professional standards established by the board and agree to abide by the NBCC Code of Ethics. NCCs work in a variety of educational and social-service settings such as schools, private practice, mental-health agencies, correctional facilities, community agencies, rehabilitation agencies, and business and industry. To qualify as an NCC, candidates must meet the minimum requirements for both education and professional counseling experience established by the NBCC. For a copy of the ethics code and further information about becoming a National Certified Counselor, contact:

National Board for Certified Counselors
5999 Stevenson Avenue
Alexandria, VA 22304
Telephone: (703) 461-6222

# AMERICAN ASSOCIATION FOR MARRIAGE AND FAMILY THERAPY

The AAMFT has a student-membership category. You must obtain an official application, including the names of at least two Clinical Members from whom the AAMFT can request official endorsements. You also need a statement signed by the coordinator or director of a graduate program in marital and family therapy in a regionally accredited educational institution, verifying your current enrollment. Student membership may be held until receipt of a qualifying graduate degree, or for a maximum of five years. Members receive the *Journal of Marital and Family Therapy*, which is published four times a year, and a subscription to six issues yearly of *Family Therapy News*. For a copy of the AAMFT's *Ethical Principles for Marriage and Family Therapists* and for applications and further information, write to:

American Association for Marital and Family Therapy
1717 K Street, N.W., No. 407
Washington, DC 20006
Telephone: (202) 429-1825

# NATIONAL ASSOCIATION OF SOCIAL WORKERS

NASW membership is restricted to those who have graduation from an accredited social-work program. For a copy of the *Code of Ethics of the National Association of Social Workers* or for information on membership categories and benefits, write to:

National Association of Social Workers
7981 Eastern Avenue
Silver Spring, MD 20910
Telephone: (301) 565-0333

# NATIONAL ORGANIZATION FOR HUMAN SERVICE EDUCATION

Members of the National Organization for Human Service Education are drawn from diverse disciplines: mental health, child care, social services, gerontology, recreation, corrections, and developmental disabilities. Membership is open to human-service educators, students, fieldwork supervisors, and direct-care professionals. For further information, write to:

National Organization for Human Service Education
Executive Offices
National College of Education
2840 North Sheridan Road
Evanston, IL 60201-1796
Telephone: (312) 256-5150, Ext. 2330

# AMERICAN PSYCHOLOGICAL ASSOCIATION

The APA has a Student Affiliates category rather than student membership. Journals and subscriptions are extra. Each year in August the APA holds a national convention. For further information or for a copy of the *Ethical Principles of Psychologists* write to:

American Psychological Association
1200 - 17th Street, N.W.
Washington, DC 20036
Telephone: (202) 955-7600

In addition to the national organization there are seven regional divisions, each of which has an annual convention. For addresses or information about student membership in any of them contact the main office of the APA or see a copy of the association's monthly journal, *American Psychologist*:

- New England Psychological Association
- Southeastern Psychological Association
- Eastern Psychological Association
- Southwestern Psychological Association
- Western Psychological Association
- Midwestern Psychological Association
- Rocky Mountain Psychological Association

The APA has a number of publications that may be of interest to you. The following can be ordered from:

American Psychological Association
Order Department
P. O. Box 2710
Hyattsville, MD  20784
Telephone:  (703) 247-7705

1. *Specialty Guidelines for Delivery of Services by Psychologists*

    a.  "Delivery of Services by Clinical Psychologists"

    b.  "Delivery of Services by Counseling Psychologists"

    c.  "Delivery of Services by School Psychologists"

    d.  "Delivery of Services by Industrial/Organizational Psychologists"

2. *Careers in Psychology* (pamphlet)

3. *Graduate Study in Psychology and Associated Fields*. Information on graduate programs in the United States and Canada, including staff/student ratios, financial-aid deadlines, tuition, teaching opportunities, housing, degree requirements, and program goals.

4. *Preparing for Graduate Study: Not for Seniors Only!*

5. *Ethical Principles in the Conduct of Research with Human Participants*

6. *Standards for Educational and Psychological Testing*. Revised standards for evaluating the quality of tests, testing practices, and the effects of test use. There are also chapters on licensing and certification and on program evaluation. New in this edition are chapters on testing linguistic minorities and the rights of test takers.

## AMERICAN PSYCHOANALYTIC ASSOCIATION

The American Psychoanalytic Association approved a code of ethics in 1975 and revised it in 1983. Some of its sections deal with relationships with patients and colleagues, protection of confidentiality, fees, dispensing of drugs, consultation, sexual misconduct, remedial measures for the psychoanalyst, and safeguarding the public and the profession. These principles of ethics can be secured by writing to:

American Psychoanalytic Association
309 East 49th Street
New York, NY 10017

# AMERICAN PSYCHIATRIC ASSOCIATION

The American Psychiatric Association has a code of ethics entitled *Principles of Medical Ethics, with Annotations Especially Applicable to Psychiatry*.  Contact:

American Psychiatric Association
1400 K Street, N.W.
Washington, DC 20005
Telephone: (202) 682-6000


# SOCIOLOGICAL PRACTICE ASSOCIATION

The Sociological Practice Association is the professional organization of clinical and applied sociologists.  Clinical sociology is sociological intervention.  Clinical sociologists have specialty areas such as organizations, health and illness, forensic sociology, aging, and comparative social systems and work as action researchers, organizational development specialists, sociotherapists, conflict interventionists, social policy implementers, and consultants.  For information regarding certification instructions and for a copy of the *Ethical Standards of Sociological Practitioners*, contact:

Sociological Practice Association
RD 2, Box 141A
Chester, NY 10918

# ETHICAL PRINCIPLES
# OF PSYCHOLOGISTS

*(Amended June 2, 1989)*

## Preamble

Psychologists respect the dignity and worth of the individual and strive for the preservation and protection of fundamental human rights. They are committed to increasing the knowledge of human behavior and of people's understanding of themselves and others and to the utilization of such knowledge for the promotion of human welfare. While pursuing these objectives, they make every effort to protect the welfare of those who seek their services and of the research participants that may be the object of study. They use their skills only for purposes consistent with these values and do not knowingly permit their misuse by others. While demanding for themselves freedom of inquiry and communication, psychologists accept the responsibility this freedom requires: competence, objectivity in the application of skills, and concern for the best interests of clients, colleagues, students, research participants, and society. In the pursuit of these ideals, psychologists subscribe to principles in the following areas: 1. Responsibility, 2. Competence, 3. Moral and Legal Standards, 4. Public Statements, 5. Confidentiality, 6. Welfare of the Consumer, 7. Professional Relationship, 8. Assessment Techniques, 9. Research with Human Participants, and 10. Care and Use of Animals.

Acceptance of membership in the American Psychological Association commits the member to adherence to these principles.

Psychologists cooperate with duly constituted committees of the American Psychological Association, in particular, the Committee on Scientific and Professional Ethics and Conduct, by responding to in-quiries promptly and completely. Members also respond promptly and completely to inquiries from duly constituted state association ethics committees and professional standards review committees.

## Principle 1: Responsibility

*In providing services, psychologists maintain the highest standards of their profession. They accept responsibility for the consequences of their acts and make every effort to ensure that their services are used appropriately.*

**a.** As scientists, psychologists accept responsibility for the selection of their research topics and the methods used in investigation, analysis, and reporting. They plan their research in ways to minimize the possibility that their findings will be misleading. They provide thorough discussion of the limitations of their data, especially where their work touches on social policy or might be construed to the detriment of persons in specific age, sex, ethnic, socioeconomic, or other social groups. In publishing reports of their work, they never suppress disconfirming data, and they acknowledge the existence of alternative hypotheses and explanations of their findings. Psychologists take credit only for work they have actually done.

**b.** Psychologists clarify in advance with all appropriate persons and agencies the expectations for sharing and utilizing research data. They avoid relationships that may limit their objectivity or create a conflict of interest. Interference with the milieu in which data are collected is kept to a minimum.

**c.** Psychologists have the responsibility to attempt to prevent distortion, misuse, or suppression of psychological findings by the institution or agency of which they are employees.

**d.** As members of governmental or other organizational bodies, psychologists remain accountable as individuals to the highest standards of their profession.

**e.** As teachers, psychologists recognize their primary obligation to help others acquire knowledge and skill. They maintain high standards of scholarship by presenting psychological information objectively, fully, and accurately.

**f.** As practitioners, psychologists know that they bear a heavy social responsibility because their recommendations and professional actions may alter the lives of others. They are alert to personal, social, organizational, financial, or political situations and pressures that might lead to misuse of their influence.

## Principle 2: Competence

*The maintenance of high standards of competence is a responsibility shared by all psychologists in the interest of the public and the profession as a whole. Psychologists recognize the boundaries of their competence and the limitations of their techniques. They only provide services and only use techniques for which they are qualified by training and experience. In those areas in which recognized standards do not yet exist, psychologists take whatever precautions are necessary to protect the welfare of their clients. They maintain knowledge of current scientific and professional information related to the services they render.*

**a.** Psychologists accurately represent their competence, education, training, and experience. They claim as evidence of education qualifications only those degrees obtained from institutions acceptable under the Bylaws and Rules of Council of the American Psychological Association.

**b.** As teachers, psychologists perform their duties on the basis of careful preparation so that their instruction is accurate, current, and scholarly.

**c.** Psychologists recognize the need for continuing education and are open to new procedures and changes in expectations and values over time.

**d.** Psychologists recognize differences among people, such as those that may be as-

sociated with age, sex, socioeconomic, and ethnic backgrounds. When necessary, they obtain training, experience, or counsel to assure competent service or research relating to such persons.

**e.** Psychologists responsible for decisions involving individuals or policies based on test results have an understanding of psychological or educational measurement, validation problems, and test research.

**f.** Psychologists recognize that personal problems and conflicts may interfere with professional effectiveness. Accordingly, they refrain from undertaking any activity in which their personal problems are likely to lead to inadequate performance or harm to a client, colleague, student, or research participant. If engaged in such activity when they become aware of their personal problems, they seek competent professional assistance to determine whether they should suspend, terminate, or limit the scope of their professional and/or scientific activities.

## Principle 3: Moral and Legal Standards

*Psychologists' moral and ethical standards of behavior are a personal matter to the same degree as they are for any other citizen, except as these may compromise the fulfillment of their professional responsibilities or reduce the public trust in psychology and psychologists. Regarding their own behavior, psychologists are sensitive to prevailing community standards and to the possible impact that conformity to or deviation from these standards may have upon the quality of their performance as psychologists. Psychologists are also aware of the possible impact of their public behavior upon the ability of colleagues to perform their professional duties.*

**a.** As teachers, psychologists are aware of the fact that their personal values may affect the selection and presentation of instructional materials. When dealing with topics that may give offense, they recognize and respect the diverse attitudes that students may have toward such materials.

**b.** As employees or employers, psychologists do not engage in or condone practices that are inhumane or that result in illegal or unjustifiable actions. Such practices include, but are not limited to, those based on considerations of race, handicap, age, gender, sexual preference, religion, or national origin in hiring, promotion, or training.

**c.** In their professional roles, psychologists avoid any action that will violate or diminish the legal and civil rights of clients or of others who may be affected by their actions.

**d.** As practitioners and researchers, psychologists act in accord with Association standards and guidelines related to practice and to the conduct of research with human beings and animals. In the ordinary course of events, psychologists adhere to relevant governmental laws and institutional regulations. When federal, state, provincial, organizational, or institutional laws, regulations, or practices are in conflict with Association standards and guidelines, psychologists make known their commitment to Association standards and guidelines and, wherever possible, work toward a resolution of the conflict. Both practitioners and researchers are concerned with the development of such legal and quasi-legal regulations as best serve the public interest, and they work toward changing existing regulations that are not beneficial to the public interest.

## Principle 4: Public Statements

*Public statements, announcements of services, advertising, and promotional activities of psychologists serve the purpose of helping the public make informed judgments and choices. Psychologists represent accurately and objectively their professional qualifications, affiliations, and functions, as well as those of the institutions or organizations with which they or the statements may be associated. In public statements providing psychological information or professional opinions or providing information about the availability of psychological products, publications, and services, psychologists base their statements on scientifically acceptable psychological findings and techniques with full recognition of the limits and uncertainties of such evidence.*

**a.** When announcing or advertising professional services, psychologists may list the following information to describe the provider and services provided: name, highest relevant academic degree earned from a regionally accredited institution, date, type, and level of certification or licensure, diplomate status, APA membership status, address, telephone number, office hours, a brief listing of the type of psychological services offered, an appropriate presentation of fee information, foreign languages spoken, and policy with regard to third-party payments. Additional rel-

evant or important consumer information may be included if not prohibited by other sections of these Ethical Principles.

**b.** In announcing or advertising the availability of psychological products, publications, or services, psychologists do not present their affiliation with any organization in a manner that falsely implies sponsorship or certification by that organization. In particular and for example, psychologists do not state APA membership or fellow status in a way to suggest that such status implies specialized professional competence or qualifications. Public statements include, but are not limited to, communication by means of periodical, book, list, directory, television, radio, or motion picture. They do not contain (i) a false, fraudulent, misleading, deceptive, or unfair statement; (ii) a misinterpretation of fact or a statement likely to mislead or deceive because in context it makes only a partial disclosure of relevant facts; (iii) a statement intended or likely to create false or unjustified expectations of favorable results.

**c.** Psychologists do not compensate or give anything of value to a representative of the press, radio, television, or other communication medium in anticipation of or in return for professional publicity in a news item. A paid advertisement must be identified as such, unless it is apparent from the context that it is a paid advertisement. If communicated to the public by use of radio or television, an advertisement is prerecorded and approved for broadcast by the psychologist, and a recording of the actual transmission is retained by the psychologist.

**d.** Announcements or advertisements of "personal growth groups," clinics, and agencies give a clear statement of purpose and a clear description of the experience to be provided. The education, training, and experience of the staff members are appropriately specified.

**e.** Psychologists associated with the development or promotion of psychological devices, books, or other products offered for commercial sale make reasonable efforts to ensure that announcements and advertisements are presented in a professional, scientifically acceptable, and factually informative manner.

**f.** Psychologists do not participate for personal gain in commercial announcements or advertisements recommending to the public the purchase or use of proprietary or single-source products or services when that participation is based solely upon their identification as psychologists.

**g.** Psychologists present the science of psychology and offer their services, products, and publications fairly and accurately, avoiding misrepresentation through sensationalism, exaggeration, or superficiality. Psychologists are guided by the primary obligation to aid the public in developing informed judgments, opinions, and choices.

**h.** As teachers, psychologists ensure that statements in catalogs and course outlines are accurate and not misleading, particularly in terms of subject matter to be covered, bases for evaluating progress, and the nature of course experiences. Announcements, brochures, or advertisements describing workshops, seminars, or other educational programs accurately describe the audience for which the program is intended as well as eligibility requirements, educational objectives, and nature of the materials to be covered. These announcements also accurately represent the education, training, and experience of the psychologists representing the programs and any fees involved.

**i.** Public announcements or advertisements soliciting research participants in which clinical services or other professional services are offered as an inducement make clear the nature of the services as well as the costs and other obligations to be accepted by participants in the research.

**j.** A psychologist accepts the obligation to correct others who represent the psychologist's professional qualifications, or associations with products or services, in a manner incompatible with these guidelines.

**k.** Individual diagnostic and therapeutic services are provided only in the context of a professional psychological relationship. When personal advice is given by means of public lectures or demonstrations, newspaper or magazine articles, radio or television programs, mail, or similar media, the psychologist utilizes the most current relevant data and exercises the highest level of professional judgment.

**l.** Products that are described or presented by means of public lectures or demonstrations, newspaper or magazine articles, radio or television programs, or similar media meet the same recognized standards as exist for products used in the context of a professional relationship.

## Principle 5: Confidentiality

*Psychologists have a primary obligation to respect the confidentiality of information obtained from persons in the course of their work as psychologists. They reveal such information to others only with the consent of the person or the person's legal representative, except in those unusual circumstances in which not to do so would result in clear danger to the person or to others. Where appropriate, psychologists inform their clients of the legal limits of confidentiality.*

**a.** Information obtained in clinical or consulting relationships, or evaluative data concerning children, students, employees, and others, is discussed only for professional purposes and only with persons clearly concerned with the case. Written and oral reports present only data germane to the purposes of the evaluation, and every effort is made to avoid undue invasion of privacy.

**b.** Psychologists who present personal information obtained during the course of professional work in writings, lectures, or other public forums either obtain adequate prior consent to do so or adequately disguise all identifying information.

**c.** Psychologists make provisions for maintaining confidentiality in the storage and disposal of records.

**d.** When working with minors or other persons who are unable to give voluntary, informed consent, psychologists take special care to protect these persons' best interests.

## Principle 6: Welfare of the Consumer

*Psychologists respect the integrity and protect the welfare of the people and groups with whom they work. When conflicts of interest arise between clients and psychologists' employing institutions, psychologists clarify the nature and direction of their loyalties and responsibilities and keep all parties informed of their commitments. Psychologists fully inform consumers as to the purpose and nature of an evaluative, treatment, educational, or training procedure, and they freely acknowledge that clients, students, or participants in research have freedom of choice with regard to participation.*

**a.** Psychologists are continually cognizant of their own needs and of their potentially influential position vis-a-vis persons such as clients, students, and subordinates. They avoid exploiting the trust and dependency of such persons. Psychologists make every effort to avoid dual relationships that could impair their professional judgment or increase the risk of exploitation. Examples of such dual relationships include, but are not limited to, research with and treatment of employees, students, supervisees, close friends, or relatives. Sexual intimacies with clients are unethical.

**b.** When a psychologist agrees to provide services to a client at the request of a third party, the psychologist assumes the responsibility of clarifying the nature of the relationships to all parties concerned.

**c.** Where the demands of an organization require psychologists to violate these Ethical Principles, psychologists clarify the nature of the conflict between the demands and these principles. They inform all parties of psychologists' ethical responsibilities and take appropriate action.

**d.** Psychologists make advance financial arrangements that safeguard the best interests of and are clearly understood by their clients. They contribute a portion of their services to work for which they receive little or no financial return.

**e.** Psychologists terminate a clinical or consulting relationship when it is reasonably clear that the consumer is not benefiting from it. They offer to help the consumer locate alternative sources of assistance.

### Principle 7: Professional Relationships

*Psychologists act with due regard for the needs, special competencies, and obligations of their colleagues in psychology and other professions. They respect the prerogatives and obligations of the institutions or organizations with which these other colleagues are associated.*

**a.** Psychologists understand the areas of competence of related professions. They make full use of all the professional, technical, and administrative resources that serve the best interests of consumers. The absence of formal relationships with other professional workers does not relieve psychologists of the responsibility of securing for their clients the best possible professional service, nor does it relieve them of the obligation to exercise foresight, diligence, and tact in obtaining the complementary or alternative assistance needed by clients.

**b.** Psychologists know and take into ac-count the traditions and practices of other professional groups with whom they work and cooperate fully with such groups. If a psychologist is contacted by a person who is already receiving similar services from another professional, the psychologist carefully considers that professional relationship and proceeds with caution and sensitivity to the therapeutic issues as well as the client's welfare. The psychologist discusses these issues with the client so as to minimize the risk of confusion and conflict.

**c.** Psychologists who employ or supervise other professionals or professionals in training accept the obligation to facilitate the further professional development of these individuals. They provide appropriate working conditions, timely evaluations, constructive consultation and experience opportunities.

**d.** Psychologists do not exploit their professional relationships with clients, supervisees, students, employees, or research participants sexually or otherwise. Psychologists do not condone or engage in sexual harassment. Sexual harassment is defined as deliberate or repeated comments, gestures, or physical contacts of a sexual nature that are unwanted by the recipient.

**e.** In conducting research in institutions or organizations, psychologists secure appropriate authorization to conduct such research. They are aware of their obligations to future research workers and ensure that host institutions receive adequate information about the research and proper acknowledgment of their contributions.

**f.** Publication credit is assigned to those who have contributed to a publication in proportion to their professional contributions. Major contributions of a professional character made by several persons to a common project are recognized by joint authorship, with the individual who made the principal contribution listed first. Minor contributions of a professional character and extensive clerical or similar nonprofessional assistance may be acknowledged in footnotes or in an introductory statement. Acknowledgment through specific citations is made for unpublished as well as published material that has directly influenced the research or writing. Psychologists who compile and edit material of others for publication publish the material in the name of the originating group, if appropriate, with their own name appearing as chairperson or editor. All contributors are to be acknowledged and named.

**g.** When psychologists know of an ethical violation by another psychologist, and it seems appropriate, they informally attempt to resolve the issue by bringing the behavior to the attention of the psychologist. If the misconduct is of a minor nature and/or appears to be due to lack of sensitivity, knowledge, or experience, such an informal solution is usually appropriate. Such informal corrective efforts are made with sensitivity to any rights to confidentiality involved. If the violation does not seem amenable to an informal solution, or is of a more serious nature, psychologists bring it to the attention of the appropriate local, state, and/or national committee on professional ethics and conduct.

## Principle 8:
## Assessment Techniques

*In the development, publication, and utilization of psychological assessment techniques, psychologists make every effort to promote the welfare and best interests of the client. They guard against the misuse of assessment results. They respect the client's right to know the results, the interpretations made, and the bases for their conclusions and recommendations. Psychologists make every effort to maintain the security of tests and other assessment techniques within limits of legal mandates. They strive to ensure the appropriate use of assessment techniques by others.*

**a.** In using assessment techniques, psychologists respect the right of clients to have full explanations of the nature and purpose of the techniques in language the clients can understand, unless an explicit exception to this right has been agreed upon in advance. When the explanations are to be provided by others, psychologists establish procedures for ensuring the adequacy of these explanations.

**b.** Psychologists responsible for the development and standardization of psychological tests and other assessment techniques utilize established scientific procedures and observe the relevant APA standards.

**c.** In reporting assessment results, psychologists indicate any reservations that exist regarding validity or reliability because of the circumstances of the assessment or the inappropriateness of the norms for the person tested. Psychologists strive to ensure that the results of assessments and their interpretations are not misused by others.

**d.** Psychologists recognize that assessment results may become obsolete. They make every effort to avoid and prevent the misuse of obsolete measures.

**e.** Psychologists offering scoring and interpretation services are able to produce appropriate evidence for the validity of the programs and procedures used in arriving at interpretations. The public offering of an automated interpretation service is considered a professional-to-professional consultation. Psychologists make every effort to avoid misuse of assessment reports.

**f.** Psychologists do not encourage or promote the use of psychological assessment techniques by inappropriately trained or otherwise unqualified persons through teaching, sponsorship, or supervision.

## Principle 9:
## Research with Human Participants

*The decision to undertake research rests upon a considered judgment by the individual psychologist about how best to contribute to psychological science and human welfare. Having made the decision to conduct research, the psychologist considers alternative directions in which research energies and resources might be invested. On the basis of this consideration, the psychologist carries out the investigation with respect and concern for the dignity and welfare of the people who participate and with cognizance of federal and state regulations and professional standards governing the conduct of research with human participants.*

**a.** In planning a study, the investigator has the responsibility to make a careful evaluation of its ethical acceptability. To the extent that the weighing of scientific and human values suggests a compromise of any principle, the investigator incurs a correspondingly serious obligation to seek ethical advice and to observe stringent safeguards to protect the rights of human participants.

**b.** Considering whether a participant in a planned study will be a "subject at risk" or a "subject at minimal risk," according to recognized standards, is of primary ethical concern to the investigator.

**c.** The investigator always retains the responsibility for ensuring ethical practice in research. The investigator is also responsible for the ethical treatment of research participants by collaborators, assistants, students, and employees, all of whom, however, incur similar obligations.

**d.** Except in minimal-risk research, the investigator establishes a clear and fair agreement with research participants, prior to their participation, that clarifies the obligations and responsibilities of each. The investigator has the obligation to honor all promises and commitments included in that agreement. The investigator informs the participants of all aspects of the research that might reasonably be expected to influence willingness to participate and explains all other aspects of the research about which the participants inquire. Failure to make full disclosure prior to obtaining informed consent requires additional safeguards to protect the welfare and dignity of the research participants. Research with children or with participants who have impairments that would limit understanding and/or communication requires special safeguarding procedures.

**e.** Methodological requirements of study may make the use of concealment or deception necessary. Before conducting such a study, the investigator has a special responsibility to (i) determine whether the use of such techniques is justified by the study's prospective scientific, educational, or applied value; (ii) determine whether alternative procedures are available that do not use concealment or deception; and (iii) ensure that the participants are provided with sufficient explanation as soon as possible.

**f.** The investigator respects the individual's freedom to decline to participate in or to withdraw from the research at any time. The obligation to protect this freedom requires careful thought and consideration when the investigator is in a position of authority or influence over the participant. Such positions of authority include, but are not limited to, situations in which research participation is required as part of employment or in which the participant is a student, client, or employee of the investigator.

**g.** The investigator protects the participant from physical and mental discomfort, harm, and danger that may arise from research procedures. If risks of such consequences exist, the investigator informs the participant of that fact. Research procedures likely to cause serious or lasting harm to a participant are not used unless the failure to use these procedures might expose the participant to risk of greater harm, or unless the research has great potential benefit and fully informed and voluntary consent is obtained from each participant. The participant should be informed of procedures for contacting the investigator within a reasonable time period following participation should stress, potential harm, or related questions or concerns arise.

**h.** After the data are collected, the investigator provides the participant with information about the nature of the study and attempts to remove any misconceptions that may have arisen. Where scientific or human values justify delaying or withholding this information, the investigator incurs a special responsibility to monitor the research and to ensure that there are no damaging consequences for the participant.

**i.** Where research procedures result in undesirable consequences for the individual participant, the investigator has the responsibility to detect and remove or correct these consequences, including long-term effects.

**j.** Information obtained about a research participant during the course of an investigation is confidential unless otherwise agreed upon in advance. When the possibility exists that others may obtain access to such information, this possibility, together with the plans for protecting confidentiality, is explained to the participant as part of the procedure for obtaining informed consent.

## Principle 10: Care and Use of Animals

*An investigator of animal behavior strives to advance understanding of basic behavioral principles and/or to contribute to the improvement of human health and welfare. In seeking these ends, the investigator ensures the welfare of animals and treats them humanely. Laws and regulations notwithstanding, an animal's immediate protection depends upon the scientist's own conscience.*

**a.** The acquisition, care, use, and disposal of all animals are in compliance with current federal, state or provincial, and local laws and regulations.

**b.** A psychologist trained in research methods and experienced in the care of laboratory animals closely supervises all procedures involving animals and is responsible for ensuring appropriate consideration of their comfort, health, and humane treatment.

**c.** Psychologists ensure that all individuals using animals under their supervision have received explicit instruction in experimental methods and in the care, maintenance, and handling of the species being used. Responsibilities and activities of individuals participating in a research project are consistent with their respective competencies.

**d.** Psychologists make every effort to minimize discomfort, illness, and pain of animals. A procedure subjecting animals to pain, stress, or privation is used only when an alternative procedure is unavailable and the goal is justified by its prospective scientific, educational, or applied value. Surgical procedures are performed under appropriate anesthesia; techniques to avoid infection and minimize pain are followed during and after surgery.

**e.** When it is appropriate that the animal's life be terminated, it is done rapidly and painlessly.

---

This version of the *Ethical Principles of Psychologists* was adopted by the American Psychological Association's Board of Directors on June 2, 1989. On that date, the Board of Directors rescinded several sections of the Ethical Principles that had been adopted by the APA Council of Representatives on January 24, 1981. Inquiries concerning the substance or interpretation of the *Ethical Principles of Psychologist*s should be addressed to the Administrative Director, Office of Ethics, American Psychological Association, 1200 Seventeenth Street, N.W., Washington, DC 20036.

These Ethical Principles apply to psychologists, to students of psychology, and to others who do work of a psychological nature under the supervision of a psychologist. They are intended for the guidance of nonmembers of the Association who are engaged in psychological research or practice.

The Ethical Principles have previously been published as follows:

American Psychological Association. (1953). *Ethical Standards of Psychologists*, Washington, DC.

American Psychological Association. (1958). Standards of ethical behavior for psychologists. *American Psychologist*, 13, 268-271.

American Psychological Association. (1959). Ethical standards of psychologists. *American Psychologist*, 14, 279-282.

American Psychological Association. (1963). Ethical standards of psychologists. *American Psychologist*, 18, 56-60.

American Psychological Association. (1968). Ethical standards of psychologists. *American Psychologist*, 23, 357-361.

American Psychological Association. (1977, March). Ethical standards of psychologists. *The APA Monitor*, pp. 22-23.

American Psychological Association. (1979). *Ethical Standards of Psychologists*, Washington, DC: Author.

American Psychological Association. (1981). Ethical principles of psychologists. *American Psychologist*, 36, 633-638.

Request copies of the *Ethical Principles of Psychologists* from the APA Order Department, P. O. Box 2710, Hyattsville, MD 20784; or phone (703) 247-7705.

# APPENDIX 4

# OTHER BOOKS BY THE AUTHOR

The following are other books that my colleagues and I have written that might be of interest to you. All of these are published by the Brooks/Cole Publishing Company, Pacific Grove, CA 93950-5098.

Corey, G. (1991). *Case Approach to Counseling and Psychotherapy*, 3rd ed. Demonstrates how theory can be applied to specific cases. The outline of theories corresponds to your textbook and manual. Readers are challenged to apply their knowledge of theories to a variety of cases. I demonstrate my way of working with these cases from each of the nine theoretical perspectives and also in an eclectic, integrated fashion. For each of the nine theories there is a central case (Ruth). Proponents of the theories write about their assessment of Ruth and then proceed to demonstrate their particular therapeutic style in counseling her. I then follow up and show how I might intervene with her by staying within the general framework of each of these theories.

Corey, G. (1990). *Theory and Practice of Group Counseling*, 3rd ed. Outlines the basic elements of group process, presents an overview of the key concepts and techniques of ten theoretical approaches to group counseling, and shows how to integrate these various approaches.

Corey, G. (1990). *Manual for Theory and Practice of Group Counseling*, 3rd ed. Similar to this manual.

Corey, G., & Corey, M. S. (1990). *I Never Knew I Had a Choice*, 4th ed. A self-help book for personal growth that deals with topics such as the struggle to achieve autonomy; the roles that work, sex roles, sexuality, love, intimacy, and solitude play in our lives; the meaning of loneliness, death, and loss; and the ways in which we choose values and find meaning in life.

Corey, M. S., & Corey, G. (1989). *Becoming a Helper*. Deals with topics of concern to students who are studying in one of the helping professions. Some of the issues explored are examining your motivations and needs, becoming aware of the impact of your values on the counseling process, learning to cope with stress, dealing with burnout, exploring developmental turning points in your life, and ethical issues.

Corey, G., Corey, M. S. & Callanan, P. (1988). *Issues and Ethics in the Helping Professions*, 3rd ed. A combination textbook and student manual that contains self-inventories, open-ended cases and problem situations, exercises, suggested activities, and a variety of ethical, professional, and legal issues facing practitioners.

Corey, G., Corey, M. S., Callanan, P., & Russell, J. M. (1988). *Group Techniques*, rev. ed. Describes ideas for creating and using techniques in groups. Gives a rationale for the use of techniques in all the stages in a group's development.

Corey, M. S., & Corey, G. (1987). *Groups: Process and Practice*, 3rd ed. Outlines the basic issues and concepts of group process throughout the life history of a group. Applies these basic concepts to groups for children, adolescents, adults, and the elderly.

To the Owner of This Book: Please Evaluate This Manual

I hope that you have enjoyed and learned from the *Manual for Theory and Practice of Counseling and Psychotherapy,* Fourth Edition. This edition was improved by the responses of many readers of earlier editions who returned this evaluation sheet. So that I can improve the next edition, please take a few minutes to complete this sheet and return it. Thank you.

School: _____
           Name of college or university         City         State        Zip Code

Department: _____ Your instructor's name: _____

  1.  What I *like most* about this manual is: _____

_____

_____

  2.  What I *like least* about this manual is: _____

_____

_____

  3.  Some ways in which I used this manual, both in and out of class, were: _____

_____

_____

  4.  Some of the manual's exercises that were used most meaningfully in my class were: _____

_____

_____

  5.  My general reaction to this manual is: _____

  6.  The name of the course in which I used this manual and the level (graduate or undergraduate):

_____

  7.  Please write specific suggestions for improving the manual, and make other comments about the book and your experience with it.

_____

_____

_____

_____

_____

_____

Optional

Your name: _____     Date: _____

May Brooks/Cole quote you, either in promotion for the *Manual for Theory and Practice of Counseling and Psychotherapy* or in future publishing ventures?

Yes _____ No _____

Sincerely,

Gerald Corey

---

FOLD HERE

**BUSINESS REPLY MAIL**
FIRST CLASS     PERMIT NO. 358     PACIFIC GROVE, CA

POSTAGE WILL BE PAID BY ADDRESSEE

ATT: Dr. Gerald Corey

**Brooks/Cole Publishing Company**
**511 Forest Lodge Road**
**Pacific Grove, California 93950-9968**

NO POSTAGE
NECESSARY
IF MAILED
IN THE
UNITED STATES

FOLD HERE